Long Range Desert Group

To
E., M. AND V.
WHO WAITED

Long Range Desert Group

W. B. Kennedy Shaw

Sometime Intelligence and
Topographical Officer, L.R.D.G.

Foreword by David Lloyd Owen

GREENHILL BOOKS, LONDON
PRESIDIO PRESS, CALIFORNIA

This edition of *Long Range Desert Group*
first published 1989 by Greenhill Books, Lionel Leventhal Limited,
Park House, 1 Russell Gardens, London NW11 9NN
and
Presidio Press,
31 Pamaron Way, Novato, Ca.94947, U.S.A.

British Library Cataloguing in Publication Data
Shaw, W. B. Kennedy, (William B. Kennedy), *d. 1979*
Long Range Desert Group
1. World War 2. North African Campaign.
Army operations by Great Britain. Army.
Long Range Desert Group & Great Britain. Army.
Special Air Service Regiment.
I. Title   940.54′23

ISBN 1–85367–024–3

Publishing History
Long Range Desert Group was first published in 1945 (Collins)
and is reproduced now exactly as the original edition, complete
and unabridged. For this edition a new Foreword by
Major-General D. L. Lloyd Owen has been added.
The text in the original volume is fragile and this
creates imperfections when reproduced and which
necessarily appear in this facsimile volume.

Printed by Bookcraft (Bath) Ltd.

Foreword

Major-General D. L. Lloyd Owen, C.B., D.S.O., O.B.E., M.C.

WHEN Bill Kennedy Shaw's masterly account of the Long Range Desert Group's work in Libya between 1940 and 1943 was first published in 1945 he gave me a copy of it. I have treasured it ever since because the kind words he inscribed in it came from a friend of such sterling quality and whose knowledge of deserts was possibly as great as that of any man then living. And I have valued it over all the years because his classic book has been out of print for far too long.

As the former Intelligence Officer of the LRDG Bill Kennedy Shaw was in a unique position to record the definitive story of that remarkable unit in which I was privileged to play a part. He wrote it at a time when the censor's blue pencil was still very active, and no details of ULTRA had been revealed. Readers today, and particularly students of military history, will find no reference in the text, for example, to Vladimir Peniakoff (or Popski as we knew him). He is disguised under the pseudonym of Penman. Equally fictitious are the codewords, given in Chapter Twelve, for the great raids of September 1942 and which are so well described in this book.

I mention these small points simply because Bill Kennedy Shaw was such an honest, humble and painstaking man that he would never mislead or exaggerate in anything that he wrote. He was far too sincere throughout his life.

When Ralph Bagnold first raised the LRDG in June 1940, he was well aware of Bill's reputation and worth from expeditions that they had carried out together in the vast Libyan desert in the decade before the outbreak of the second world war. In 1927 Bill, together with Douglas Newbold also on leave from the Sudan Government service, had made a quite astonishing journey of a thousand miles on a camel across southern Egypt. A splendid photograph of his small caravan of camels is reproduced in the book (illustration no. 2).

The knowledge that he gained in those pre-war years together with his shrewd, incisive mind gave the author of this book the ideal qualifications for his appointment as unit Intelligence Officer. He excelled at it.

The success of every Patrol sent out on operations was due in no small measure to the sound briefing, which he always gave to its leader before that Patrol went out. And his disarmingly mild manner helped to extract every scrap of information from Patrol leaders on their return. This often was the source of much invaluable intelligence for the staff at Eighth Army headquarters, which was always hungry for up-to-date and accurate news.

Bill Kennedy Shaw was a genius at his work; and this is reflected in his factual and exciting chronicle of LRDG activities. His profound respect for the uncompromising harshness, and the beauty, of the desert show up so well in his brilliant description of it. For those reasons alone this book is as readable today as it was when it first appeared.

After the defeat of the Axis powers in North Africa, Bill left the LRDG to make further use of his unrivalled understanding of the people. He served with the British Military Administration in Tripolitania as their adviser on Arab affairs until he returned to England in 1944.

After the war he became Agent to Lord Bledisloe at Lydney Park in Gloucestershire until ill-health, brought on by some virus that had infected him in the Middle East, forced him to give up an active life. Ultimately his eyesight failed him before he died in Lichfield in April 1979.

Bill Kennedy Shaw will ever be remembered as one of that distinguished band of enthusiasts, who explored the largely unknown and uncharted wastes of the desert west of the Nile between the two World Wars, and who were led by Ralph Bagnold.

Today, in his 94th year, Brigadier Bagnold is the President of the LRDG Association of which I have been proud to be the Chairman since it was formed in 1945. We keep alive the memories and experiences of those war years through the annual Newsletter of our Association. But the real story will live forever in Bill Kennedy

Shaw's evocative and stirring narrative of the Long Range Desert
Group in the desert. It is extraordinarily well told.

DAVID LLOYD OWEN

SWAINSTHORPE, NORWICH,
        1989

' Then we do nothing ? ' said Hugh.
' We wait,' said De Aquila. ' I am old, but still
I find that the most grievous work I know.'

Puck of Pook's Hill

VIII

Preface

THERE are no two ways about deserts—either you dislike intensely being in them or you find their attractions hard to resist. I belong to the latter class and since 1927 the Libyan Desert, its history, exploration and archæology, its politics and everything that concerns it, has been one of my chief interests in life. In it at various times I have spent about three and a half years and have travelled by camel, car and aircraft at least forty-five thousand miles.

As Intelligence Officer of the Long Range Desert Group from July, 1940, until February, 1943, I took part in some of the operations of the first year and later, as a less active spectator at Group Headquarters, saw most of the game.

So if I have not written an accurate account, even if not a readable one, of the work of the L.R.D.G. in Libya, I have only myself to blame.

But even so I shall have made mistakes. To some I shall have given too much honour : to some too little. Of both I ask forgiveness.

My thanks are due to many friends who have described to me their adventures, and also to those who have written parts of this book and to whom acknowledgment is made in the appropriate place.

W. B. K. S.

TRIPOLI—HEBRON—MA'ADI
1943

My guides, sniffing the air like dogs, led me from crumbling room to room, saying, ' This is jessamine, this violet, this rose.'

But at last Dahoum drew me : ' Come and smell the very sweetest smell of all,' and we went into the main lodging, to the gaping window sockets of its eastern face, and there drank with open mouths of the effortless, empty, eddyless wind of the desert, throbbing past. . . .

' This,' they told me, ' is the best : it has no taste.'

Seven Pillars of Wisdom

Contents

Acknowledgments

MY THANKS are due to the New Zealand Government for permission to reproduce some of Capt. Peter McIntyre's drawings ; to the New Zealand Public Relations Service who allowed me to consult their archives ; to Mr. G. W. Murray and to Mr. H. Rowntree for help in preparing the maps and to 'Abd el Hamid Eff. Mukhtar who drew them ; to the Army Film and Photographic Unit for leave to use their photographs, and to other friends who have given me illustrations for this book but of whose names I have not, I regret, a complete record.

W. B. K. S.

Illustrations

[1] From *Libyan Sands* by R. A. Bagnold, by kind permission of the author and Messrs. Hodder & Stoughton.

MAPS

NORTH EAST AFRICA

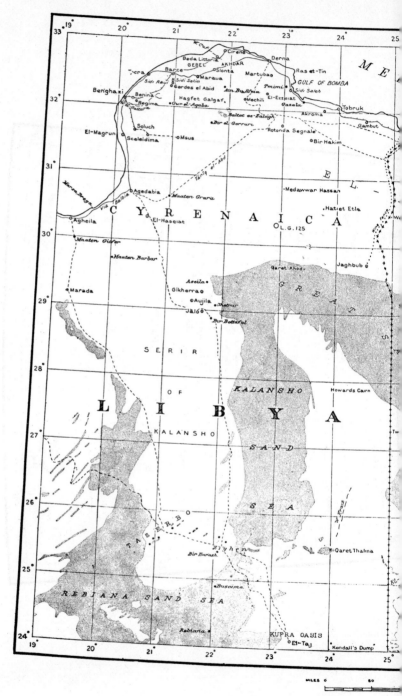

EGYPT AND LIB

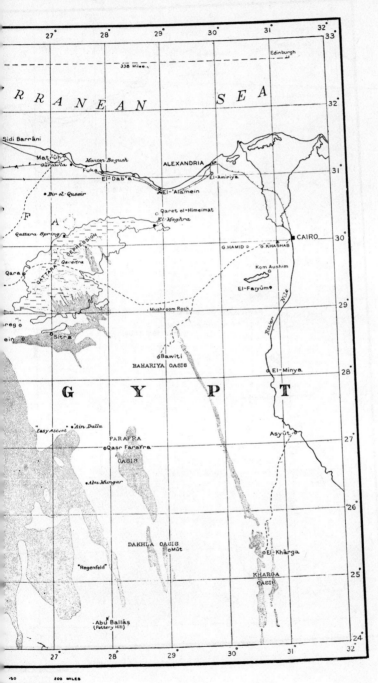

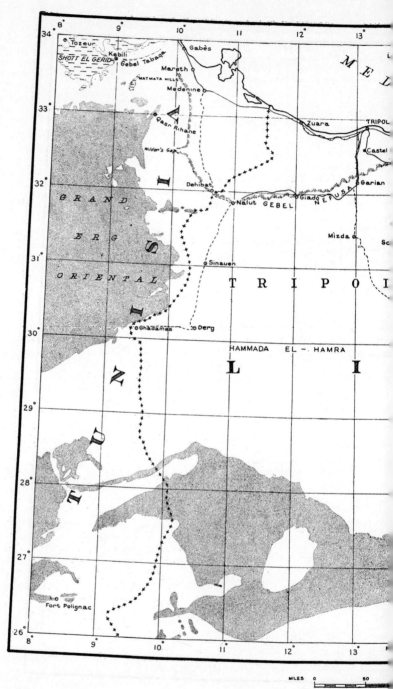

EGYPT AND

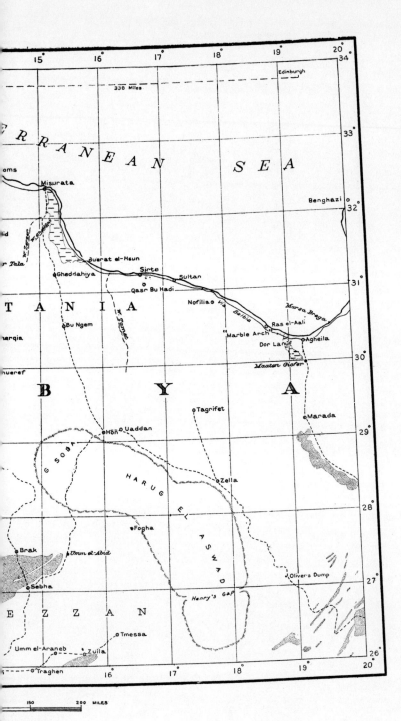

STERN SECTION

Long Range Desert Group

CHAPTER ONE

ORIGINS

IT IS a drab, faded, little book, bound in one of those unattractive colours which seem to be reserved for the publications of His Majesty's Stationery Office. On the outside cover is a stern warning about keeping it in safe custody and disclosing the contents only to authorised persons. It has no date but " internal evidence," as the critics would say, shows that it was published in 1919.

Its title is hardly more exciting than its appearance—" Report on the Military Geography of the North Western Desert of Egypt," by Captain Claud H. Williams, M.C., 1/1st Pembroke Yeomanry, attached No. 5 Light Car Patrol.

The first sentence of the Preface is commendably to the point : " The object of this report is to place on record any information in my possession, gathered in the course of desert patrolling during the past three years, that may be of military value in the future."

You will ask why I quote all this. I do so because on the experiences described in this book many of the achievements of the Long Range Desert Group were founded.

Few people now remember the Light Car Patrols. The men who made them are forgotten though some of their names are still on the maps : " Williams' Pass " ; " Ball and Moore (1917)," written alongside a desert route ; " Owston's Dump " ; " Davidson's Pass." The others have vanished before the proper conservatism of the official cartographers who have found Arabic equivalents for the old names. " James' Peak " is now " Qur Hadid " ; " Williams' Dunes " have become " Ghard Misa'ada"; and " Partridge's Gap " is " Fassulet Rammak." But though

11

their names may be forgotten they have a place in L.R.D.G. history.

In 1915, as in 1940, Egypt was in danger of attack from the west. Sayed Ahmed esh Sherif, the Senussi leader, had joined the Turks against the hated Italians, and at the end of 1915, with enemy money and equipment and directed by Turkish and German officers, the Senussi forces advanced as far as Matruh. For more than a year they threatened Egypt with invasion. The simplest way to deal with the threat might well have been to pay each Arab £5 a month more than he was being paid by the Germans, but Britain adopted more conventional methods of warfare and thousands of troops, badly needed in Palestine and elsewhere, were tied up in the Western Desert.

The greater part of these troops were horsed Yeomanry, unable to operate far away from ample supplies of water and fodder, so along the Mediterranean coast the Yeomanry engaged the Senussi while in the waterless desert of the interior the Light Car Patrols, specially organised and equipped for this sort of job, guarded the desert frontier and the oases. They were our pioneers. They invented the sun-compass and made the first condensers for their boiling radiators. With simple methods of survey they ran their traverses far into the desert, going out beyond the range of the old camel-explorers. The cars they used were Fords, the original Model T, certainly the best then available but hardly one which would be chosen to-day. Williams in his book praises the " oversize three and a half-inch tyres," a pathetic comparison with the ten-inch sand tyres which the L.R.D.G. always used. But in spite of all these difficulties the Light Car Patrols did their job, showing for the first time what cars could achieve in desert travel. It is a pity no one wrote their story.

But if men forget the desert remembers. Often during our journeys around the Qattara Depression or Bahariya or south-westwards towards 'Ain Dalla we would find the trace of their narrow wheel-tracks across the gravel or the black, rusted food-tins at their old camps.

In 1917 the Senussi were driven out of Egypt and the next

year the Light Car Patrols were disbanded. The desert lay undisturbed.

A quarter of a century later history was being repeated. From the west the Italians menaced Egypt. Though more mobile than the horse and camel-borne units who had fought each other in the Western Desert in the Great War, neither the Italians nor the British who opposed them could move their forces any great distance inland, for it was by sea and along the coastal roads and railways that they received their supplies.

But this time the inner desert was more important than in 1915. For the British in Egypt, in addition to a possible attack from the west, had to face the Italian armies on the east, in Eritrea and in Abyssinia. The Italian forces in the Middle East greatly outnumbered ours ; there were only 2500 British and 4500 Sudanese troops in the Sudan in 1940 with no tanks, seven aircraft and hardly any guns, whereas there were about 500,000 Italians in Abyssinia and it was only General Wavell's stupendous bluffing and his ability to move his small reserves between Egypt and the Sudan rapidly and at the right moment that saved the Middle East.

Communications between Egypt and the Sudan lay through the Red Sea, or along the Nile Valley—by train to Aswan, by river steamer from Aswan to Wadi Halfa, and thence southwards by train. At any moment the Red Sea might have been made unusable by the enemy navies and the Nile Valley route was open to attack from the west.

Seven hundred miles west of the Nile is the oasis of Kufra. There, secure from attack behind the twin barriers of Sand Sea and Gilf Kebir Plateau, with plentiful water and good communications to the coast and to Hon, the enemy could build up a considerable force. Beyond Kufra is 'Uweinat with its good though limited water and its landing grounds. From 'Uweinat to Wadi Halfa is a three days' run over excellent going. In the summer of 1940 a force of a hundred or two determined men could have attacked and taken Wadi Halfa, wrecked the dockyard and the railway workshops, sunk any river steamers or

barges and made a mess of the Egypt-Sudan line of communications at that point

From Kufra, too, is the line of approach to the Chad Province
of French Equatorial Africa through Sarra and Faya. And
through the Chad Province ran the West Africa-Middle East
air route, the chain of airfields between Takoradi and Cairo
along which so many hundreds of aircraft were flown
when the Mediterranean was closed. An Italian force moving
down from Kufra and, farther west, from Murzuk in June,
1940, winning over the hesitant French and capturing Fort
Lamy, would have been very hard to dislodge at a time when
we needed every man and truck for the defence of Egypt and
the Sudan.

So there was a real need to know what the enemy was doing
in the inner desert. Being Italian he was in fact doing nothing,
but we were not then entitled to gamble on that.

How was this need to be met? After the Light Car
Patrols had been disbanded official interest in the inner desert
lapsed and in the early summer of 1940 there was no military
force in Egypt capable of reaching Kufra from the Nile Valley.
But the nucleus from which such a force could be created did
exist.

For ten years and more before the Nazi war Major (now
Brigadier) R. A. Bagnold had been the acknowledged leader of
a small band of enthusiasts who found enjoyment in exploring the
Libyan Desert. Their expeditions, beginning in the late 'twenties
with week-end trips from Cairo to Siwa or Sinai, had grown
into large-scale explorations in the 'thirties, journeys of five
thousand and six thousand miles during which we covered
most of the desert between the Mediterranean and the northern
Sudan.

Our expeditions were all private ones, paid for by those who
took part in them, and they cost about £20 a head per thousand
miles. From so-called " official quarters," in a typically British
way, we received little or no attention, though I remember being
sought out in London during the Sanctions " flap " of 1935 by a

harassed staff officer from the War Office who asked me whether
I thought the Italians would be able to move an armoured force
along the escarpment from Sollum to Matruh. As I had never
seen an armoured force I expect my advice was of little value,
and in any case the problem was solved by a surrender to
Mussolini's blusterings. There was an exception, however, in the
Royal Geographical Society from whom we received constant
support and encouragement. The R.G.S. had a real share in
the successes of the L.R.D.G.

During those years we re-learned the lessons of the Light
Car Patrols and added new knowledge of our own. Bagnold
perfected the sun-compass, invented rope-ladders (now replaced by sand-mats) and steel channels (of which more later)
for " unsticking " cars from sand, and with them forced his
way far into the Sand Sea which Williams and his men had
hardly touched.

About thirty men and women shared in those pre-war
journeys, but six or eight of them had a much greater knowledge
of the desert than the rest, having served for many years in Egypt
with the Army or, like Clayton, in the Egyptian Government
Survey. At the outbreak of war with Italy only one or two of
these men had been sent to the Middle East. None were engaged
in work directly connected with the desert. Had the Germans
been in our place would they not have seen the war with Italy
as at least a very considerable probability, have gathered these
men together and set them to work in the country of which they
knew so much ?

In fact it was a fortunate accident which brought L.R.D.G.
into being. In October, 1939, Bagnold was on his way from
England to take up some routine post in East Africa. In the
Mediterranean, still open as Italy had not yet come down from
her seat on the fence, his ship was involved in a collision and put
into Alexandria for repairs. During the delay Bagnold visited
Cairo where General Wavell heard of his arrival and had him
transferred to his own Command.

You may read in the newspapers of a year or two later, when

they were first allowed to write about L.R.D.G., that the moment Italy declared war the Army sent for Bagnold, the man who knew more than any one else about sand, saying to him, " Make us a Long Range Desert Group." The only true part of this tale is about the sand.[1]

In November, 1939, and again in January, 1940, Bagnold made proposals for such a force but it was not until after Italy had declared war on June 10th, that his scheme was adopted. On this third occasion Bagnold put forward his plans on June 19th ; on the 23rd they were approved ; on August 5th L.R.P.[2] left Cairo on its first training trip and on the 27th was ready for action. But much had happened before then.

At the beginning of the war I was in Palestine in the Colonial Service. In September, 1939, I had written to the Middle East Command offering to serve in an area of which I had much experience, but had been told that it was considered inadvisable to take me off the job I was then doing—which was helping to censor the Palestine newspapers. In June, 1940, Bagnold came up to Jerusalem and asked me to join his new force. This was a chance which comes only once in a lifetime. Here was the Army proposing to pay me to do what I had spent a lot of time and money doing for myself before the war. In two weeks I was out of the Colonial Service and into the Army.

Meanwhile Bagnold had begun to collect a few more men who knew the Libyan Desert. Clayton soon arrived from Tanganyika. He had spent eighteen years in the Egyptian Desert Survey and had a knowledge of the desert which was unsurpassed. Of the other " desert trippers " of pre-war days Harding Newman was in Egypt but the Military Mission would not let him go, and Prendergast was in England and did not join us till six months later. But Bagnold had found Mitford, an R.T.R. officer who

---

[1] I refer those who wish to know just *why* sand gets into their bully stew to *The Physics of Blown Sand and Desert Dunes* by R. A. Bagnold, O.B.E., F.R.S. (Methuen, 1941.)

[2] During the first six months the unit was called " Long Range Patrols," but for the sake of clearness I have used the title L.R.D.G throughout.

knew Egypt well, and who, besides Clayton, was one of the few
Englishmen who had been to Kufra.

Arrival in Cairo put time back ten years. It was just like the
preparation for a " Bagnold Trip " in the 'thirties and the same
friends helped us as they had helped us then. Since maps of
Libya and suitable technical equipment were not at the time
available from Army resources Rowntree printed the maps for
us at Giza, we borrowed theodolites from Black at the Physical
Department or from Murray at the Desert Surveys, and
Harding Newman " wangled " sun-compasses for us out of the
Egyptian Army. When we wanted information we went to
Hatton or Bather at the Egyptian Frontiers Administration or to
Jennings Bramly at Burg el 'Arab. Shapiro at Ford's did rush
jobs on the cars ; school-mistresses gave us books of Log. Tables
and racing men their field-glasses, and in half-forgotten shops in
the back-streets of Cairo we searched for a hundred and one (to
the Army) unorthodox needs.

The first big problems were men and machines. All our early
journeys had been made with Ford 15-cwt. " pick-ups," first the
Model T, then the Model A, the best car Ford ever made, and
later with the V 8's. Though the load which these could carry
was enough to give a range of twelve hundred odd miles for peace-
time exploring, their capacity was far too small for the guns,
ammunition, mines and all the paraphernalia of war, and so
Bagnold proposed to use 30-cwt. trucks. I was doubtful if these
would be able to cross the sand seas over which we should have
to operate, but Bagnold was right. The huge tyres now made—
we used 10.50 × 16's—and the higher horse-power engines
enabled us to cross almost any dunes with loads up to two
tons.

The Army had no suitable cars in Egypt but Bagnold and
Harding Newman managed to collect them ; some from the
Chevrolet Company in Alexandria and others from the Egyptian
Army. At Ordnance Brigadier Richards, a very good friend to
L.R.D.G., gave us a high priority for the necessary alterations
and by the middle of August all were ready.

R.D.G.

After machines men. The New Zealand Command in the Middle East were asked if they would provide officers and men for three patrols and on the 1st July they agreed to do so. It must have been a hard decision to take. It involved a small but continuous liability against their own then scanty forces, and also the placing of New Zealand troops directly under British command. I think they never regretted the decision ; certainly no one else ever did.

A newspaper article once described L.R.D.G. as "the bravest, toughest and brainiest unit of Britain's great desert army." "When," it went on, "the decision was taken to organise the Long Range Desert Group for operations behind the enemy lines a call was sent out to all units of the desert army for volunteers. The call stated ' only men who do not mind a hard life, with scanty food, little water and lots of discomfort, men who possess stamina and initiative, need apply.' "

The second sentence is hardly accurate as the initial recruiting was confined to a few units only, and modesty compels a denial of the first, but the qualities were some of those we needed. Brains, initiative, reliability, endurance and courage were probably of equal importance, though the L.R.D.G. man did not need his courage so often as the unfortunate infantryman suffering constant bombing and shelling up on the coast. But when, caught by enemy aircraft in open desert, he did need it—he needed it badly. Toughness without intelligence was of no use to us, nor was extreme youth essential; speaking without statistics I should say that the twenty-five-year-olds or the nearer-thirties lasted longest and did best.

There can be no doubt whatever that much of the early and continued success of L.R.D.G. was due to the speed and thoroughness with which the New Zealanders learned desert work and life. For it is not enough to have learned how to operate, in the military sense, in the desert, though that may be half of the battle. Naturally the driver must be able to drive in conditions entirely new to him, the signalman to keep in touch, the navigator to find his way, the gunner to have his sand-filled Vickers ready for instant use. But there is more to it than that. To exist at all in the Qattara Depression or in the Sand Sea in June or in the Gebel Akhdar in February is in itself a science which practice develops into an art. The problem is to make yourself so much master over the appalling difficulties of Nature—heat, thirst, cold, rain, fatigue—that, overcoming these, you yet have physical energy and mental resilience to deal with the greater object, the winning of the war, as the task presents itself from day to day.

Most of the first New Zealanders were from the Divisional Cavalry—the " Div. Cav."—farmers or the like in civil life, and with a maturity and independence not found in Britishers[1] of similar age. Physically their own fine country had made them on the average fitter than us, and they had that inherent superiority which in most of a man's qualities the countryman will always have over the townsman. Many were owner-drivers at home and therefore naturally disposed to take care of their cars ; regarding them as a thing to be preserved rather than, as was sometimes the British attitude, as the property of an abstract entity, " the Government," whose loss or destruction was small concern of theirs.

I had never met New Zealanders before ; all the knowledge I had of them were my father's words of the last war—that they were the finest of the troops from the Dominions. Closer acquaintance showed that one should always believe one's father. To me they always seemed to have a real sense of what our Empire could be to them. The untravelled Englishman, so long as he gets them, is little interested where his bread and butter comes from. The New Zealander on the contrary has a very real appreciation of where his butter (and mutton) go to. And it is not merely commercially that he sees what the Empire stands for. How often have I heard a man express the hope that after the war he might have a chance to go to England—to " home." To hear a New

---

[1] There seems to be no word for " dwellers in the United Kingdom." Throughout this book only the context will show whether " British " means this or " men of the British Commonwealth of Nations."

Zealand farmer's comment on the Labour Government one would imagine that the country could look forward to nothing but instant and utter ruin, but having discounted all that it seemed to me, an outsider, that New Zealand approached most nearly to that true democracy which so many of us profess to be fighting for and which so few understand.

Occasionally it fell to a British officer to command a New Zealand patrol. Knowing the conventional opinion held by the New Zealanders of the average Englishman this was a task approached with some misgivings. But if you could show that your first object was to get on with the job, and that you knew as much or even a little more than they did about doing it, then the patrol, awarding perhaps the high praise that you were " not such a bad sort of bastard after all," would achieve all and more than you could ask. And to distract attention from your own shortcomings you could always resort to a diversion—to start a discussion on the relative merits of the North Island and the South Island or invite, if you had time to spare, a description of pig hunting in the woods round Lake Waikikamukau.

In the L.R.D.G. we had one immense advantage—all our men were volunteers drawn, at times, from as many as fifty units of the Army. There was never any lack of them and always a long waiting list ; in the early days it was said that a vacancy was worth a " fiver." It was common enough for men to go down in rank when they joined. Captains came as lieutenants ; sergeants as privates ; driver-mechanics gave up their trade pay. The best stayed for years ; the worst left very quickly. For example, an unhappy choice who arrived in Siwa one Christmas Day. By evening he was calling the Second in Command by his Christian name ; worse—being familiar with the Sergeant-Major; worse still—telling his future patrol just how L.R.D.G. work should be done. It was a surprised and injured man who left for Matruh at 7.30 a.m. on Boxing Day.

A balance sheet of serving in the L.R.D.G., drawn up from the point of view of the average soldier, would probably read something like this :

Assets.	*Liabilities.*
The best food in the Middle East.	The strain of operating almost continually behind the enemy's lines.
A job which was always interesting and often exciting.	Never returning to base for a long refit and rest, and suffering as a result from weariness, desert sores and occasional *cafard*.
Almost complete freedom from drills, guards and fatigues.	
A minimum of being "mucked about."	

Living as we usually did two hundred miles or more from the nearest other troops and being under direct command of either Middle East[1] or Eighth Army, we escaped those periodical inspections which involved other units in days of feverish preparation and a two-hour wait on a hot parade ground until the (relatively) Great Man arrived. I recollect being inspected once by a Secretary of State for War and twice by a Commander-in-Chief, Middle East. Lesser mortals, such as Divisional or Brigade Commanders, did not bother us.

[1] I use the phrase "Middle East" both in its geographical sense, i.e. the countries of the Middle East and also, as all the Army used it, to mean G.H.Q. Middle East in Cairo. The context will usually make it clear in which sense it is used.

CHAPTER TWO

PREPARATION

HAVING found men and vehicles the next thing was to turn them into a fighting force. There were so many things to be arranged —training in cross-desert driving, special equipment, alterations to the cars, navigation, rations, signals, Intelligence.

The Military Historian will find the War Establishment for L.R.D.G. in the archives of Middle East H.Q. Briefly, the first (L.R.P.) patrols consisted of two officers, about thirty men, eleven trucks, eleven machine-guns, four Boys anti-tank rifles, one 37 mm. Bofors gun, with pistols and rifles to taste. Later on we got better arms and many more of them. The Lewis gave way to Brownings and Vickers K's, and the Boys and Bofors to .5 Vickers and 20 mm. Bredas. And later the patrols were halved in size to become one officer and 15-18 men in five cars, the whole unit being organised as : Group H.Q. ; " A " (New Zealand) Squadron ; " B " (Guards, Rhodesian and Yeomanry) Squadron ; Signal Troop, and L.R.S.[1]

The alterations to the trucks were based on the experience of pre-war journeys of exploration—more leaves in the springs ; condensers for the radiators ; doors, windscreens and hoods removed ; and special fittings for wireless, guns, water-containers, sand-channels and the rest. The trucks, so-called 30 cwts., actually carried something like two tons, with a standard range (in time) of three weeks' rations and water and (in distance) of 1100 miles without re-fuelling. One truck in each patrol carried a Bofors or Breda gun mounted in the back ; machine-guns, as the photographs in this book show, were mounted on a central pillar or on tube mountings round the sides of the cars. At the beginning Bagnold made experiments in armouring the trucks

[1] Light Repair Squadron R.A.O.C.

but the extra weight of metal reduced the range of action so much that he abandoned the idea.

Knowing that we should often get no fresh meat or bread or vegetables for weeks or months on end we needed a special ration scale. In the back numbers of the *Geographical Journal* were the scales which Craig and Harding-Newman, the quartermasters of our peace-time journeys, had drawn up, and which long experience had proved to be admirable. Using these and the kinds of food provided by the Army in the Middle East I increased the amounts of some, reduced others, and sent the result to the medical people.[1] They returned it saying that the calorific value was 5000 (or was it 500?) points too high but that as " most of it would probably be lost in inefficient cooking " the scale was approved, and so it remained till the end. Later on, David Stirling's men, all the British troops in Kufra, and one or two other units who could manage it, got themselves put on the L.R.D.G. ration scale, to the envy of those who had failed to do so.

Most men in L.R.D.G. were specialists in something and of all these experts the signalmen were probably the most important, though the navigators ran them close. For what was primarily a reconnaissance unit good signals were essential. Without them a patrol, three or four hundred miles away from its base, could neither send back vital information nor receive fresh orders. If signals failed the best thing to do was to come home.

And looking back now I realise how seldom they did fail. We were far too often unkind to the signalmen. We cursed them for having to halt at given times to " come up " for Group H.Q.; we disliked their poles and aerials which might advertise to the enemy the presence of a patrol ; we scoffed at their atmospherics, skip-distances and interferences ; we blamed them when they could not " get through " and when the ciphers would not come out ; we were impatient of their " check and repeats," forgetting the regularity with which they kept communication.

Lack of rainfall and wind erosion—the climatic influences

[1] See Appendix 5.

which, after thousands of years, have formed the desert landscape
—have deprived it of recognisable landmarks by which one can
find one's way about and therefore a L.R.D.G. patrol had to be
able to navigate as a sailor does at sea. Navigation and the
teaching of navigators were my special concern and a subject to
which, so it seemed, the Army had given no thought or training.
Do not mistake navigation for map-reading. Map-reading is
fully taught in the Army, but map-reading presupposes maps and
in Libya there was the rub. A map of the country in which
L.R.D.G. worked would have delighted him who wrote :

> " I never see a map but I'm away
>   On all the journeys that I long to do,
>   Over the mountains which are marked in grey,
>   Up all the rivers which are shown in blue,
>   And into those white spaces where they say—
>   Unknown." [1]

The country was divided into four classes :
(1) A little, well mapped, all in Egypt.
(2) A lot, badly mapped, all in Libya.
(3) Some of which maps had been printed but with nothing
on them.
(4) Some of which no maps existed, at any rate not on a scale
at which one could plot a course.

In the beginning, for the country west of the Egyptian
frontier, we had only the blank sheets printed for us at the
Survey of Egypt or the reproductions of captured Italian maps.
The former naturally had nothing on them ; the latter far too
much.

The Italian maps of Libya must, I think, reflect the Italian
national character in its aspects of bombast and self-assurance.
There was no nonsense about the petty details of topography on

---

[1] In spite of diligent inquiry I have been unable to trace the author or the
original version of these lines which I may have misquoted.

these sheets. Many of them were obviously based on air observation (but not on air survey), and after a few flights across the country the cartographer had roughed in a range of mountains here and a sand sea or two there. The mountains were all high as became the dignity of Fascist Italy. Making our way anxiously towards an obviously impassable range of hills, we would find that we had driven over it without feeling the bump. But I have a certain grudging admiration for Captain Marchesi of the Instituto Geografico Militare, the equivalent of our Ordnance Survey, who made the 1/100,000 map of Jalo. Marchesi, I am sure, was a realist. Jalo, he felt, was a one-eyed hole of which no map was really needed. The sand was soft and the day hot, so why worry? Marchesi put his feet up on the mess table, shouted for another drink, and drew his map. It is just possible that the absurd inaccuracies were a deep plot to mislead our attacking forces, but it seems hardly likely that the Italians had thought of that as long ago as 1931.

In time, after repeated journeys, we began to collect enough material to make our own maps. Map sheets conforming to the Egyptian 1/500,000 series now extend across Libya : look at the bottom of the sheet and on many of them you will find, below the " Compilation Diagram," the words " Surveyed by L.R.D.G." This became more true after Lazarus had joined us. Bagnold had applied for a Survey officer R.E. to be attached to L.R.D.G. and in the summer of 1941 he materialised in the form of Ken Lazarus, a Colonial Office surveyor in peace-time, who had been doing work for the gunners in East Africa and Abyssinia since the war began. There cannot be many instances of continued survey work behind the enemy lines in war-time. Lazarus with his small Survey Section of two or three cars would go out from Kufra or Siwa and return weeks later with enough material to add a new sheet to the maps of Libya which we were making for the Italians.

Besides topography my other main job was Intelligence. The *Concise Oxford Dictionary* contains the definition " Intelligence Department, engaged in collecting information especially for military purposes." At Middle East, in so far as Libya was con-

cerned, the collection was not a very extensive one in the summer
of 1940. It would seem elementary to have copies of all the
standard works of reference, geographical journals, and military
histories published by a country with which there was every
chance of one shortly going to war, and also to have at least one
copy of all the maps which that country had issued. But coming
from Palestine to Cairo in July I could find at Middle East no
copies of books which, as a matter of course, I had at home, and
the Survey of Egypt were the only people who had a full set of
maps. In two years' time our Intelligence work in Libya, and
particularly at the H.Q. of the Eighth Army, was probably as
good as anywhere in the world, but at the beginning there seemed
to have been a great lack of foresight and preparation.

Nothing in the way of Intelligence interests the modern
commander more than " going." In the L.R.D.G. no question
was asked us more often than " What's the going like there ? "
To deal with this and other geographical problems there was
created in 1941 a special section of the " I " branch at Middle
East called G.S.I. (Topo.),[1] which Stuart Menteith soon turned
into a very efficient concern. In the inner desert and far into
Libya most of his information came from L.R.D.G. For the
areas nearer the coast he used other sources and by the end of
1941 had produced good coloured maps of all the country from
Sirte to the Nile.

Now there is no good reason that I know of why such maps
should not have been printed long before the war for all the
country east of the Libyan frontier. The Egyptians would not
have prevented us. Who would ? And even inside Libya much
might have been done. There are several customary methods by
which nations spy out each other's territory in peace-time.
Exploration and archæology are two of them, witness the survey
of Southern Palestine made by Newcombe, Lawrence and
Woolley in 1913 which provided Allenby with so much useful
information. Missionaries, scientific research and tourism are
others. The Italians themselves used all these against us in

---

[1] General Staff Intelligence (Topographical).

Arabia, Palestine and Abyssinia and they would have found it hard to object to a British Museum botanical expedition to central Cyrenaica or an investigation by the Royal Anthropological Institute of the skulls of the Arabs of Marmarica.

But if the British had done little the Italians, with far greater opportunities, had done less. There are well over fifty thousand Italians in Egypt with whom they should have been able to organise a superb system of intelligence, yet their information about the Western Desert army was pitiful, and about our forces in the Sudan in 1940 even worse.

Starting from scratch, in five weeks the L.R.D.G. had been created. I do not think that any one except Bagnold could have, achieved this. Some had the necessary knowledge of the Army, others the necessary experience of the desert, none had both. And what is more, I think no one had also the vision to see just what was needed for the job, backed by the driving power and the importunity to extract this from Middle East. Most of the people on the staff at G.H.Q. in Cairo with whom we had to deal were all out to help. But a few of them, accustomed to supplying the long-standardised wants of a peace-time army, found some of our requests difficult to understand. We asked, for example, for sandals while every one else wore boots ; for an Egyptian shop-keeper's whole stock of trouser-clips, because there was nothing else to be had for holding maps to map-boards ; for Nautical Almanacs, yet we were not sailors ; for 10-ton Diesel lorries, but we were not R.A.S.C. ; for a 4.5 howitzer, usually given only to Gunners ; for Arab head-dresses ; for an apparently scandalous quantity of tyres (most Army vehicles ran on roads or passable tracks) ; for two aircraft ; for a paraffin-worked refrigerator, to preserve the M.O.'s vaccines in the heat at Kufra.

Moreover in those early days the Staff were not very desert—or distance-minded—some wag nicknamed them the Short Range Desert Group. Once we had occasion to seek some new theodolites to replace losses in action. The officer who controlled them was indignant. What on earth did we want theodolites for ? Were we Sappers ? He himself had made a march of twenty miles in the Sinai Desert and using a prismatic compass had been only four hundred yards out at the end of his " plot." When we said that he would still have been five miles out at the end of four hundred he began to see the point.

Three years later, looking back to 1940, one saw how sound Bagnold's original conception had been. With a few minor changes the organisation had stood the test of time and battle. That was like Bagnold ; he did not make many mistakes. In the words of an exasperated New Zealander, sternly bidden on a hot August afternoon to abandon the pretence that he had just checked the pressure of his tyres and to pump them up to 25 lbs. front and 39 rear—" The trouble with this joker is that he's always —— well right."

CHAPTER THREE

FIRST SORTIES

By September, 1940, L.R.D.G. was ready for action, and from that date until the fall of Tripoli in January, 1943, there were few occasions when at least one patrol was not out in the desert, usually far behind the enemy's lines. As I have explained, L.R.D.G. was first formed to keep an eye on what the Italians were doing in the inner desert far south of the coast, and reconnaissance of one sort or another continued to be the most important part of our work. We could have risked, and sometimes did risk, a patrol in some desperate offensive action, but patrols took time to train and build up and to continue to do this would have entailed too heavy losses, working as we did with unarmoured cars and at such great distances from a base.

What sort of a country was it, this Libya, the finest specimen in Mussolini's collection of deserts, in which we were to spend most of the next three years?

The Libyan Desert is roughly the same size as India, an area twelve hundred miles by a thousand, with two natural boundaries —the Nile on the east and the Mediterranean on the north, and two artificial ones—the beginning of the sub-desert country of the Sudan in about latitude 16° and the Tibesti Mountains on the south, and the political frontier of Libya on the west. The northern half, down to about latitude 26°, is limestone and the southern half sandstone. Above the generally flat desert surface rise the plateau of the Gilf Kebir, the six thousand foot massif of Gebel 'Uweinat and the rough basalts of Gebel Soda and the Harug el Aswad. Huge areas are covered by sand seas—those called Egyptian, Kalansho, Rebiana and Murzuk, the first about the size of Ireland and all normally regarded as impassable to cars.

Enough rain falls each year to make a fairly fertile coastal

29

strip, twenty miles wide in Tripolitania and in the Gebel Akhdar and narrowing to a mile or two at 'Agheila and 'Alamein. Over the rest of the desert no rain falls except an occasional local thunderstorm once every ten or twenty years. Scattered over it are a number of oases, fed by artesian water, ranging from poverty-stricken hollows like Zella or Tazerbo to the magnificent date-groves of Dakhla and Siwa. The population is confined to the oases and the coastal strip, at an average density of about one man to the square mile, and is mostly Arab in the north and mixed Arab and negro in the south.

The sun shines on most days, shrivelling you to a cinder in summer and putting but little warmth into the winter winds. The temperature may reach 120° F. in the shade in June and fall a degree or two below freezing in winter. A country which recalls the Arab saying, " When God made the Sudan he laughed."

That is a dull, text-book description of the Libyan Desert which will not, I fear, give the reader that picture of the desert which I should like to put into his mind. I cannot describe the desert effectively in words ; photographs show flatly and without contrast no more than a fraction of its immensity, and I have met only one artist who could paint its shapes and colours.

There are really two deserts in Libya, or one semi-desert and one real desert. The former is the narrow strip along the Medi-terannean where the Eighth Army fought and sweated and shivered ; where the wheels of a hundred thousand vehicles had churned the clay surface to a fine powder which relentlessly made its way into eyes, nose, mouth, hair, food, engines and guns ; where swarms of flies made life a burden. Early in the war this strip came to be called the Western Desert—inaccurately, for the western desert of Egypt is all the country west of the Nile, but the name stuck and cannot be changed now. Most men who fought there hated it and will carry that hatred all their lives.

But not one man in a thousand had been fifty miles south of the coast into the real desert in which L.R.D.G. operated and which, to make this story plain, should have some distinctive name of its own—The Wilderness, The Solitude, The Waste. The desert, as Dan said of the sea, is all right in the middle : the edges are the sorrowful parts.

Although in it one saw Nature at her hardest, yet it was a country which many of us, I think, in time began to love. Its attraction for me was that it was so clean. Clean of people, and there are many dirty ones, in every sense of the word, in the Middle East : clean of flies : clean sand instead of clay or lime-stone dust. Also because it was quiet, at times so silent that you found yourself listening for something to hear. And it was beautiful too, not at midday when the hills look flat and lifeless, but in the early morning or late evening when they throw cool, dark shadows and the low sun makes you marvel at the splendid symmetry of the yellow dunes. A psychologist would say, perhaps, that to take pleasure in deserts is a form of escapism, a surrender to the same impulses which made hermits of the early Christians, a refusal to face the unpleasant realities of modern life. He may be right; there are a lot of things in this life worth escaping from, even if only for half an hour at the end of the day's run of an L.R.D.G. patrol.

I have read nothing that conveys better the pleasant feeling of isolation which the real desert induces than the words of my friend, Douglas Newbold, written in an account[1] of his explorations in the southern Libyan desert in 1923 :

"The knowledge that there were no human beings save vagrant shepherds within several days' march, and that these rocky uplands were as untrodden as the craters of the moon produced a feeling of remoteness from human affairs, such as has inspired the climbers of peaks . . . to endless flights of fancy. There is no better description of the sensation than the few words in stiff Latin of Professor Conrad Gesner who, led to mountaineering in the middle of the XVIth century by his study of mountain vegetation, wrote :

"'Nihil hic auribus molestum esse potest, nihil im-

[1] "A Desert Odyssey of a Thousand Miles," *Sudan Notes and Records,* Vol. VII., No. 1.

portunum, nulli tumultus aut strepitus urbani, nullae hominum
rixae. Hic in profundo et religioso quodam silentio ex prealtis
montium jugis ipsam fere celestium si quae est orbium
harmoniam exaudire tibi videberis.' "

I think it is difficult for any one who lives in an European
climate and who has never seen a real desert to form a picture
of just what it is like. It may help to realise that in a country
where rain never falls there are none of those things which are
directly attributable to rain—streams, lakes, hedges, woods,
crops, river-valleys—nor any of those which are indirectly the
consequence of it—roads, villages, towns, railways, canals. The
result of thousands of years of this sort of climate has been to
produce a landscape in which cars can move in most directions
at will, restricted only to a relatively small degree by escarpments
and sand seas.

But Libya had not always been like this. Ten thousand years
ago the climate was kinder, there was more rain and men lived
in what is now desert, hunting ostrich and antelope and keeping
milk cattle. Often we found traces of them—paintings and
engravings on the rocks and stone implements at their camping
places. Then the climate began to change, the rainfall failed
and the desert people moved in to the oases or the Nile Valley.
There must be many places which we passed through on L.R.D.G.
journeys where no man had been for five thousand years.

Clayton was the first to cross the Libyan frontier. It was
known that all the supplies for the garrisons at Kufra and
'Uweinat went down from Jalo and he wanted to get on to the
track and see something of the traffic. Instead of crossing the
Sand Sea from 'Ain Dalla he decided to go from Siwa to Two
Hills. This route leads through some of the worst of the Sea but
Clayton knew it well from his surveys south of Siwa and from
the days when he was demarcating the international boundary
in 1929. So he went to Siwa by way of Matruh, arriving incognito
as " Captain Smith." The Italians were then in Jaghbub and if

they had heard that Clayton who, as their Intelligence ought to have told them, was believed to be in Tanganyika, was actually in Siwa, they might well have started adding two and two together. But Siwa knew Clayton as well as Clayton knew Siwa and I doubt if the incognito deceived any one.

At Siwa he borrowed six trucks of the Egyptian Frontiers Administration to help as petrol carriers for the first part of the journey. The Sudanese crews were happy to get a trip into the desert and worked like blacks (which they were) in " unsticking " the cars in the next few days. The precise point on the map at which they turned back to Siwa is not recorded and they may, or may not, have been the only Egyptian Army troops to operate in Italian territory during the war.

By August 11th Clayton had crossed the Sand Sea to Two Hills and, pushing into unexplored country, was making discoveries that were to be of great use to us later on.

For a hundred miles westwards from the edge of the Egyptian Sand Sea stretches a level gravel plain of excellent going. Having crossed this Clayton found himself in another Sea of which we had never heard. The Italians may have known of it but they never troubled to show it on their maps and certainly had never crossed it. All day on the 12th Clayton's party forced their way through these new sands, over range after range of complicated dune lines with unpleasant cross-dunes in the valleys. By evening they were near the western edge along which runs the Jalo-Kufra route and here for three days in the hottest weather of 1940 they kept a 24-hour watch.

Why they saw nothing we only learned some time later. The beaconed route with tall iron posts at every kilometre does run along the edge of the sands, but when continued use cut up the gravel surface and made it soft the Italians had gradually abandoned this and started to use a line farther and farther west and as much as twenty miles from the beacons. But though he saw no traffic the discoveries of this reconnaissance were some of the most useful that L.R.D.G. ever made. For many months afterwards, coming from both Cairo and Siwa, we used this route

R.D.G.

across the gravel plain guarded by the horseshoe of sands to the north. Across it we used to pass between Siwa and Kufra in 1941 ; over it ran the Kufra-Siwa air route with its chain of landing grounds and emergency dumps of water ; in 1942 Easonsmith's raid on Barce and Mayne's attacks against the enemy's lines of communication before 'Alamein profited by this knowledge.

One other short reconnaissance made at this time is worth mentioning, not so much for its results, which were small, but for the originality of the idea, which was Clayton's.

We were anxious to know what the Italians were doing at 'Uweinat ; in what strength they held their two posts and to what extent they were using the landing grounds. A reconnaissance by car would be difficult to carry out unseen, for the bad going close to the mountain forces one to keep some distance out on the plain where cars can easily be spotted by sentries. The ideal method would be on foot, but in the heat of August the distances to be covered made this out of the question, so Clayton fell back on the idea of using camel transport. But as the camel would have had to cross three or four hundred miles of arid desert before reaching the objective he bought a camel in Kharga, folded it into a lorry and sent it off, peering disdainfully over the tail-board, to 'Uweinat. Two Arabs went with it, old employees of Clayton's in his surveys before the war. They stayed there a week, obtained some useful though negative information, packed their camel into the lorry again and returned safely to the Nile.

Before we could operate in the area round Kufra and 'Uweinat we had to make dumps of supplies along the Libyan frontier for the distance from Cairo was too great to send out patrols self-contained from there. So while Clayton was going out west from Siwa I took .the 6-ton Marmon-Harringtons of the Heavy Section to make a dump of petrol beyond 'Ain Dalla on the edge of the Sand Sea.

It was almost exactly ten years since I had been at 'Ain Dalla. Then we had come from Bahariya in three Ford cars, a party of six men under Bagnold. We had hoped to get right across the

Sand Sea to the Gilf Kebir but the southern sands had defeated us. However, we did force our way sixty miles west of 'Ain Dalla, beyond the line of Rohlfs' route in 1874, and far enough to show that at any rate along this latitude the dunes were not impassable.

The place had not changed in ten years. There were the same stunted palms, the same rickety wooden hut where we had stored our spare petrol in 1930, and the same pipe tapping the warm spring water half-way down the slope. Across the soft gravel of the wide depression in which the spring lies I could see the narrow wheel tracks of our former visit leading to the point where we had struggled up the northern cliffs.

In the months to come 'Ain Dalla was of immense advantage to L.R.D.G. Many will remember with pleasure the sweet waters of its unfailing spring on blistering summer days, but greater still was its strategical importance. The 'Ain Dalla route was our " underground road " to Libya ; a patrol could leave Cairo, pass by the Pyramids and disappear over the shoulder of Gebel Khashab with the certainty that till it was over the frontier it could travel unseen. And 'Ain Dalla was the junction of the routes to Kufra via Big Cairn and to 'Uweinat via Pottery Hill, both guarded by sand seas which the Italians would never expect us to cross.

This time we had a bathe at the spring and pushed on westwards towards the Sand Sea. In 1932, Clayton had found a way up the western cliffs of the depression on to the desert plateau on which the Sand Sea lies, and named it " Easy Ascent." So it was to his small party of Fords, but after some months use by L.R.D.G. the sand slopes broke up and Clayton swore that he would never put the word " easy " on his maps again. Even now it was too steep for the Marmon-Harringtons, so we made a dump at the foot of the pass, well hidden behind an outlying rock. Easy Ascent dump was used till April, 1941, whenever patrols went across the Sand Sea, and according to the Dump Book there are still 1200 gallons of petrol there for any one who cares to collect them.

We still had another trip to make to pick up the rest of the

3500 gallons of petrol at Mushroom Rock where the three patrols, which had come, but with us, on a training run from Cairo, had dumped their surplus petrol. On the second journey southwards to 'Ain Dalla one of the Marmon-Harringtons cracked its main chassis member. I went on with the other two cars, intending to return and ferry the load forward for I thought that we should have to abandon the broken vehicle where it was. However, I did not know New Zealanders, still less "Arch" McLeod, a year later "A" Squadron staff-sergeant fitter and I dare swear the best fitter in the Middle East. The next day we were washing at 'Ain Dalla when there was a distant roaring towards the eastern cliffs and out of the haze came the abandoned truck. McLeod had cut a bit off the tail of the chassis, plated the crack and hurried after us only a few hours behind.

And so back to Cairo.

At the beginning of September L.R.D.G. set out on its first big job.

The Italians, after three months of hesitation, had at last shown some initiative and advanced across the Egyptian frontier to Sidi Barrani. In the inner desert they might also be on the move and so Bagnold planned a thorough examination of all the routes leading to Kufra from north and south. By watching the tracks and traffic and by taking prisoners if possible he hoped to learn what the Italians were doing. All three patrols were taking part.

I was with Bagnold and his small H.Q. party, and with us was Mitford's W patrol. On September 5th we left Cairo by the usual route to 'Ain Dalla, filled up there with water and with petrol at Easy Ascent. Easy Ascent was still easy and all fourteen trucks got quickly to the top where we slept. At dawn next day Bagnold and I started ahead to pick a route. Across "El Qantara"—the Bridge between two wide sand-filled basins—and for fifteen miles beyond was easy going over gravel and flat sand. Then at one of Clayton's small survey cairns on a ridge-top we hit the first great "breaker" of the Sand Sea.

There is nothing like these sand seas anywhere else in the world. Take an area the size of Ireland and cover it with sand. Go on pouring sand on to it till it is two, three or four hundred feet deep. Then with a giant's rake score the sand into ridges and valleys running north-north-west and south-south-east, and with the ridges, at their highest, five hundred feet from trough to crest.

Late in the evening when the sands cool quickly and the dunes throw long shadows the Sand Sea is one of the most lovely things in the world ; no words can properly describe the beauty of those sweeping curves of sand. At a summer midday when the sun beats down all its shapes to one flat glare of sand and the sand-drift blows off the dune crests like the snow-plume off Everest, it is as good an imitation of Hell as one could devise. It was across 150 miles of this dead world that Bagnold was proposing to take for the first time a force of heavily loaded trucks.

To begin with it was easy. In the morning when the shadows fall you can see the shape of the dunes and steer accordingly ; but by nine o'clock the shadows have vanished and only the feeling of the pit of your stomach tells whether you are going up or down.

Then I had to remember the lessons of five years before, of the last time I had been here when we made the first crossing from 'Uweinat to Siwa. Gradually I recalled them—always keep height so that you can turn downhill when a soft patch comes and profit by the slope to get through it ; ribbed sand, butter-yellow, is generally hard and safe ; shining purplish patches are usually liquid bogs ; never brake hard to stop or the wheels will dig in ; change down early before the slope begins and charge it in second gear. When we passed out of the stony ground we could let down the tyres so that the lower pressure gave an extra inch or two on the bearing surface of the tread. It was a common belief that the sand was harder in the early morning but the real explanation was that at that time the tyre pressure was lower ; in the heat of midday the pressure would rise considerably.

After twenty miles we came to a huge dune barrier, a mile wide and three hundred feet high, in which there seemed to be no gap. Bagnold decided to rush it and went at speed for a low place in the crest. Being an old hand at this game he slowed at the top and so could turn sharply and stop at the brink of the fifty-foot precipice where the west-facing slope of soft sand fell away below. When you know how to do it you can topple the car gently over the edges of these slopes and plough down them, axle-deep and in first gear, to the bottom, But in a flying leap from the crest the car turns over and over and in the next two years one man was killed and a back and more than one limb broken on these unseen sand slopes.

So we turned south and hunted for a gap in the dune range, finding one which took us a few miles farther on, only to be held up again for two hours and more while the patrol pushed its way across a soft patch between two high crests.

By now we were through the country where there were gravel patches between the dunes. The whole world was sand, millions of tons of it, and no stone, no bush, nothing living save an occasional Painted Lady butterfly and a few pied wagtails (why always wagtails?) whose life in this coverless waste must have been made a misery by the hawks which live always in the dunes and prey on the passing migrants.

In their arrangement the dunes form a repetition sequence. From the summit you plough down a mile-long slope with many soft patches to the foot of the next range to the west, then turn north or south searching for a crestless slope which will lead over the next range, up this and then through the whole process again.

For the leading cars " sticks " were frequent and inevitable. At one moment you would be doing a steady thirty miles an hour to the reassuring whine of the tyres; the next halted dead in five yards with the car up to its axle in a dry " quicksand." Then to continue to use the engine in low gear was fatal for the back wheels would dig a grave from which release could only be achieved by unloading. The first thing was to decide whether to go back or forwards to the nearest patch of " solid " ground. Then, using sand channels and sand mats and with a dozen sweating and cursing men, the truck would be extricated two yards at a time.

In the Western Desert during the war thousands of Army cars carried slung alongside them a pair of these ∧_____∧ section, perforated steel channels yet probably not one man in as many thousands knew their origin, so for the sake of history I record it here.

In the spring of 1926 Bagnold had been up to Jerusalem from Cairo by car across the Sinai Desert and in the Mitla Hills through which the pass led up from the Canal he had trouble in crossing the steep-sided water runnels. Before setting out on another journey some months later he looked round for a solution :

> " It was thought that the best answer to the difficulty of the vertical water banks would be to carry light portable ramps to be laid like bridges for the wheels, so as to avoid the necessity of digging down the banks to make a road. After unsuccessful experiments with corrugated iron beaten into channels Bader discovered, by nosing round among the old-iron shops of Cairo, a stock of strong rolled-steel troughing designed in the war for roofing dug-outs. We bought a couple of these, five feet long, to carry with us. Actually the road was found to be so much improved that the channels were not wanted once. They were carried home and lay about at the back of the mess garage for the next three years till accidentally, as shall be told, they paved the way very literally for our later expeditions."[1]

That was in 1929, in the eastern edge of the Sand Sea near 'Ain Dalla when :

> " Every few miles one or other of the two lorries would get stuck in the soft ground, the back wheels sinking in and merely spinning round, digging themselves even deeper as long as they were forced to turn. If it had not been for these old steel channels we must have given up after the first three days and gone back to Cairo. They were the salvation of the

[1] R. A. Bagnold, *Libyan Sands*.

expedition. They proved an unfailing way of extricating a car or lorry which no amount of pushing could move. The mode of operations was as follows. With our hands or with shovels sloping grooves were dug out between the front wheels and the back, reaching down to the lowest point of the back tyres sunk in the ground. In these grooves the channels were laid with their rearmost ends almost underneath the tyres. Then, when the clutch was let in, the back wheels at once began to grip firmly on the steel on which they rolled forward easily up the slope. By the time the front ends of the channels were reached, the lorry had attained sufficient momentum to carry it for some distance beyond. The great thing was to keep the speed up once it had started moving." [1]

We used these original channels of Bader's over thousands of miles before the war. Now I think they are lost and have missed what ought to be their final resting place—the Imperial War Museum.

[1] *Middle East General Order 108, published 4.2.44.*

108. INVENTIONS.

    In accordance with para. 3, Standing Orders for War, M.E.F., it is recorded that Brig. R. A. BAGNOLD developed, in collaboration with other officers as stated below, the following inventions or applications of existing principles to military purposes :

(a) *Sand Channels.*

    Devised in 1929 and subsequently adopted, with modifications, as standard desert equipment.

(b) *Sand Mats.*

    Devised in 1929 in collaboration with Major P. A. CLAYTON, in the form of rope ladders with bamboo rungs, subsequently modified by the substitution of canvas for rope, and adopted as standard desert equipment.

(c) *Sun Compasses and Land Navigation.*

    Designed for land navigation and used by Brig. BAGNOLD in 1927. The original form of precision instrument has been used by specialist desert units since 1940, and was the forerunner of the modified designs which have been generally used for desert course setting.

    Brig. BAGNOLD collaborated with Lt.-Col. V. F. CRAIG and Maj. W. B. KENNEDY SHAW in formulating precision methods of desert navigation and route plotting.

(d) *Expansion Tank for Conservation of Radiator Water.*

    Used by Brig. BAGNOLD in 1926, and subsequently adopted as standard desert equipment.

(e) *Composite Ration Pack.*

    The use of a ration pack to provide a varied daily ration for a standard small number of men was instigated by Brig. BAGNOLD for specialist desert units in 1940, and this principle has since been generally adopted.

After about a hundred miles from 'Ain Dalla the dunes become lower and you enter an area of rolling sand " downs " and the last twenty miles are easy, fast going with no " sticks."

It took us two days' hard work to get to Big Cairn on the western edge of the Sea. Here on the Libyan frontier Clayton had built his last survey cairn when he carried his triangulation across from 'Ain Dalla in 1932. The dunes peter out into the gravel plain between the two sand seas, with Big Cairn five feet high and conspicuous because it is the only feature in a featureless waste.

Here we unloaded all the spare water and petrol and while Bagnold stayed to mark out a landing ground Mitford took his patrol back for another load from Easy Ascent.

It is only in this latitude, in a belt ten or twenty miles wide, that the Sea is reasonably easy to cross from east to west. Farther south near the Gilf Kebir and north near Siwa the high sand ranges would make this impossible. Our tracks were still easy to see but would vanish in the first wind, and I wanted to mark this route permanently. Coming across we had put empty petrol tins on every crest and strewn our camp rubbish along the way, and to make the route still clearer I collected boxes of stones at Big Cairn and from the back of a truck tossed them out the whole 150 miles back to Easy Ascent, dropping one just as the last went out of sight. On the sand a stone the size of a fist shows up for two hundred yards ; the sand never blows over it and so the route was marked for all time. Coming back with full loads we did the crossing in six and a quarter hours.

While we were ferrying supplies across from 'Ain Dalla Clayton and Steele had been moving 7000 gallons of petrol through the most difficult part of the Sand Sea from Siwa to Big Cairn. There all the patrols parted ; Clayton set off for Tekro and the French frontier, 600 miles away; Mitford for the area north of Kufra, and the long-suffering Steele turned back to Siwa for another load.

I went with Mitford. Across the gravel plain to the eastern edge of the Kalansho Sand Sea was easy going, but on the morrow when we were in the sands began what were, I think, the three most unpleasant days of my life.

After sixteen years in the Middle East I was beginning to think that I knew something about heat. I had had some experience—five years in the Sudan ; the Red Sea in the hot weather ; a summer at Beisan in the Jordan Valley 300 feet below sea level ; Cairo to Khartoum by train in June—all these had qualified me to lie against any one about the temperatures I had known. But I had not before this met a Libyan *qibli*.

Many countries have their hot winds ; the *khamsin* of Egypt, the *sherqiya* of Palestine, the *harmattan* of West Africa. Add all these together and blow them, with sand to taste, northwards out of the gates of Hell and you may begin to know what the *qibli* is like at Kufra in the summer.

You don't merely feel hot, you don't merely feel tired, you feel as if every bit of energy had left you, as if your brain was thrusting its way through the top of your head and you want to lie in a stupor till the accursed sun has gone down.

It started on September 16th. All that day we struggled across the Kalansho sands and at evening reached the Jalo-Kufra track. The next day was worse, for a southerly sandstorm blew as well and the driving grains pricked face and legs like needles. We visited two of the landing grounds on the Jalo-Kufra air route and wrecked the petrol pumps, fuel tanks and wind indicators, the latter small iron aircraft pivoting to the wind on a pipe. No Italians were moving on such a revolting day. West of L.G.3 is a crashed aircraft with the fuselage set up on end, a landmark for miles around. I remember we spent midday at the base of it, crouching under tarpaulins stretched between the cars for shade.

Up on the coast, where the wheels of ten thousand vehicles had churned up the desert surface, dust-storms were common enough and made life a misery, but in the real desert of the south sandstorms, which in fiction so often overwhelm the hapless caravan, are less frequent and fairly harmless, especially if they come on a north wind.

The worst I ever experienced, on the west side of the Gilf Kebir in April, 1935, was blowing in gusts of up to 60 m.p.h., but though it whipped our skin and took the paint off the cars, we could travel for most of the day with the sun-compass, for the sand grains are heavy and rise only 10-20 feet above the ground. and so cannot darken the sun as does a dust-storm in the north.

In Siwa in the summer of 1942 we had a dust-storm the like of which even the oldest inhabitants could not remember. It came about six in the evening, a solid wall of " cloud " 2000 feet high, stretching from horizon to horizon, pouring down the northern scarp into the depression. It hit " A " Squadron mess first, a mile north of the Rest House where we were living, and they telephoned saying it was too dark to read. With us all was still. A moment later it had reached us, as a 40 m.p.h. storm of fine dust, penetrating everywhere and bringing the thermometer, which had been 102° at tea-time, down to 80° in a few moments.

Having judged from the car tracks the amount of traffic on the Jalo-Kufra route we moved on westwards to examine that between Tazerbo and Marada. That afternoon was, I think, the worst of all. At camp, Beech was slightly delirious from heat-stroke and I remember Croucher, who was navigating in the second car behind Mitford, telling me that for the last twenty miles he found himself saying, to the rhythm of the tyres on the sand, " If he doesn't stop I shall go mad. If he doesn't stop I shall go mad. If he doesn't . . ."

After supper on days like this many men would be sick, for one's stomach refused to carry on under such conditions, and we had not then learned the anti-*qibli* pick-me-up, equal parts of rum and lime-juice, invented, I think, by the Rhodesian patrol coming down from Big Cairn to Kufra in May, 1941, when they met what was probably the worst *qibli* in L.R.D.G. history. In 1940 we had Chevrolets, but the Rhodesians were then in cab-over-engine Fords in which the hot blast from the engine swept straight up into your face and the engine casing had to be insulated to prevent the skin from being burnt off your leg.

The water ration was then six pints a day, one in tea at breakfast, two in tea in the evening, one in lime-juice at lunch, and two in your water-bottle to be drunk at will. In winter this would have been ample, and good enough in ordinary summer weather, but now it seemed nothing. In those days conversation was an interesting thermometer. When the temperature reached a certain height drink became the only topic and each man had his own ideas about making his water ration go further. There were the small sippers and the large gulpers. One would put his water out on a tin plate in the shade and accept loss by evaporation in exchange for the resulting coolness ; another would save up for a drink of Eno's and water in the evening and a third spare a few drops to wet a handkerchief to put against the back of his neck. A more elaborate plan was to have a Thermos which, left open to cool its contents by night, gave a cold drink the following day.

The water consumption of the cars was kept at a minimum by a simple condenser. From the top of the radiator, the overflow pipe of which was blocked up, a rubber tube led into a two-gallon can bolted to the running-board and half-filled with water. When the water in the radiator boiled the steam condensed in this can, and when it had ceased boiling the vacuum in the radiator would suck the water back and fill it up again. If all the joints were air-tight there would be no need to " top up " the radiator for hundreds of miles.

The next day we turned south towards Tazerbo. The track was marked every kilometre with posts, ten foot high angle-irons which threw a patch of shade about three inches wide. This was the time of the autumn migration and at the foot of every post was a bird, crouched and gasping. Most of them were some sort of dove or pigeon and on those three days they must have died in thousands. The moment we stopped they flew under the cars in dozens, striving to find shelter from the terrible sun and wind. We put water out for them but they seldom drank it ; they seemed to have decided, rightly, that it was not worth the effort to keep alive, and died.

Two days later, on September 20th, L.R.D.G. went into action for the first time in the bloodless battle of Landing Ground No. 7. While we were following the track to Kufra near the L.G. there appeared, churning slowly through the soft sand, two six-ton lorries of the firm of Trucci and Monti, the fortnightly convoy to Kufra.

One burst of Lewis gunfire over their heads ended that great battle and we had our first prisoners—two Italians, five Arabs and a goat, and our first booty—2500 gallons of petrol, a nice line in cheap haberdashery and, best of all, the bag of official mail. As a result of this incident the Italians, as we learned later, gave a ground and air escort to all convoys to Kufra, thus wasting vehicles, aircraft and fuel which they could have used better elsewhere.

In the days that followed we rejoined Bagnold and " R " patrol at Wadi er Riquba ; hid the Trucci lorries in the Gilf Kebir where they still are ; were seen but not attacked by the Italian Air Force from Kufra and joined up with Clayton for a reconnaissance in force of 'Uweinat.

Near Wadi Sura Ballantyne and I left the patrols to take the prisoners and mail back to Cairo. With three trucks we cut through the Gilf Gap and up to Pottery Hill, heading for 'Ain Dalla. This was a fascinating journey for me as from Pottery Hill to 'Ain Dalla I had to find a way over country which no cars had ever crossed before and which had only been partly explored by camel, by Rohlfs in 1874 and by Wingate working out from Dakhla in 1933.

Sixty miles north of Pottery Hill we passed Rohlfs' cairn at Regenfeld where, more than half a century earlier, one of the strangest events in Libyan exploration had taken place. In 1874 the German Rohlfs, the greatest of the camel-explorers of last century, set out from Dakhla to reach Kufra. Sixty miles west of Dakhla he struck the edge of the Sand Sea, the nature of which was then quite unknown. The dunes run north and south and Rohlfs, travelling westwards, had to cross one of these 300-foot high sand ranges every few miles. For some days he struggled on, until at a point 110 miles from Dakhla he halted to rest his camels for a day. The outlook was gloomy, the country ahead was unknown, the camels were tiring and water running short, there seemed no alternative but to return. Then, while Rohlfs and his two companions, Zittel, the scientist, and Jordans the surveyor, were debating what they should do, it began to rain. This was little short of a miracle for no cautious meteorologist would predict that rain will fall in the inner desert more often than once in about twenty years. But on that February day in 1874 it poured ; the Germans filled their water tanks, watered their camels, and abandoning hope of ever reaching Kufra, turned northwards along the dune lines to Siwa. Rohlfs named the place " Rainfield " and on a low ridge between the dune lines built his cairn.

With little trouble we found a new route to 'Ain Dalla which was used regularly by the patrols for the rest of that autumn.

In Cairo we delivered the prisoners to the Detention Barracks at Abbassia. Tommy Farr of 216 Squadron had come back with us ; he had accompanied the patrol from Cairo nominally to prospect for suitable landing grounds, but actually as part of a plan of Bagnold's to make the R.A.F. more inner-desert-minded against the day when we might need their help during our operations. With a month's beard he might have been mistaken for anything and the sergeant-major at the barracks, pointing to him, asked me, " Is that one of your prisoners, sir ? " Like a slow-witted fool I answered, " No, that is a R.A.F. officer," otherwise we might have had the laugh on Tommy from the wrong side of the prison bars.

The capture of the Kufra mail gave us a reputation rather out of proportion to the value of its contents. From Cairo to Kufra is 650 miles in a straight line, farther than from Land's End to John o' Groats. The story got about. " Good Lord," said the Staff, " how do these fellows do it ? " In clubs and messes the tale became exaggerated. People asked it if were true that we had raided Graziani's headquarters up on the coast and stolen his ciphers. And so it laid for us the foundation of a reputation which we never lost.

We got a pat on the back from one whose praise we valued :

GENERAL HEADQUARTERS,
MIDDLE EAST,
CAIRO.
1st October, 1940.

DEAR BAGNOLD,

I should like you to convey to the officers and other ranks under your command my congratulations and appreciation of the successful results of the recent patrols carried out by your unit in Central Libya.

I am aware of the extreme physical difficulties which had to be overcome, particularly the intense heat.

That your operation, involving as it did 150,000 truck miles, has been brought to so successful a conclusion indicates a standard of efficiency in preparation and execution of which you, your officers and men may be justly proud.

A full report of your exploits has already been telegraphed to the War Office, and I wish you all the best of luck in your continued operations, in which you will be making an important contribution towards keeping Italian forces in back areas on the alert and adding to the anxieties and difficulties of our enemy.

Yours sincerely,

A. P. WAVELL.

Meanwhile the patrols were out again. Mitford went off to attack 'Uweinat where among the giant boulders at the base of the six-thousand-foot mountain were two Italian posts, at 'Ain Zwaya on the west and 'Ain Dua on the south. At each *'ain* there is good water and a landing ground, and this made 'Uweinat a useful base for the enemy. From it they could chase our patrols, send aircraft across the Sudan to Eritrea and keep an eye on the French down towards Faya.

Mitford was spotted by aircraft before he got to 'Ain Dua and bombed for an hour or more but had no casualties. Air attack was the one real danger to L.R.D.G. ; this was the first time we had experienced it and Mitford was fortunate, for in the next three years we came to learn how destructive and unpleasant it could be.

There is little cover in the desert where there is no vegetation and where the sand-charged wind rounds off all the natural features into smooth shapes which give no shadow. Moving cars, throwing up dust, are easy to spot, but if you could hear or see the aircraft first and stop, you would probably escape notice for stationary trucks are hard to pick up. Taking it all round we were amazingly lucky. Again and again I have heard men tell how aircraft passed over them unseeing when they had heard them first and halted or when they themselves had stopped for a moment for some trivial reason.

What you did when the pilot had spotted you depended on the country. If it was broken you could wedge the cars into small gullies or between rocks where they were difficult to see and to hit when seen, and where the men could find cover. Bombing never did much harm ; the casualties always came from ground straffing. If the patrol's fire was hot enough it might keep the enemy high up and prevent him from pressing home the attack, but it takes a good man to keep his gun going from an unarmoured truck against a fighter diving to attack. Yet it was done often enough.

When caught by aircraft in flat, featureless desert the plan was to keep moving and to split the patrol up and watch what the enemy would do. If he bombed it was fairly easy. The driver kept moving with a spotter up on top of the truck behind, and when the latter saw the bomber getting on his line or the bombs begin to fall he shouted, the driver turned sharply right or left and all might be well.

Mitford attacked 'Ain Dua on October 31st and found it held by a small garrison of Libyan troops in a strong natural position In the morning and again in the afternoon a detachment of

W patrol on foot fought a hide-and-seek battle among the house-size boulders, while from out on the plain the Bofors and the Boys rifles kept the enemy's heads down. A number of them were killed and wounded : L.R.D.G. had no losses and gained for Sutherland the first New Zealand M.C. of the war and for Willcox the M.M.

It was part of Bagnold's plan to keep the enemy guessing where L.R.D.G. would turn up next, and so the day before Mitford's skirmish at 'Ain Dua Clayton, five hundred miles away to the north, attacked the fort at Aujila. The unfortunate Italians could not reasonably expect us to turn up there and when Clayton appeared a Libyan soldier strolled out to greet him and was too astounded to speak when told to hand over his arms. A couple of Bofors shells into the fort sent a cloud of pigeons out of the tower and the Italian garrison over the back wall, scuttling to the palm groves. A few days before Clayton had pushed up north-west of Aujila to mine the road within seventy miles of Agedabia ; this, as we learned a year afterwards, destroyed half a dozen or more Italian trucks. A week later he was back in Cairo, having travelled 2100 miles in 15 days.

We had one last crack at 'Uweinat that autumn. In November Steele went down with R patrol to mine the route to Kufra and see what else he could pick up. On the western landing ground he found a Savoia S.79 bomber and burnt it, as well as 8000 gallons of petrol in drums stacked nearby. A faint popping from the garrison at 'Ain Zwaya was the only Italian reaction. Buried in the sand a mile or two away were three tons of aircraft bombs and Steele, who always liked playing with explosives, had a day out.

The spring at 'Ain Zwaya is not at the foot of the mountain but three-quarters of an hour's climb up a boulder-strewn gorge. The Italians had run a pipe down from the spring to a tank on the plain and, as we knew from the prisoners taken in September, kept a small pumping party up at the top. So while Steele was burning bombs and bombers I went off with three men in an attempt to cross the mountain on foot from the north and capture

R.D.G.

a couple of the pumpmen for the sake of the information they could provide.

It is easy to underestimate the difficulty of climbing on 'Uweinat though I should have known better. Bagnold and I had tried to reach the top in 1930 but started our climb too far to the east to cover the distance in the one day available. In 1932 we succeeded, much to the annoyance of the Italians when they found our summit cairn three years later on what they thought was the first ascent. The western end is heartbreaking climbing. The huge smooth boulders are as big as cottages and you spend hours, making little forward progress, scrambling over them and groping in the caverns in between. This time we spent two days and two nights on the mountain but failed to get to the spring in time and had to turn back to keep a rendezvous with Steele.

Meanwhile in Cairo Bagnold had been doubling the unit. In December a Guards patrol, half Coldstream and half Scots, was formed under Crichton-Stuart ; McCraith collected a Yeomanry patrol from the Cavalry Division in Palestine and Holliman took over the Rhodesians.

Holliman had spent September down south with the Marmon-Harrington six-tonners adding to the line of dumps along the Libyan frontier. Before the war his journey would have been a major expedition ; he went by rail to Aswan, drove along the west bank of the Nile to Wadi Halfa, and then started ferrying petrol four hundred miles across the desert to the Gilf Kebir where we needed a dump for operations south of Kufra.

The transport of petrol for long distances over bad going was a difficult problem. Until the capture of Benghazi for the second time gave us a supply of German " Jerricans," we carried our petrol in four-gallon, non-returnable tins, packed two to a wooden case. At the beginning of the Libyan war, when wood for cases was plentiful, this method was fairly satisfactory, but later on, when the strong wooden cases were replaced by cardboard boxes or by plywood crates the loss of petrol by leakage was very high. Sand stuck to the damp tins and made a sort of grinding paste ; this and careless loading at railhead and at dumps soon punctured the thin metal. Twenty-five per cent was a normal loss and on long journeys across rough country it would be much higher : enough petrol must have been wasted in the Western Desert in this way to run all the buses in London for months or years.

The four-gallon petrol tin, the *safiyha* of Egypt or the *tanaki* of Palestine, is one of the commonest objects of everyday life in the Middle East. It meets many needs—to bring water from the village well ; to grow aspidistras on verandas ; to provide the raw material for the tinsmith ; to build houses in " tin-town " slums. For all these and many other uses it is as well suited as it is unsuitable for the transport of petrol in a desert war. It was unfortunate that the Army had equipped itself in peace-time only for a war in England where petrol-pumps abound.

The strong, unleaking, returnable " Jerrican," by contrast, is an outstanding example of intelligent design followed by good production. We, or the Americans, imitated it with the " Amerrican," but omitted to copy the most important item—a good pouring lip. The " Jerrican " had one disadvantage ; it provided no wood for cooking meals.

Holliman picked up his petrol at Wadi Halfa. It was probable that the Italians had a spy there—they were fools if they had not —and the departure of some thousands of gallons of M.T. petrol into the desert might make him think. So it was explained in Wadi Halfa that the petrol was being sent out for the use of the R.A.F. at the landing ground at Selima and was therefore packed in aviation spirit cases. Unfortunately this proved too much for the local agent of the Shell Company who knew very well that aviation petrol must go into boxes marked aviation. He filled them accordingly which was not so good for our engines when the mistake was discovered later on. To add to the deception Holliman and his party were fitted out with R.A.F. caps, the only characteristic part of their nondescript clothing.

A stranger meeting a L.R.D.G. patrol returning from a month's trip in Libya would have been hard put to it to decide to what race or army, let alone to what unit, they belonged. In winter the use of battle dress made for some uniformity, but in summer, with a month-old beard thick with sand, with a month's dirt (for the water ration allowed no washing), skin burnt to the colour of coffee, and clad in nothing but a pair of torn shorts and *chapplies* (the N.W. Frontier pattern sandals imported by Bagnold) a man looked like a creature from some other world.

It was interesting to watch all the established ideas about sunstroke being exploded. At the beginning we were given the large, quilted army topees, which on their first trip inevitably fell beneath a case of rations or a gun magazine and were reduced to pulp. Then we tried the Arab head-dress of *kafiya* and *aqal* which were good for keeping out driving sand but stuffy in the hot weather and apt to get entangled in the engine or in guns. Finally most men, in summer as well as in winter, used nothing more than " caps, comforter " with few if any cases of sunstroke resulting, though heatstroke was another matter.

CHAPTER FOUR[1]

MURZUK

BETWEEN September and November of 1940 we had harried the Italians from Jalo in the north to 'Uweinat in the south. The next time we appeared in that area they would presumably be more ready for us, and Bagnold was looking round for new targets.

In July and August, far away in the French Central African colonies, heated discussions had been taking place. Petain had signed the armistice with the Huns in June, and in Africa soldiers and civil servants were wavering. Generally speaking, the older men with more to lose were for Vichy, and the younger for de Gaulle.

At the end of August a *coup d'état*, in which Général de Larminat and Capitaine Moitessier were the leaders, had scotched the Vichy-istes at Brazzaville, but some weeks before M. Eboué, the stout-hearted Governor of the Chad Province, had declared for de Gaulle. Colonel d'Ornano, Capitaine de Guillebon and the younger officers were wholeheartedly with M. Eboué, and the visit of General de Gaulle himself in October set the seal to their enthusiasm.

In November Bagnold, with the idea of a raid on the Fezzan in mind, went to Fort Lamy, the headquarters of the Chad Province. His proposal for a combined Anglo-French operation was greeted with enthusiasm ; d'Ornano, commanding the troops at Fort Lamy, was determined to go on the raid himself. The French in Chad wanted to take some immediate step to implement their recent change of politics by military action against the Italians, and to justify themselves in the eyes of their own people

[1] I am indebted to Major M. D. D. Crichton-Stuart, M.C., Scots Guards, for allowing me to read his account of the Murzuk operations which has not yet been published.

and of the native population. They would show the world, and the " gens de Vichy " in the other French colonies, that the Free French in Equatoria had both the will and the means to fight.

Bagnold and d'Ornano quickly got to details and before he left Fort Lamy Bagnold had written out the operation order for the raid into the Fezzan.

The main objective was to be Murzuk, a thousand miles as the crow flies from Cairo and 350 from the nearest French post in Tibesti. Murzuk is the capital of the Fezzan, in time past a great centre of Saharan trade. To-day its trade has dwindled to nothing but it is an important garrison town and road junction.

At such a distance from our bases the raid could be nothing more than a " hit and run " affair ; even if we took Murzuk we could not hope to hold it for more than a day or two. But in addition to the damage we might do the raid would make the Italians waste petrol, transport and aircraft in chasing us out again.

We had a fair idea of what we should find at Murzuk—a native town with two or three thousand inhabitants, a small fort, two or three aircraft at the aerodrome and a garrison of about fifty Italians and a hundred and fifty Libyan troops. Various Italian books on the Fezzan gave a rough idea of the layout of the town and barracks, and I had got some useful information from Libyan prisoners of war taken at Sidi Barrani early in December, at the beginning of Wavell's spectacular advance into Libya.

On the afternoon of December 26th G and T patrols left Cairo. Clayton commanded T patrol and the whole force and Crichton-Stuart the Guards. In all there were seventy-six men and twenty-three cars.

Outside Cairo on the Mena road Anderson, the Senussi Liaison Officer, was waiting for us with Sheikh 'Abd el Galil Seif en Nasr. After the Italo-Turkish war of 1911 the Arabs in Libya resisted Italian penetration long and bitterly ; at the beginning of the Great War they drove them back to the shelter of a few towns on the coast and when the Italians began to reconquer the country in 1922 the Arabs took up arms again. During all that time the Seif en Nasr family were among the leaders. They are the paramount chiefs of the great nomad tribe, the Awlad Suleiman, with a name for courage and leadership which still lives in Tripolitania.

'Abd el Galil himself was the veteran of a score of battles. It was the desperate charge of five hundred horsemen of the Awlad Suleiman led by him and his brother which turned the tide at Qasr bu Hadi in 1915 and gave the Arabs the victory over the Italians. He had fought his last fight at Garet el Hawaria north of Kufra, where in January, 1931, the power of the Senussi in Libya was finally broken. Then the family had been forced to flee from Libya and for the last ten years 'Abd el Galil had been living in Egypt. His brother, Ahmed, had taken refuge with the French in Chad, and at that time was raising a *goum* from among his followers to fight the Italians again.

At that stage in the war there could be no question of inciting the Fezzan tribes to rise against the Italians. An unsupported rebellion would do more harm than good, and in any case the fighting qualities of the sedentary Fezzazna are almost negligible. We took the Sheikh with us partly as a guide and partly because we hoped it would disturb the Italians if the news got round— " 'Abd el Galil Seif en Nasr is back."

Edmundson, the New Zealand M.O., had a spare seat in his car so 'Abd el Galil rode with him. A big man, sixty years or more, with a fine, fierce face which reminded me of Kennington's pictures in the *Seven Pillars of Wisdom*, and with one claw-like hand shot to pieces in some desert battle, he chewed tobacco and spat incessantly and the doctor's temper for the day varied with the direction of the wind.

For me nothing ever dulled the excitement of those departures from Cairo in the autumn of 1940 when we had our base there. The change from the town to the desert was instantaneous, dramatic. Yesterday you were enjoying the very considerable comforts of war-time Cairo. To-day from Abbassia or the Citadel you drove through the crowded streets, along the Mena causeway, past the hideous architecture of the roadside villas, past the gardens and mango-groves, past the camels and dragomen at the Pyramids, through Mena camp on to the Faiyum road, and off the road again to the northern shoulder of Gebel Khashab. In the soft ground round the Gebel a car or two would be sure to stick ; during a fortnight in Cairo the drivers had lost their " hands," and waiting for them to come on you looked back to the Nile Valley—on the right the Pyramids, behind them the green streak of the richest soil in the world, beyond again the tall houses of Cairo with Saladin's Citadel above them, and, filling the eastern horizon, the cave-riddled Moqattam Hills.

Driving on when the trucks had been " unstuck " in half a mile you were in another world. A treeless, plantless, waterless, manless world, almost featureless too save for poor, nondescript Gebel Hamid ahead, appearing and disappearing over the rolling gravel, and farther on the long dune lines of Qatania and Rammak, their saw-toothed sand peaks like a string of battleships in line ahead at sea.

From Cairo we followed the well-known route to 'Ain Dalla, up Easy Ascent—not so easy now that it had been cut up with the passing of many cars—across the Sand Sea to Big Cairn to refuel there from the dumps laid down in September. Then the sands had been scorching by day; now it was bitterly cold and there was ice on water-bottles at dawn. From Big Cairn across the dividing *serir*, through the second Sand Sea of Kalansho, over the Kufra track unseen, and then in country unknown to us through the sands north-west of Tazerbo.

On the tenth day we reached a point a hundred miles south-east of Wau el Kebir. From there Clayton went south to Kayugi to collect the Free French party and the petrol which they had brought for us by camel over the mountains from Bardai.

While Clayton was away I took three cars of T patrol to map the Italian route believed to run from Wau el Kebir through the Eghei Mountains to Kufra. As the map shows, north-south lines of communication are good in Libya, but east-west are bad, hindered by the basalts of the Harug and by the Dohone Plateau which stretches north-east from Tibesti. For many years the only known route westwards from Kufra lay round the Rebiana Sand Sea north of Tazerbo and then to Bir Ma'aruf and Wau el Kebir. But we had heard rumours of a new route which the Italians had found through the Eghei Mountains, and in March, 1940, Monod, the Saharan explorer, sent up by the French on camels from Tibesti, had found their car tracks and the lines of empty *fusti* which marked the Tereneghei Pass. This route might be useful to us in future operations and if the Murzuk raid failed and we had to " beat it," a withdrawal through the hills would be more pleasant, with aircraft overhead, than across the bare Kalansho gravels.

We traced the route eastwards half-way through the hills, but then, following the wrong track, branched off for fifty miles to the south and had no time to finish the job.

In the Tereneghei Pass, where the Italian route cuts through the mountains, Monod had found a deposit of amazonite, an attractive green stone which was the " emerald " of the Garamantes who, according to Herodotus, were the ancient inhabitants of the Fezzan. The deposit had been worked since very early times and the Tibbu still use it to obtain material to make crude pendants and amulets. I had hoped to be able to visit the place but our wrong turn prevented us. A year later Lazarus surveyed the pass more accurately and brought back some specimens of the " emeralds."

It was a good trip : the Eghei Mountains, a jumble of sandstone, basalt and granite, are a blank on the maps and one of the few unexplored areas of North Africa. Except for the Italians' tracks we saw no sign of life ; even the Tibbu seldom visit these barren hills.

When we got back to camp, Clayton and the French were there—Lieut.-Colonel d'Ornano commanding the troops in Chad, a " Beau Geste " figure, tall, monocled, in turban and burnous ; Capitaine Massu from Zouar and Lieutenant Egenspiler from Fort Lamy, and with them two French sergeants and five native troops.

On January 8th we started again for Murzuk. The original plan had been to attack Wau el Kebir first where there was a small post, but Clayton wisely decided against this for it was essential to reach Murzuk while the Italians were quite unaware that we were even in Libya.

The next day, moving north between Wau el Kebir and Wau en Namus we saw the first men since leaving Cairo, three wandering Tibbu with their camels. The chances of their bothering to go in to the nearest Italian post and report us were very slight, but we kept half a mile away and sent one of the French natives, also a Tibbu, over to them to say that we were an Italian patrol seeking a new route between Wau en Namus and Fogha.

'Abd el Galil was quiet and sad all that day and I thought he must be unwell, but he explained that we had passed a place where, years before, the Italians had shot eleven of his tribesmen. In the past, in years of good rains, they had grazed their camels over this country, but the Italians, wishing to keep a tight grip on these nomads who were their chief opponents, had since then forced them to move up north nearer to the coast.

Late on the 9th there was a hitch, for we struck very fresh lorry tracks on a beaconed route north of Tmessa. We were still 150 miles from Murzuk and any enemy who came along this route again could not fail to see our tracks. So we turned back without crossing and camped a mile away, and at dawn all twenty-three cars were driven across the route following exactly in each other's tracks, and then a party of men, walking backwards, swept over the wheel-marks with the skirts of their sheepskin coats while others scattered gravel to restore the desert surface. When it was finished our car tracks were almost invisible but the job took too long to do often.

It is said that a nomad Arab will look at a month-old camel track and tell you that it was made by a white Bishari she-camel five months gone in calf and ridden by a middle-aged Arab missing two fingers of his left hand! We could not claim such precise gynæcological data regarding our Italian opponents, but car-track lore was important in L.R.D.G. Age and direction were the two vital points. The sharpness of the tread-impressions and the steepness of the sides of the track marks told you their age, and on sand you could guess the direction from the small ridges thrown up alongside the wheel marks. And on uneven ground with small drainage lines the track marks were rather wider where the weight of the car had flattened the tyre as it hit the bottom of a short slope, and this showed whether the car was moving up or down hill. In broken country where the going was difficult one could be certain of the direction of travel by following the tracks for a mile or two and noticing small obstacles crossed by the driver who had come upon them unseen but which he would have swerved to avoid if, approaching from the opposite direction, 'he had noticed them some distance ahead.

I remember one visitor to Kufra being sceptical of the knowledge we claimed. Dick Croucher took him out in a car near the landing ground to demonstrate but he remained unconvinced, and finally disputed hotly Dick's assertion that the track before them ran from left to right. Dick persisted, but the visitor would not agree. " How can you be so certain ? " he demanded. " Well," said Dick, rather bored by this time, " it was made by that car standing there in which we have just driven out."

On the morning of January 11th, still unseen, we hit the Sebha road ten miles north of Murzuk. From a ridge a few miles farther south we could see the palms and, what was better still, the wireless masts at the fort and the roof of the hangar. Not a soul was in sight so we picketed and mined the road on the Sebha side and had an undisturbed lunch, while Clayton made his last plans and I built a sand-plan of Murzuk from what could be seen and from what I already knew.

While this was going on the sentry reported aircraft. There was a moment of despair that we should be discovered at the last minute of the eleventh hour, but, as we learned later, it was only a bomber returning from a flight to Ghat.

Lunch over, we set off to finish the last two miles of the journey which had begun in Cairo eighteen days and 1500 miles before. Clayton led in his 15-cwt., then Hewson with one troop of " T " patrol, and then the rest—a quiet procession of cars, down the scarp on which we had halted, through some broken ground, over a low ridge and into the outskirts of the town. I wondered if the Italians had had the foresight to put even one machine-gun post on the Sebha road. Luckily they had not, and we had achieved the advice of their own Machiavelli :

"Those enterprises are best which can be concealed up to the moment of their fulfilment."

The road seemed to lead to the fort so Clayton followed it. At a well by the roadside a group of natives gave the Fascist salute and cried " Bon giorno." A little farther Clayton overtook Signor Colicchia, the postmaster, bicycling towards the fort, and hustled the terrified official on to his car as a guide. Ahead I could now see the fort, partly hidden by trees and with some after-lunch strollers around it. The surprise was complete.

Then things began to happen. Hewson swung off the road to the left and opened fire on the strollers ; the Guards turned to the right and started to engage the fort. I was with Bruce Ballantyne with the other half of T patrol who were to tackle the airfield. The hangar was now out of sight, so from a group of natives outside a hut I seized a Sudani for a guide and pushed him on to the truck. No doubt he thought he was going to be murdered and he was paler than I should have thought a black man could be. He was too scared to speak and soon fell off, but by now we could see the hangar and were racing to beat the landing ground guards to their machine-gun posts. Bruce with two trucks got there first and most of them surrendered without firing, but he killed the last man, still fumbling with his rifle, with a quick shot through the head.

Out of the corner of my eye during this confusion I had seen Clayton's car crossing the aerodrome and wondered how he had got there. A few minutes later he joined us with his car full of bullet holes and d'Ornano's body in the back. Round the corner of the hangar he had run into a machine-gun post which one of the bolder Italians had manned. Beside him, in the front seat, Adams's Vickers gun had jammed, and before Clayton could slam the gears into reverse d'Ornano on the back had been killed with a bullet through the throat and also an Italian Air Force sergeant whom Clayton, having handed over the postmaster, had roped in as another guide. No doubt the Italians thought we had shot him in cold blood, but this is the truth about his death.

We got the Bofors going on to the gun post and the hangar and before long the twenty odd Italians had had enough of it and one of them appeared on the roof waving a white flag. Three dead or dying Libyans and one wounded Italian were their casualties. In the middle of it all I remember seeing, shuffling with half-bent knees across the landing ground, that so familiar African sight, a string of old women carrying firewood bundles on their heads.

Meanwhile at the fort, where Hewson had been killed and Wilson and three other men wounded, the patrols were successfully containing the garrison and a lucky mortar bomb had set the tower ablaze and burnt the flag and flagstaff. In the middle of the attack a touring car drove up to the gate. In it was the Italian commander who had probably been out to lunch and also, as some said afterwards, a woman and child. One shell from the Guards Bofors put an end to them ; it was unfortunate about the woman and the child but people should arrange their lunch parties more carefully.

In the hangar were three Ghiblis (Colonial bombers) and finding a portable re-fuelling tank which was full I set the Libyan prisoners to pump petrol over the aircraft. I remember being surprised to find them fitted with Lewis guns ; such are the mysteries of the international armaments business. As we were finishing Clayton came back from the fort saying that the garrison continued to hold out and that as the main objective, the destruction of the aircraft and hangar, would be achieved he proposed to withdraw. From what we heard afterwards the fort was probably on the point of surrendering, for that evening the French

native troops said that they had heard cries of " Nitla burra.
Nitla burra " (" Let's get out ") from the Libyans. They may
have been insisting on an offensive sortie, but it seems more likely
that they had had enough.

Ballantyne had moved his trucks and prisoners away from the
hangar and we laid a trail of petrol to the door. One match
struck and before we were off the landing ground the hangar
was ablaze and the bombs and ammunition exploding. As we
moved out of the town a few minutes later I looked back to see
the roof collapsing on to the aircraft within. Of the twenty odd
Italian prisoners sitting downcast on the edge of the landing
ground we kept four of the most intelligent-looking and, for lack
of transport space and rations, let the rest go, to the disgust of
the French who would happily have cut their throats.

We left the town by the same road. In the ditch lay the
postmaster's bicycle which I picked up and tied to the back of
Beech's truck, thinking it would be useful for riding to the office
in Cairo, but though Beech carried it for three weeks it was
finally lost to me, burnt with its former owner in the action at
Gebel Sherif.

A cold sandstorm was blowing when we buried Hewson and
d'Ornano by the roadside just outside the town, with the shivering
Italian prisoners standing dejectedly by and wondering, I expect,
if graves would soon be dug for them. Their countrymen in
Murzuk showed no signs of pursuit and we camped that night at
Dlem, where the villagers turned out and received 'Abd el Galil
with enthusiasm. In the base wireless room in the Citadel in
Cairo the faintly-heard dots and dashes of our No. 11 set were
giving Bagnold the news, good and bad.

This range—it is a thousand miles from Murzuk to Cairo—
taxed the abilities of the signalmen to the uttermost. The No. 11
wireless set which we always used was not designed to cover more
than twenty miles reliably, and as we habitually used it over
600, 800 or 1000 our signalmen were in a class apart. The
average trained army signalman, on joining L.R.D.G., would be
put back to school for a month or two by Tim Heywood (for

more than two years our signal officer) before he was good enough to be sent out with a patrol, and in that time had to learn to pick up very weak signals from a background of atmospherics and interference.

He also had to learn L.R.D.G. " procedure." Procedure is a standardised way of sending signals and, since a good signalman can recognise his distant colleague merely by the way he dots his dashes, in much the same way as we recognise handwriting, the characteristic Army procedure was easy enough to distinguish. There was no harm in using this in places where the enemy would expect it, such as behind the British lines, but an intelligent Italian D.F.[1] operator, hearing Army procedure in the direction of Murzuk when the front line was at Tobruk, could reasonably be expected to sit up and take notice. So L.R.D.G. used French commercial procedure, complete with call-signs, indicator-groups, etc., and thus the watchful Italian, hearing a station calling where no station ought to be, would (or might) assume that he was merely listening to Algiers ordering a dozen of champagne and two barrels of oysters from Tunis.

Murzuk had been the main objective and now we must turn southwards towards the Chad Territory, doing what damage we could en route to the outlying Italian posts and suffering, as we then supposed, the inevitable air attack. The results would depend largely on whether these posts had wireless and could be warned by Murzuk of our coming.

The first post, Traghen, was believed to have none, and this was confirmed by two camel policemen captured while out on patrol on the outskirts. (Two and a half years later I had a friendly reunion with one of them in southern Tripolitania.) We had approached from the west and on the eastern edge of the village the mud fort showed up clearly. So one of the policemen was sent in with a message that they must surrender in ten minutes or be shelled. For ten minutes we waited among the thin palms. A quarter of an hour had almost passed and Sanders,

[1] Radio Direction Finding.

the T patrol gunner, was moving up his Bofors when a confused hum of noise arose on the edge of the village. Was this a garrison of unexpected size massing for a sortie ? Then a small crowd left the western gate. Gradually it came nearer across the open ground, an extraordinary procession. With banners flying and drums beating the *mudir* and his elders were coming out to surrender the village in traditional Fezzan manner. Trailing behind the crowd were a few sheepish-looking Italian carabinieri.

The rest of the great battle of Traghen was a picnic. While 'Abd el Galil held court by the well we went through the fort for arms and papers. I was sorting the contents of the office cupboards when Clayton brought in the Italian N.C.O. to make him open the safe. In it were some thousands of lire and I took enough to buy eggs and dates in the village and left the rest. Clayton went out and the Italian's eye caught mine. "Pity to leave that for the Government," it said, " it might come in useful even in a prison camp."

Traghen had been easy game and after lunch we moved on to Umm el Araneb. The track lay over a bare, stony plain with no cover at all and I wondered if the aircraft would catch us here. It was hot and bumpy in the back of the doctor's truck where I was travelling to be near 'Abd el Galil who knew the country. Wilson was beside me on a stretcher and his leg was hurting him badly ; once he begged us to stop, the only time I heard him complain in his 3500-mile journey which ended in the Scottish General Hospital in Cairo sixteen days later.

At Umm el Araneb things were different. The fort had wireless and the postmaster who had been sent on ahead in one truck to parley with the garrison soon turned back with machine-gun bullets whistling round him. With unarmoured cars and no gun bigger than a 37 mm. Bofors it was useless to hope to take the stone-built fort, well sited above slopes of soft sand, so we turned southwards for Gatrun and Tejerri.

It had been arranged with the French that while we were raiding Murzuk their Camel Corps, Sarazac's Groupe Nomade de Tibesti, should move up from Tummo and attack Tejerri. On the approach march his Tibbu guides had deliberately led him astray, and during the delay had sent word to warn the Italians, so Sarazac's night attack failed. The reason for this was that there are many Tibbu living in Tejerri and Gatrun and it was clear that they had no intention of having an invasion on their doorstep. Uninterested, like most Africans, in the futilities of their European overlords, they preferred the *status quo*.

The patrols had no better luck at Gatrun where the garrison was awake and the Italian Air Force had at last got going, though their bombs fell nowhere near their target. So, on January 14th, Clayton ended his operations and we turned southwards towards Zouar.

As far as Tummo there is a roughly marked track. There we halted for a day with the Groupe Nomade's reserve section and, during the night, Sarazac returned from Tejerri. At times in L.R.D.G. we used to consider ourselves tough, but the life of those French Méhariste officers made one think again. With nothing more than a roll of bedding to spread on the ground they were away for months on end even from the small comforts of their desert posts. We knew that in a few weeks we would be back in the civilisation of Cairo. But the life of the Groupe Nomade is the life of its camels. Camels must follow the changing grazing and the men must follow them, and Sarazac, having finished his operations, would move at once to the scanty pasturage of the Afafi Hills. Added to this—Pétain and Laval being what they were—these men were outlaws from their own country, lost after years of service in the most desolate area of the Central Sahara, having had no home leave for years and with no prospect of leave for years to come. And, perhaps worst of all, with never a word of news from their families in France. Mail day roused no interest in Tibesti.

At Tummo the doctor's 15-cwt. broke a half-shaft for the nth time and for lack of spares had to be towed. The Guards did the job and dragged the car 900 miles to Faya, a magnificent piece of driving by Roberts and probably a record feat of salvage over roadless desert. It was a point of honour in L.R.D.G.

R.D.G.

never to abandon vehicles which could possibly be recovered. (This may seem obvious enough, but after the retreat to 'Alamein enemy prisoners of war reported that about three-quarters of the Axis transport was British, running on the million or so gallons of petrol we had left behind in Tobruk).

As well as salvaging our own cars we made up, in the course of time, a good collection of those which other units had left strewn about the desert. We had most amusement out of the Commandos' three-tonner which they abandoned by the trackside on their way to Jaghbub in the spring of 1942. After it had stood there for some weeks Philip Arnold, our most energetic scavenger, collected it and put it into use at Siwa. Some time later, another Commando 3-tonner, going to Sollum to fetch supplies for them in company with some L.R.D.G. trucks, was lost in circumstances for which we were partly to blame. As a gesture we gave them back their own unrecognised lorry, but the best of the joke came later when, re-fitting in the Delta, they obtained a replacement from Ordnance and gratefully returned to us their own truck.

To save distance and petrol we left the Bilma track and cut across country from Tummo to Zouar-ké, the mouth of the gorge running up to Zouar. This stretch of the journey led through territory of the Niger Province of French Equatoria which had clung to Vichy when the Chad Province declared for de Gaulle, and when we crossed fresh car tracks there were scornful references from Massu to " le lieutenant de Vichy " who, with a patrol based on Djado, was wandering aimlessly through these barren hills. It was as well, perhaps, that we never met him and so avoided a diplomatic incident. More interesting to me was the finding of an empty iron food container, marked " Riz," and the date and name of some firm in Marseilles, which had lain there since the French first occupied Tibesti before the Great War.

Three days' rough travelling over unexplored desert—" terrain chaotique sans ni eau ni pâturage " as the map properly described it—brought us to the magnificent rocks of Dourso which stand sentinel where the western foothills of Tibesti come down to the fringing sands of the Grand Erg de Bilma. In the heat haze to the north was the ten thousand foot cone of Toussidé, the landmark for travellers coming from the west.

I loved this country of castle-like rocks with *ril*, gazelle and bustard plentiful among the thin acacias and the red-brown gravel underfoot. There are no camp fires in the world like those, smokeless and sweet-smelling, which the desert acacias make. We clambered over the deserted Camel Corps post at Zouar-ké and I found a good neolithic polished axehead for the Museum in Khartoum.

Massu was our generous host at Zouar. He had been wounded in the leg at Murzuk, treated his wound with the end of a lighted cigarette, and said no more of it till days afterwards.

On the 20th Bagnold arrived by air from Faya and the next day he, Wilson and I left for Fort Lamy. Noël was flying us in " le vieux Bloch," an antiquated bomber which should have been condemned years ago. After each flight Noël refused to take it up again but always did so in the end, and it carried us to Fort Lamy on a hot afternoon, in three and a half hours' flying at about two hundred feet to make the most of the visibility of a mile or less, over a fantastic landscape where *barchan* dunes gave place to miles of flat acacia scrub, then *dom* palms, then open forest land with many cattle and then Fort Lamy, orderly rows of grass huts on the banks of the Shari above Lake Chad.

Waiting at Fort Lamy for transport to Cairo and watching every day tens of aircraft passing eastwards on the Takoradi-Khartoum-Cairo route, I realised how great a service our Free French allies had done us in keeping open this vital supply line.

CHAPTER FIVE

THE TAKING OF KUFRA

ON THE WAY south from Zouar to Fort Lamy Bagnold and I stopped for an hour or two at Faya to discuss with Colonel Leclerc the operations against Kufra in which L.R.D.G. was to take part.

I did not see much of d'Ornano before he was killed, but all we heard of him from the French showed that he had been an inspiring leader. After his death Leclerc succeeded him, and it is no insult to d'Ornano's memory to say that they did not lose by the change.

Modern war does not seem to produce good songs, perhaps because men march so little and it is while marching that songs are born. Nor does it throw up many outstanding leaders, probably because the movement of large mechanised forces is too impersonal an affair. But among the leaders whom the African campaigns *did* produce Leclerc takes a high place.

He had the career of the normal French regular officer—cadet at St. Cyr ; commissioned into the Cavalry ; back to St. Cyr as an instructor ; a captain at the beginning of the war. In the Battle of France he was wounded and taken prisoner. Before the Germans had moved him to a prison camp he escaped to a neighbouring château owned by some of his relations. (The name Leclerc conceals his real name—le Vicomte de Haute Coque.) Walking out of the front door in plain clothes he saw a German soldier riding on his wife's bicycle and asked the man to let him have it back. The Nazi handed it over and Leclerc rode off towards the coast. Later he reached England and joined de Gaulle who sent him to the Cameroons to organise resistance to the Vichy authorities there. From the Cameroons he passed up to Chad and became military commander of the Province. His own men thought the world of him and we, knowing him less well, had great admiration for his achievements. Youngish, fair,

68

high-coloured, with a deep, rich voice, he was a man to whom
the English gave their most insulting and yet most generous
compliment, " He might almost be an Englishman." Now, in
January, 1941, he was at Faya planning the advance on Kufra.

To one of Rommel's generals, von Ravenstein, is ascribed the
saying that North Africa is a tactician's paradise and a quartermaster's hell. The following table gives an idea of the problem
before Leclerc :

" Crow-fly " miles from Kufra.	
	Kufra, garrison about 400 strong.
95	Bishara Well, filled in.
200	Sarra Well, filled in.
365	Tekro, nearest water to Kufra.
565	Faya, base for expedition.
1015	Fort Lamy, H.Q. Chad Province.

Where, beyond Fort Lamy, his supplies came from I do not
know, but Duala in the Cameroons, 700 miles away, seems to be
the nearest port on the Atlantic coast.

His native troops were mostly Saras from Fort Archimbault,
with French officers and N.C.O.s, all good fighters. The great
difficulty was supplies and transport for at that stage in the war
the British had little to spare from the Middle East for operations
which were of relatively minor importance. Wavell was in the
middle of his first advance into Cyrenaica with forces absurdly
inferior in numbers to the Italians. So for weeks Leclerc and his
transport officers had been combing the scrap-heaps of Chad to
equip his force. He took us down to the workshops to show us his
portée 75 ; outside were a row of derelict Lafflys whose wheels
had gone to equip the rather less ancient Matfords.

It was agreed that Clayton's two patrols should be placed
under French command for the Kufra operations. They would
form the advance guard of the force from Faya and on the way
north would reconnoitre 'Uweinat where the Italians had had
a post. As events proved, the Italians had added one more to

their series of strategical mistakes and evacuated 'Uweinat ; a strong raiding force based there and operating against Leclerc's lines of communication would have been most awkward for him.

The Italians[1] certainly knew that an attack on Kufra was coming. Their wireless interception had noted new stations working to the south and their spies also should have warned them, for the French " security " was none too good. For some weeks past in Faya " Vers Koufra " had been the greeting in the streets and the toast in the mess.

On January 26th the L.R.D.G. patrols left Faya, moving northwards in a sandstorm across rough rocky country to Wan-yanga Kebir and thence to the frontier post at Tekro.

On January 31st Clayton with T patrol reached Gebel Sherif, sixty miles south of Kufra, the Guards patrol having remained in reserve near Sarra. At half-past three that afternoon he was attacked in a valley in the hills by an Italian motorised patrol.

As far as L.R.D.G. had an " opposite number " in the Saharan Command this was the Italian Auto-Saharan Company. These companies, of which the Italians had six or seven, were designed some years previously by Graziani for desert warfare, and in his initial instructions he laid particular stress on the importance of their working in very close co-operation with air-craft. At Gebel Sherif his foresight and training bore fruit.

Clayton had eleven cars and thirty odd men, and the enemy five cars and forty-four men and, to their great advantage, four 20 mm. Breda guns, one of the best weapons the Italian Army has produced. Overhead, with three aircraft directing operations, was Captain Moreschini, one of their Saharan veterans. The enemy entered the valley from the north and opened heavy and accurate fire, and it was not very long before three of our trucks were burning and Beech and two of the Italian prisoners on his truck killed. (I have a copy of an article in an

[1] In what follows all facts relating to the Italians are taken from Lt. Minutillo's report on the action at Gebel Sherif, found later at Kufra.

Italian paper [1] accusing us of shooting the prisoners, but they died under their own fire.) Beech had gone down fighting. When Mercer Nairne, the Liaison Officer with the French, came to the place ten days later his body was lying by his gun, and it is probable that many of the enemy casualties were to his credit ; they had three killed and two wounded by their own admission.

Clayton drew his remaining trucks out of the valley intending to counter-attack from the south, but now Moreschini came in with bombs and machine-gun fire. Clayton was wounded and taken prisoner and the rest of the patrol withdrew towards Sarra.

But not quite all of it. In addition to Adams and Roderick who were captured with Clayton four men remained at Gebel Sherif.

One of the patrol vehicles was driven by Moore, a New Zealander, and with him were Easton and Winchester from the Guards patrol and Tighe, an R.A.O.C. fitter. When the truck caught fire and the bombs and ammunition started to explode they left it and ran up into the rocks for cover. The rest of the patrol assumed that they had been killed or captured and so at 4 p.m. on the afternoon of the 31st these four men and the remaining Italian prisoner were crouching among the rocks of Gebel Sherif in a situation which was far from pleasant.

Not far away, on the plain at the hill's foot, were the Italians with an aircraft landed beside them. Although they had admittedly had the best of the fight they seem to have lost their nerve for they made no search for Moore and his party, did not bury the dead, and apparently hardly examined the scene of action, though Minutillo officially reported that our losses were " 4 morti accertati sul terreno (e forse qualque altro brucciato con la machine) "—which was quite untrue. After having collected Clayton they set off in haste for Kufra—" alle ore 18 s'inizia la marcia notturna di ritorno percorendo a bussola una rotta di sicurezza. Il 1 febbraio alle 4 del mattino la colonna é a Cufra."

[1] *Popolo d'Italia*, 18.10.41.

During the night, shivering among the rocks, Moore and the others discussed what they should do. The alternatives were not attractive. To make for Kufra, seventy miles away, and surrender to the Italians, or to follow the tracks of the patrol southwards in the hope that they would be picked up. It was largely due to Moore's encouragement and inspiration that they chose the latter. They decided not to surrender.

So at dawn on February 1st this was the position. Moore—wounded in the foot. Easton—wounded in the throat. Tighe. Winchester. An Italian. A two-gallon tin of water with a bullet hole through it near the top and containing about one and three-quarters gallons. No food. The clothes they wore ; everything else had been burnt in the trucks.

This is the record of the next ten days :

February 1st.—Walking southwards following the tracks of the patrol. At some period during this day the Italian disappeared and was picked up later by his own people.

February 2nd and 3rd.—Walking. The night temperatures here at this time must have been near freezing and it was almost impossible to get any sleep and rest.

February 4th.—Tighe beginning to tire: he was feeling the effects of an old operation. They found and ate some lentils thrown away after a meal on their way north.

February 5th.—Tighe could not keep up so he was left with his share of the water in a bottle which they had picked up. Later, when he came to drink it, he found that something the bottle had contained had made the water salty and almost undrinkable.

February 6th.—Sandstorm. The car tracks almost obliterated and very hard to follow. (In the soft sand of the desert, where your foot slips back at every step, one pace is equal—in effort—to three on a hard road.) The first three reached Sarra, 135 miles from Gebel Sherif. At Sarra is a well, two hundred feet deep, which the Italians had filled in, with a few mud huts nearby. In them they found some waste motor oil and bathed their feet and also made a fire out of odd bits of wood. There was no food.

February 7th.—Three walking on. The tracks still hard to see. Tighe reached Sarra and sheltered in the huts, unable to follow the others. On the ground he found *one* match. It did not fail and he got some comfort from a fire.

February 8th.—Three walking on. Tighe at Sarra.

February 9th.—Late on the evening of the 9th a party of French with Mercer Nairne reached Sarra from the north. They were returning from a reconnaissance of Kufra which I shall describe later on, and had visited Gebel Sherif, buried Beech and the Italians, and called in at Sarra. The Sarra-Kufra track is wide and ill-defined and the northward-bound French had missed Moore and the others. In a hut they found Tighe, weak but conscious. (Imagine his feelings when he heard the sound of their cars !) With his first words he told them of the others ahead. The French tried to follow their footmarks in the sand but in the dark this was impossible and they had to wait till dawn. Meanwhile the others had been walking on. Easton had dropped behind. During the day a French aircraft sighted Moore and Winchester and realised, I suppose, the plight they were in. The ground was too rough for a landing, but the pilot circled round and dropped food and a canvas bag of water. The food Moore and Winchester could not find ; the cork of the water bag was knocked out in its fall and when they got it only a mouthful or two remained.

February 10th.—At first light the rescue party left Sarra. They followed the three men's footsteps and after a time one set turned vaguely off to the west. At the end of them they found Easton, fifty-five miles from Sarra, lying on the ground but alive. Fortunately the French had with them a doctor who took Easton back to Sarra and all that day strove to save his life. But help had come too late and at seven in the evening he died. He kept his sense of humour to the end. The French

made some tea for him, weak and sweet. Easton drank it and
smiled, " I like my tea without sugar," he said.

Meanwhile another party was following Moore and
Winchester. Sixty-five miles from Sarra Winchester could
not continue and Moore gave him half the remaining water—
one mouthful—and pushed on. Here the French found him,
near delirium but able to stand up when he heard their cars.
Ten miles farther south they overtook Moore, then about 210
miles from Gebel Sherif and marching steadily southwards.
He felt confident that in three days he could reach Tekro, the
nearest water, eighty miles ahead, and was slightly annoyed,
so Mercer Nairne told me, at being prevented from proving
that he could.

There is a fitting line in Tennyson's *Ulysses*—

" To strive, to seek, to find and not to yield."

While Moore and those with him were marching southwards
" T ' patrol, returning from Gebel Sherif, had met ' G   patrol
and Leclerc. The situation was now much changed. The Italians
in Kufra were on the alert;   'T ' patrol had lost half its vehicles,
and all the cars were showing signs of the wear of their long
journey from Cairo. They, American Chevrolets, had almost
earned the " tribute to British workmanship " which the publicity
people at Middle East awarded them in the Press " puff " issued
after the raid. So Leclerc decided to form a temporary base at
Tekro, reopen Sarra well, make a reconnaissance in force of
Kufra and to let our patrols return home. One T patrol
truck, Ballantyne's " Manuka," stayed with the French, with
Kendall and its crew to help them in navigation ; the rest of the
L.R.D.G. force returned to Cairo by way of 'Uweinat and
Kharga, having travelled 4300 miles in the 45 days.

The French reconnaissance party, sixty Europeans and thirty
natives in fifteen Bedford trucks, reached Gebel Zurgh, five miles
south of Kufra, on February 7th.

That night two parties entered the oasis. Geoffroi with

twenty-five men on foot went into Giof, the Italian administrative centre among the palms below the fort. It was quite deserted for, as was learned later, all the Italians retired into the fort at night. All except one, for Geoffroi turned east along the road to the hamlet at Buma and in the radio direction finding station, which four months later was our mess, found one sleepy Italian. He was taken prisoner and the station wrecked.

Meanwhile de Guillebon with three cars had gone to the airfield. de Guillebon—tall, silent, blonde, efficient—was then and for long afterwards Leclerc's staff officer and one of the most able men in the strangely-assorted Chad force. The airfield was deserted and he burnt the one aircraft he found there. This at last roused the Italians in the fort who started shooting wildly and firing green Verey lights. Now it so happened that a green Verey light was the signal " en avant " to the French reserves at Gebel Zurgh, and a few minutes later, to the dismay of de Guillebon and Geoffroi, the twelve Bedfords with headlights full on came roaring into the oasis. Between Gebel Zurgh and the palmeries lie soft sand and hummocks and soon things became chaotic. The Bedfords stuck badly ; " Manuka " tore her sump off on a rock, overturned and had to be abandoned and burned ; the Italians in the fort fired all they had got.

But by dawn the situation was restored and the Bedfords started back to Tekro, not without losses from aircraft on the way. Beyond Sarra, as I have described, they found Moore and his companions.

Leclerc now determined to attack. The reconnaissance had been most useful for the French now knew the lie of the land and it was clear that the Italians' courage was normal. His force was : 101 Europeans, 295 natives, 26 fusils-mitrailleuses (L.M.G.s) 4 M.G.s, 2 37 mms., 4 mortars and one 75 portée.

The advance guard left Sarra on February 17th. On the 18th and again on the 19th the Bedford patrols of Geoffroi and de Rennepont under the leadership of Leclerc fought it out with the Auto-Saharan Company in the broken ground north of the fort. The text-books (with diagrams) would, I think, have called

it a " pretty little action " in which the French out-manœuvred
the Italians. Geoffroi was heavily bombed on the second day
but, by evening, the Auto-Saharan Company was making off to
Tazerbo and never appeared on the scene again.

This was the turning point and Kufra was lost to the Italians.
If they had not shut themselves up in the fort and lost their only
mobile force, the Auto-Saharan Company, this chapter might not
have been written, for Leclerc's supply columns, toiling along
through the soft sand from Bishara, were a very vulnerable
target, and in the oasis itself, if they had retained their mobility,
they might have made things very unpleasant for the French.
As it was it was only a matter of time. Ceccaldi put his 75 in a
ruined house near the market place and lobbed twenty to thirty
shells a day into the fort and by night the French roamed the
oasis at will on offensive patrols. The Kufrans left their homes
each morning for the palm groves and returned to sleep when the
day's fighting was over.

This went on till February 28th. On that morning a Libyan
soldier brought a note down from the fort asking for an arrangement by which each side should place their wounded in an area
on to which no fire should be directed. There was something
almost mediæval about this request, reminiscent of Saladin's siege
of Kerak in the twelfth century when Reynaud de Chatillon, the
besieged Crusader, sent out word that one of his knights was to
be married on the morrow and asking for a three days' lull in the
bombardment of the bastion in which the bridal chamber lay.

Leclerc replied that he would only treat with an officer in
person so at four that afternoon an Italian officer with a white
flag came out to repeat the request, which was refused. Before
returning to the fort he asked, " for my purely personal information," what the terms of surrender would be.

Leclerc then realised that the Italians were finished and put
the screw on. The patrols became more active and Ceccaldi
doubled the output from his 75. At dawn on the 1st March a
white flag was flying over the fort. The Italian rule over Kufra,
which had lasted ten years and forty days, was over.

The Italians were inclined to bargain for terms but Leclerc, as the French account says, " brusque les choses " and drove his car into the fort. In the courtyard the garrison paraded—64 Italians, 352 Libyans—leaving behind them 53 M.G.s and 4 20 mm. Bredas. They were terrified of the French native troops and begged that none of them should be allowed into the fort, so all day the French priest, le père Bronner, stood sentry at the gate protecting the representatives of a great colonial empire.

Even after the flight of the Auto-Saharan Companies the Italians could have held out in Kufra for weeks, but they had no heart in the job. In the signal room at the fort was a copy of the commander's last message :

" We are in·extremis. Long live Italy. Long live the King Emperor. Long live the Duce. Rome I embrace you."

Positions are not held on such stuff as this.

When the Italians took Kufra from the Senussi in 1931 their victory was hailed as a great achievement in desert warfare and in good " Q " work. And so it was, though the Senussi had no aircraft, no mechanical transport and no artillery. In 1941 the Italians had all these and yet were beaten by Leclerc whose supply problem was infinitely more difficult than theirs had been.

The Italians made no attempt to retake Kufra and from that date until the end of the war in Africa did nothing more than a a little bombing which cost each side four or five aircraft and us an equal number of casualties. For seven months in 1941 and for another seven months in 1942 Kufra was an invaluable base for L.R.D.G. We owed a great deal to Leclerc and his men.

CHAPTER SIX

By THE END of April, 1941, Group Headquarters and R, S and T patrols were at Kufra and Mitford had G and Y at Siwa as a detached squadron under the command of Desforce, the predecessor of the Eighth Army. On the coast the front line stood at Sollum and the siege of Tobruk had begun.

We had come to Kufra by our old route from Cairo to 'Ain Dalla, across the Sand Sea to Big Cairn and thence south-west-wards, and on the morning of April 20th first saw the eastern palm groves of the oasis. We halted for breakfast on the rolling sand beyond the airfield and Bagnold, as became the Military Commander Designate, shaved and changed his shirt.

For a desert enthusiast like myself the first sight of Kufra was a never-to-be-forgotten event. For Kufra, till the Italians took it, was a story-book oasis, unattainable, remote, mysterious, the last goal of all African explorers.

Like many other Libyan oases it lies at the southern foot of an east-west scarp, in a long trough hollowed out by the wind action of thousands of years till the desert surface had been lowered to meet the water table. Virtually no rain falls in the Libyan Desert so it is something of a mystery where the ample water supplies of the oases come from. The theory which holds most favour with geographers is that the water which has fallen as rain in the Tibesti Mountains or in the area of Lake Chad percolates under pressure through the sandstone strata which lie under the desert and comes to the surface in the oasis-depressions.

From the high wireless masts in the Italian fort at Et Tag, built over the ruins of the Senussi *zawia*, you could see the whole oasis—thousands of date palms, thinly scattered on the upper slopes and thicker around the salt marshes ; the mosque and

market place at El Giof ; the two sapphire-blue lakes as salt as
the Dead Sea, though you could dig a well of sweet water five
yards from the margin ; the tiny patches of cultivation, laboriously
irrigated by donkey-hauled leather buckets from shallow wells.

Of course the place was poor, without the palms life would
have been impossible. There is no limit to what this wonderful
tree provides for its owners—dates for food ; palm-wine for
drink ; timber for building and firewood ; leaves for thatch,
baskets, mats and sandals ; fibre for ropes.

After some initial severity the Italians had done well by
Kufra—built a school, a hospital, a market and a mosque, though
the Arabs, preferring their old Senussi building, thought nothing
of the latter and readily and rather surprisingly lent it to us for
a ration store. The Italians collected no taxes and their introduction of motor transport did something to reduce the isolation.
For it is difficult to exaggerate the loneliness of the oasis. In
English geographical equivalents, taking Kufra as London, the
nearest places where you could be sure of finding another human
being who would give you a drink of water were Rebiana
(Salisbury), Bzema (Coventry) or Tazerbo (Liverpool), while to
be certain of a glass of beer you must go to Benghazi (Berlin).

Kufra—the Secret of the Sahara! When the Italians occupied
it all its romance was ended, but sitting there that April morning,
while the advance party went in, I could think back over a
century of its history.

Back to its first discoverer, a Majbri from Jalo, looking, no
doubt, for the inevitable lost camel which has led to so many
desert discoveries. (Ask any nomad in North Africa where he is
going and nine out of ten will answer, " I'm looking for a camel
I've lost." Having found it he hobbles it with an entirely
inadequate piece of rope and so is soon looking for it again.)

And back to the great Sayed Mohammed el Mahdi es Senussi
who from Kufra had raised the Senussi to the peak of their power.
Back to Rohlfs the German, in 1879 the first European to visit
it, barely escaping with his life. Beyond the palms stood Qaret
en Nasrani, the " Christian's Hill," where he had camped his

first night. And, forty years after Rohlfs, to Lapierre and his companions, captured in the Fezzan when the tribes rose against the Italians in 1914 and kept prisoners of the Senussi in Kufra for five weary years. Back to Hassanein and Rosita Forbes coming by camel from Jaghbub in 1921 and to Hassanein again, two years later, setting out alone from Kufra on the greatest African camel journey of our century to discover Arkenu and 'Uweinat. To Bruneau de Laborie passing from Chad to Cairo in 1924. And lastly to that fateful January morning in 1931 near Hawari when Arab freedom in Libya ended and their great leaders fought their last fight—'Abd el Galil Seif en Nasr ; 'Abd el Hamid Bu Matari ; Suleiman his brother and Saleh el Ateiwish. A century of great men and great deeds.

And now they were dead or forgotten and I looked across the palms and the patches of salt marsh to the bomb-shattered hangar at Buma and the wireless masts towering over the remains of the Senussi *zawia* on the hill at Et Tag, and the Italian brothel by the roadside below the fort.

After breakfast we moved in and sought a camping place. There were some half-ruined mud and stone houses at Buma and we put the Headquarters and Signals into these. For an officers' mess we used the D.F. station which Geoffroi had half-burned down in February, and I collected the local masons and started to build sleeping quarters alongside the mess, a series of hermit-like cells whose design pleased me greatly. I learned, too, a tip to scotch all the queries of Army auditors—to pay wages in French francs and in Italian lire converted from Egyptian pounds and keep all the accounts in Arabic on the excuse that my Arab clerk of works understood nothing else.

The French, who had been there since March, wanted to be relieved of garrisoning Kufra and the Sudan Defence Force, who were to take over from them, could not arrive till July, so L.R.D.G. filled the gap. Bagnold became Military Commander and Steele and Holliman took their patrols out to Tazerbo and Bir Harash, for whoever holds the Zighen gap holds Kufra against attack from the north.

Life in Tazerbo was not pleasant. The thermometer climbed steadily towards 120°F in the shade ; from dawn to dusk the flies were beyond belief ; every afternoon it blew a sandstorm ; scorpions and snakes added to the hazards of existence. (The story of the Sand Viper, Libya's deadliest snake, found gargling in its hole after biting a South Islander, is encouraged in Auckland but rejected by reliable authority in Christchurch.)

At Bir Harash, where the Rhodesians dug themselves a swimming pool and where there were no flies, life was more pleasant. The absence of flies was a good example of the effects of camp cleanliness ; under Holliman, when one appeared, the whole patrol turned out to slay it. I well remember his fury when in August we halted for a day at Harash which the S.D.F. had then occupied and the flies were so bad that we moved ten miles out of the place from dawn till dusk. But even so life at Harash was a " desert-island " sort of existence ; for three months the Rhodesians lived there, sixty miles from the nearest human beings, sheltering under their cars among the few stunted palms, and patrolling daily across the Zighen gap.

From Kufra the French were gradually withdrawing their garrison to Faya, but many of them stayed on long enough for us to make a lot of friends. They were a strange crowd these outlaws from France, the officers of the Régiment des Tirailleurs Sénégalais du Tchad, reckless, gay in spite of their misfortunes, and with one object in life—to get their teeth into the Boche. Yet for all their dash and courage one could not but notice some of the traits which must have helped to bring France to the Armistice —a spirit of *Je m'enfoutisme* about the dull things like discipline, good " Q " work and the maintenance of vehicles, aircraft and equipment which go so far to win modern battles. On the march they poured in oil, petrol and water and drove furiously to the horizon—*suive qui peut*.

In addition to the garrison they had a bit of an air force, some worn-out Lysanders (" Les Lisandaires "), which were all the British could or would spare then, and a few ramshackle French machines. Of the latter the museum piece was the

R.D.G.

antiquated ambulance—le Potez Avion Sanitaire. But though the aircraft were a strange assortment tied together with string, there was nothing wrong with the pilots, amongst whom we counted many good friends. Their methods may have been unorthodox but they could teach our airmen a thing or two about desert flying.

With Mahé, whom we knew best, I had some interesting flights. L.R.D.G. Headquarters reached Kufra in the middle of April, coming across the Sand Sea from 'Ain Dalla. Dick Croucher had left Cairo a few days earlier with an unwieldy party of two overloaded 10-tonners and some of our cast-off Chevrolets, carrying Barnes, the Political Officer, and his Libyan police. He took the longer route through Kharga and round the southern end of the Gilf Kebir, but should have reached Kufra about the same time as we did. So when he had not turned up three days later something had to be done about it, and Bagnold sent me off with Mahé to look for him.

We took off at dawn in one of the decrepit Lysanders, Mahé piloting and I in the back, separated from him by the long-range petrol tank and squatting on a green enamel bath stool plundered from the Italian officers' quarters in the fort. Like most of the gadgets in the Lizzie the intercom telephone was broken and its place was taken by a small bag tied on to the end of a stick in which we pushed notes to each other. Mahé's English was worse than my French, so French was the official language for the operation. He also had a string tied to each arm with which I " drove " him like children playing horses.

Looking for a dozen cars in the desert is like searching for the proverbial needle but we knew roughly the line Croucher would take : up the west side of the Gilf Kebir till he was level with Kufra and then due westwards. It was six years since I had seen this side of the Gilf and Mahé did not know it at all, but I hoped to be able to recognise the flat-topped outlier of Point 1020 and then turn south along the cliffs.

We had not been off the ground long before the wind rose, and by the time we were nearing the Gilf visibility was very bad.

I could recognise none of the familiar landmarks, and we only found the cliffs when they loomed unpleasantly close out of the haze. We turned south and followed them for a time, rather like a man in a dark passage putting out a hand to feel for the walls, but it was clear that the chances of seeing Croucher were far smaller than of getting lost ourselves. Mahé passed me a note : " Si vous n'êtes pas absolument sûr de notre position il serai mieux de rentrer à Koufra." I was absolutely sure of nothing but a keen desire to be on the ground again, so we turned to Kufra on a guessed bearing and luckily hit off the sharp tooth of Qaret et Tawila, the good landmark south of the oasis. Later in the day, when the visibility was better, we went out again and saw Croucher near Wadi Firaq. We dropped a message saying that water and food were on the way out from Kufra. It was lucky that we found him for he was down to about the last pint.

Eighteen months later on a December afternoon I was at almost exactly the same spot, returning to Kufra from Cairo in a Hudson. It was one of those occasions (late evening in the Sand Sea is another), when the desert repays in the beauty of a few short hours a hundred days of choking heat, bitter wind, driving sandstorm, thirst and discomfort. We came over the Gilf at about 6000 feet to a view which you get once in a lifetime and thereafter strive in vain to keep in the brain's eye. One hundred and twenty miles away to the south-west was 'Uweinat with Arkenu to the right of it and the sharp tooth of Kissu behind, and the air was so clear that I could pick out the individual peaks which we had got to know so well climbing the mountain with Bagnold for the first time in 1932. To the south-east a black pimple in a vast sand plain was Gebel Kamil, named by Prince Kemal el Din, the Egyptian explorer, after his father. Far to the north I could see plainly the giant dune lines of the Sand Sea running down to the northern end of the Gilf plateau where (on my birthday as I remembered) in October, 1930, we had spent some hot and anxious hours bogged in soft sand between two dunes. I have always collected views, as others collect poems or postage stamps—Kitty's Leap at Erkowit ; the

Bosphorus above Anatoli Hissar ; the Jordan Valley from Kawkab el Hawa ; Salisbury Plain from the Second Hawthorn Bush (a family favourite that one) ; the Cyprus coast from Kantara Castle—and that December afternoon over the Gilf takes a high place in the collection.

Apart from some local patrolling to get to know the country, the first two months at Kufra were quiet, for we could not leave our outpost tasks and petrol was scarce. The " Q " problem at Kufra was an unending difficulty. Lines of communication were always long in Libya, but that from Wadi Halfa broke all records. 650 miles it was, the distance from Dover to Land's End and back, with two water points en route, a journey of a week or more, over sand plain, dune lines, rock and gravel, and in the summer in a temperature that would make the fortune of the most inefficient publican.

The Sudan Defence Force was responsible for supplying Kufra, and to begin with had very little idea—and small blame to them—of what they were up against. Tony Browne went down to Wadi Halfa at the end of April to guide the first convoy up. The first stage was from the Nile to Selima, loveliest of all Libyan oases, then to the desert well at Bir Misaha, and then 400 waterless miles to Kufra. Lonsdale was in charge of the transport and got the first seventy tons through on May 13th ; a great achievement in the face of countless difficulties—heat, soft sand, worn-out trucks, inexperienced drivers. Gradually things improved as the drivers became more desert-minded, but the expense was always colossal ; I think it cost £1 to put a gallon of petrol into Kufra. By the end of June twenty 10-tonners had been added to the convoys and things were going better.

It was during the time we were at Kufra that the L.R.D.G. air force began to come into its own.

In January of 1941 Prendergast had arrived from England to join the unit as second-in-command. He had great experience of desert travel—with Bagnold in the early days ; in Egypt and Palestine ; in Iraq and Iran ; with the War Office Experimental

Column from Cairo to the Uganda frontier and back in 1933 ;
and for many years commanding a Motor Machine-Gun Båttery
in the Sudan Defence Force. In addition he had about a thousand
flying hours to his credit as a private aircraft owner, many of
them in Egypt and the Sudan.

He saw at once how valuable aircraft would be to L.R.D.G.,
based on Kufra and needing quick contact with G.H.Q. in Cairo,
and set about to make an air force of his own.

At the beginning there were many difficulties. The R.A.F.,
perhaps naturally enough, were very sticky. They could not
spare us men or machines and did not at all like the idea of an
independent unit like L.R.D.G. having its own aircraft. Their
view was that all military aeroplanes in the British Empire must
be under R.A.F. control, and for a time they refused to give us
numbers or allow us to paint the roundels on the wings, without
which we should have been shot down immediately. In the end
they were only dislodged from this attitude by Very High
Authority.

Finally, after much negotiation, Prendergast got two aircraft
—the Big Waco and the Little Waco—bought from Egyptian
private owners. (" Waco " stands, I think, for Western Aircraft
Corporation of Ohio.) Prendergast flew one and Barker, a New
Zealand pilot who had at one time worked with Kingsford Smith,
the other. There was no ground staff, the pilots did the maintenance in their spare moments, and, the R.A.F. still being
" difficult," an Egyptian aircraft company did the bigger jobs.
The Wacos were single-engined, cabin machines, cruising at
about 140 and 115 m.p.h. respectively, and carrying two men
easily and three at a pinch. The payload was small, because
when you are flying round the inner desert alone in a single-
engined aircraft without wireless, you must have a navigator as
well as the pilot. Not only did you want to be sure of your
destination but at all times you had to be on the pre-arranged
course, so that a rescue party could have a reasonable chance of
finding you in the event of a forced landing or a crash. Both
aircraft carried bubble-sextants and chronometers and more than

once, when doubtful of their position, landed to check the course
with a " fix " on the sun.

The Wacos earned their keep over and over again—in visits
to Middle East and to Army Headquarters from Siwa, Kufra,
Jalo and Hon ; in bringing in wounded men and taking spare
parts out to the patrols. And it says a lot for the skill of the
pilots and navigators that there was never a disaster or anything
approaching one.

In August of 1941 Prendergast took over command of the
unit from Bagnold who was promoted to a staff job at G.H.Q.,
Middle East, and from then until the end of its operations in
Africa Prendergast remained O.C., L.R.D.G.

The most important of a general's qualities, says General
Wavell,[1] is " what the French call *le sens du practicable*, and we
call common sense, knowledge of what is and what is not possible.
It must be based on a really sound knowledge of ' the mechanism
of war,' i.e. topography, movement and supply. These are the
real foundations of military knowledge, not strategy and tactics
as most people think."

It was in his *sens du practicable* and his care for supply that
Prendergast's success in commanding L.R.D.G. lay. Topography
and movement he could in great measure leave to the patrol
commanders, to concentrate, with much attention to detail, on
ensuring a flow of supplies from our very distant bases, and on
deciding, among the many and strange tasks which we were
asked to undertake, the difficult question, " Is it an L.R.D.G.
job ? "

For the commander of so small a force, the equivalent of
about half an infantry battalion, O.C. L.R.D.G. was in a strange
position. He never commanded the whole unit in action and
often was not within five hundred miles of the scattered sections
of it which were engaged. From that distance, and with no more
knowledge of the situation on the spot than was contained in a
brief signal, he had to take decisions and issue orders which might
make or mar a month's work by a patrol.

[1] *Generals and Generalship.* The Lees Knowles Lectures, 1939.

In July, the Sudan Defence Force took over the garrison duties at Kufra and we were free to be L.R.D.G. again.

On the coast, the front line, as far as it was a line, was then at Sollum with Tobruk in our hands. Bagnold had suggested to G.H.Q. at Middle East that, in anticipation of future operations in Tripolitania, it would be useful to know something about the Sirte Desert, the area inland from the Mediterranean coast between Buerat el Hsun and 'Agheila, and L.R.D.G. was told to make a plan for a reconnaissance. This was one of the first tasks of a kind in which we later became specialists ; long range topographical or " going " explorations far behind the enemy lines.

T patrol did the job with Ballantyne in one party and Ellingham and I in the other. "Going" reconnaissance means the production of a picture of the country as seen through the eyes of the force which is to follow after—tanks, transporters, 3-tonners, 10-tonners or whatever they may be. The R.A.F. want to know about possible landing grounds ; Sappers demand information about water supplies ; "Ops" will ask how many miles in an hour their columns can do and whether movement is possible on a wide or narrow front. Thus the mapping must be reasonably accurate, especially of any impassable obstacles and of landing grounds.

We left Tazerbo on July 30th in blistering heat and, on the second day out, 120 miles south-east of Marada, in what was later to be the " Middle Lift Wadi," the advanced base for the Sudan Defence Force's attack on Jalo in 1942, left an unfortunate support party under " Doc " Edmundson to frizzle for ten days until we returned.

We crossed the Marada track half-way up towards the sea, at a point where eighteen months later Tony Browne guided the New Zealand Division round to outflank Rommel at 'Agheila, and then split into two parties. Ballantyne took the southern and Ellingham and I the northern, and between us we collected information which proved very useful in the next two years. The Italians never seemed to go any distance inland and, as it was midsummer and the grazing had dried up, most of the Arabs were up on the coast, so the journey was uneventful, though after so many months of *sand* sea there was a thrill in turning north one evening west of Nofilia and coming within sight of the real thing. Remembering my Xenophon, I scrawled " Km. 6297 Θάλαττα, Θάλαττα " in my traverse book, and then, recollecting someone's phrase about the " rude smattering of the classics which deceives no one," felt a pedant and scratched it out.

Prendergast, with an eye on future operations, had suggested that we should attempt to get right up to the coast road, the Via Balbia. We tried east of Sirte and found little cover and the going rough, but farther east, south of Ras el Aali, discovered better ground and an easy way down to the road.

But that is another story.[1]

On reconnaissance jobs of this sort one day's routine differed little from that of another for four out of five were spent on the move. Before dawn the cook had lit the fire and for a few minutes you could lie, watching the eastern horizon brighten and the stars pale, in that most luxurious period of any day—when you are awake but need not get up. Then—"*Come* and get it." Porridge, a sausage and a half, tea (tapping the empty petrol tin to make the tea leaves sink), biscuits, " margarine with butter content " (content not stated), jam. I kept the last half-inch of tea to wet the sand I cleaned my plate with—a clean, quick operation in the sandstone desert but muddy and messy with the fine limestone dust in the north. After breakfast the start could be leisurely for until the sun had risen twenty degrees or so above the horizon it would not throw a sharp shadow on the sun-compass dial. Moving on, in open, " air " formation with an aircraft spotter up on the back of the truck, the first hour or two would be cool and you drove coated and bare-headed, then towards nine or ten, hitting you on the ridge tops in waves of warm air, the heat began. In summer by eleven (sun time) it would be scorching and soon after, with the sun almost vertical and its shadow too short to reach the graduations on the compass, there was an

---

[1] From this point onwards the reader will find many references to the " Road Watch." What that means is explained in Chapter 13.

excuse to stop. If the enemy was far off and there was no need for camouflage a tarpaulin stretched between two cars gave good shade, and so you lay for the midday heat, not sweating for sweat dried as it reached skin surface, dozing or talking of the unfailing summer noontime topic—drink. Only the wireless operator had to stir himself, listening in case Group Headquarters had a message, and the navigator following the sun, falsely pale and cool through the smoked glass screen of the theodolite, on its climb to the meridian.

By one o'clock the sun-compass could be used again and the patrol moved on. This was the best part of the day, for after 3 p.m. it would at least be growing hourly cooler, and in this Sirte desert the on-shore breeze would begin to blow. Towards sunset you camped, in low ground to hide the cooking-fire and car lights and near a sand drift if there was one for soft sleeping and good plate cleaning. Then supper—bully stew, tea and rum (in the early months before supplies in the Middle East ran short) ; drew to-morrow's water-bottle ration ; heard the B.B.C. news at 8 p.m. ; scraped a hole for your hip-bones and so to bed, to listen to the hammering of the fitter busy with the day's repairs ; the tapping of the wireless operator's key ; and the " Coming. Coming. UP " from the navigator to his booker as a star moved past the cross-hairs in the theodolite telescope and the hour, minute and second of Greenwich time were noted down.

Navigation in the desert has two parts—a " dead reckoning " course by compass and speedometer, and an " astro-fix " by observations of stars or sun to check the accuracy of the D.R. position. A magnetic compass is not much use in a car. The magnetism of shifting loads, changing gear levers and varying engine speeds makes such a compass almost impossible to compensate accurately ; the only way to get a correct bearing is to stop and walk a few yards away from the car. In our long journeys this would have meant frequent delays so we used sun-compasses whenever the sun shone—and occasionally with the moon !

The sun-compass was ideal for the job.[1] Without worrying about the induced magnetism of the car or the earth's magnetic field it gave directly the true bearing which had to be plotted on the map.

For the astro-fix observations we used theodolites. Before the war I had spent many desert nights sitting for hours cramped on an empty petrol tin before the car's headlights, working out the elaborate formula which ended—if all went well—in a latitude and longitude. But by 1940 things were easier, and this, thanks to the progress of aviation. In an aircraft at night, when you are taking star shots with your bubble sextant, it is no use if it takes you an hour to compute the results, for by that time, travelling at 200 m.p.h., you may be over the next continent. So the airmen had produced books of tables which greatly reduced the former labour and which would give a " fix " which was accurate to within a mile or so. Though this would shock the professional surveyors, it was accurate enough for our needs, for in the desert if you can land up within a mile of the well, oasis, road or fort for which you are aiming, there will be plenty of signs round about to lead you in to the actual spot.

There were, of course, occasions when the sums went wrong and a page of careful calculations showed one to be in Alaska or in St. Paul's ! Then the weary navigator must unpack his theodolite, find new stars and do his work over again.

And navigators were weary. They well earned the shilling a day which in 1942 the War Office approved to be paid to those who had passed the test for the new army trade—Land Navigator. Sitting all day beside the driver in the navigating car, with one eye on the sun-compass, the other on the speedometer and the third on his watch he would record the course and the distance run, seizing his chance between the joltings of the truck to write

[1] The sun-compass consists of a horizontal circle, divided into 360 degrees, with a central needle casting a shadow across the graduations. By rotating the circle, which is fixed to the dashboard of the car, throughout the day to correspond with the sun's movement through the sky, the shadow is made to indicate the true bearing on which the car is travelling.

down each bearing and mileage. At halts, crawling under the car for shade or crouching with his back to the winter wind, he must plot his course up to date in order to be able at any moment to show the patrol commander the position. And, at night, when the rest of the patrol were (more or less) comfortably in. bed, sharing with the tired wireless operator the light of a hooded inspection lamp, he must chase Arcturus or Aldebaran through the flapping pages of the Astronomical Navigation Tables, Volume G.

In time, goaded by Bagnold, the Army came to realise that there must be something in this navigation business after all, but not before one formation, ordered to march on a given bearing, disappeared from the battle along the grid line of the same value, which is not at all the same thing.

So the L.R.D.G. (but not Surveys or Military Training), became the Middle East experts in navigation. Bagnold wrote the two training pamphlets on the subject, and Browne, Croucher and I at various times conducted courses in navigation for officers and men from units of the Eighth Army. The first of these I took at Matruh in the spring of 1942, and did not complete without a passage of arms with an angry major of Field Security who was convinced that the torches we flashed to read the theodolite angles would bring a blitz on to the town. The lecture room was the battered parish hall of the Greek Church and, having no seats, I borrowed the pews out of the adjoining church, to the righteous indignation of the Church of England chaplain who had taken it over and the temporary dislocation of Sunday matins.

A couple of weeks after the completion of the Sirte reconnaissance Middle East gave us another similar task. They wanted a report on the country between Jalo and Agedabia, as seen through the eyes of a force of all arms with A.F.V.s and 3-tonners. Especially they wanted information about water supplies and possible landing grounds.

Though we did not know it at the time this was all part of the plan for the November offensive. It was intended to bluff the enemy into thinking that we were massing a large force at Jaghbub with which to advance on Jalo and thence up north to cut the coast road at Agedabia. Later, in the autumn, a number of tanks and lorries appeared in Jaghbub ; cars drove up and down all day raising the dust in feverish activity, and a " Divisional " wireless station poured out bogus messages.

The Rhodesian patrols did the job, Holliman with S1 covered the northern part of the country near Agedabia, and Olivey, with whom I went, the area round Jalo. We finished the reconnaissance without incident, zigzagging over the country and filling up old whisky bottles with samples of water, all very nasty, from the wells. They went in to Cairo and I suppose somebody analysed them.

Fortunately we had brought an Arab guide with us from Kufra, for the Italian maps were hopelessly inaccurate, and without him it would have been almost impossible to locate the actual wells. This old man never failed us, though it was eleven years since he had been in that area. On the way up from Kufra he was quite out of his depth for the speed of the cars threw out all his calculations, made at the two-and-a-half-mile-an-hour speed of walking camels, but within a few miles of a well he became interested and alert, stared at the half-remembered landmarks and led us straight to some three-foot waterhole scratched in the sand.

One of these was Bir Bettafal, the only good well near Jalo, to which the Arabs go out to fetch sweet water, for even in Jalo itself the wells are brackish. I hoped we might pick up some information here about Jalo, and we were in luck for we caught two Arabs with camels just about to leave. One was a precocious and rather unpleasant youth, the Arab equivalent of the English boy who recognises the make of every motor car at a glance, but he knew a great deal about the garrison of the oasis. He had been to an Italian school and was glib in descriptions of " contra-aerea " and " anti-carri " guns. As he said he had a married sister at Kufra it did not seem much hardship to take him back there for the sake of the information he could give.

The following January, when we were in Jalo, I met his father, a charming man, head of the big Majbri family of Bishara amongst whom I had some friends in Egypt. He welcomed the British but was rather resentful of some who had carried off his son from Bir Bettafal the summer before. I sympathised deeply and have wondered since if he ever found out.

Middle East wanted the results of the Jalo reconnaissance as soon as possible, so when the reports and maps were ready I took them to Cairo by air. The journey was a good example of L.R.D.G. aviation, typical of the flights which Prendergast and Barker had been making regularly for the past few months.

There are safer methods of travel than flying across the heart of the Libyan Desert in single-engined aircraft without wireless, and so we had done what we could to improve matters. The R.A.F. came to Kufra from Cairo by way of Wadi Halfa, but the Wacos were slow and the longer journey would have meant a day wasted. So earlier in the summer Prendergast had made a more direct air route of his own, to join the Nile at Asyut, and had laid out a chain of landing grounds and stocked them with petrol, oil, water and food.

From Kufra to the Gilf Kebir the route followed the track of supply convoys to Wadi Halfa, and if one had a forced landing there the chances of being picked up were quite good. But from Wadi Sura to Kharga was 400 miles of unfrequented desert and along most of this stretch we had made a depot of water and biscuits every fifteen miles.

There were three of us in the Little Waco ; Barker, Arnold navigating, and myself. We took off as soon as it was light enough to see, hoping to get the worst part of the journey over before the September day reached its hottest. Before we had gone far the sun was up and we were flying into its eye, unable to see anything ahead. How much has been written of the glories of the desert dawn and how grudgingly we admired its beauty that summer at Kufra, longing for the moment when the scorching 14-hour day would end.

To the south were the two flat-topped hills which marked Kendall's Dump, alias " Twenty-Four—Twenty-Four," where the latitude and longitude of those numbers cross. Here we had a landing ground, and here on his first arrival at Kufra Bagnold had built up a dump of food and petrol, foreseeing the possibility of having to evacuate the oasis in a hurry and make his way back to the Nile.

Thirty minutes later we were at the Gilf and turned south along the cliffs. Three thousand feet below, halted in a bunch, were a dozen Mack 10-tonners on the last lap of their run from Wadi Halfa. They must have taken us for a roving C.R. 42 for they scattered in an instant like a herd of lumbering elephants surprised at the first shot.

At Wadi Sura we circled the landing ground to check position and then turned east across the Gilf. The Gilf is, with Gebel 'Uweinat, the most striking feature of the southern desert. On the west the cliffs, almost impassable, rise for a thousand feet above the plain to the flat plateau at their top. This is a relic of some earlier desert surface now suspended high above the surrounding country, preserved from erosion by the harder sandstone strata of its surface layers. The 100-mile stretch across the Gilf was the least pleasant of the journey ; at the worst after a forced landing exactly in the middle one would have to walk fifty miles to the landing ground at either end. And because of the difficulty of getting cars up on to the plateau we had made no dumps of food and water there.

We crossed the Gilf and landed—with a bump—at our new landing ground at Gebel Ailam, filled up with petrol and oil and left a note in the post-box to say we had passed by. The bump was no fault of Barker's, for on a featureless, sandy surface in the glare of a summer day it is terribly difficult to judge height and you may well land fifteen feet above ground—or below it.

From here on to Kharga was the most difficult stretch of the flight. The plan made by Prendergast was that in the event of a forced landing we should come down on the car tracks, walk to the nearest water and wait for a rescue party. This meant flying low enough to see the tracks, which by now, with the sun casting little side-shadow, were only visible at about 300 feet, and so being unable to go up to the cool air at 6000. For 200 miles we stared down at the faint wheel tracks, Arnold peering out at one side and I at the other, now seeing them for a few moments, now losing them again.

A hundred miles from Kharga was the last emergency landing ground which I had marked out in June. Prendergast, flying to Cairo a few weeks earlier, had been unable to find it, for in all this desert good landmarks are very scarce. There had been some jesting at my expense and it was up to me to prove that the landing ground really existed. By now in the glare and the heat haze we had lost the car tracks for good and I was doubtful of picking up the one landmark I remembered, a dog's tooth hill standing on a broken ridge, for in the desert a landscape first seen in the light of early morning looks entirely different when the shadows are falling the other way. However, the hill showed itself and we landed for oil for the over-heated engine.

In the air again there was no need to continue track-following for the great limestone scarp beyond Kharga showed clear ahead, and we could go up to 6000 feet and keep the engine temperature down. Below us to the left was the broken country round " Aviator's Grave " ; the record on the 1/500,000 map of some forgotten tragedy of the last war, now nothing but a few square yards of desert within a fence of rusty barbed wire and the inevitable blackened food tins scattered beside.

From Asyut, where the Nile was in flood across the valley and where the Shell agent produced cold drinks and biscuits, it was two hours easy going to Cairo over the weird landscape of the Eastern Desert where the *wadis* and their many-branched tributaries look like a scale model in a geography class designed to illustrate the progress of erosion.

The War Office and Middle East were pleased with the information we had collected.

GENERAL HEADQUARTERS,
MIDDLE EAST FORCES.
29*th September*, 1941.

MY DEAR BAGNOLD,
    I have received the following message from the C.I.G.S. :

"I am very impressed by the work done by your Long Range Desert Patrols. Their latest reconnaissance is a fine example of their skill and daring. I would be grateful if you would convey my warmest congratulations."

I am very glad indeed to forward this message and will be grateful if you will add my congratulations on a very fine performance, one of many that the Group have done, and convey the contents of this letter to all concerned.

              Yours sincerely,
                  C. J. AUCHINLECK.

Col. R. A. BAGNOLD.

CHAPTER SEVEN

" A " SQUADRON AT SIWA

WHILE T and G patrols were returning from Murzuk and, later on, while the incidents described in the last chapter were taking place, other patrols were busy in the north.

Wavell's advance into Cyrenaica in December, 1940, had cut off the Italians in Jaghbub. His strategy was to contain the garrison there so an Australian cavalry regiment guarded the northern approaches and Steele with R patrol watched the western side, while the Italian broadcasts turned Castegna, their commander in the oasis, into a national hero for resisting attacks which were never made. R patrol sat outside Jaghbub for six weeks with only a fine haul of brandy from an Italian convoy coming in from the north-west to mitigate cold, boredom and days of driving duststorm. T patrol relieved them at the beginning of March and Jaghbub fell to a fierce assault by the Australians a few days later.

Jaghbub is the Holy City of the Senussi, for here beside the white-domed mosque is buried Sayed Ibn Ali es Senussi, the founder of the sect. For generations it was the centre of Senussi learning, and pilgrimage to the tomb of the Sayed brought the pilgrim a reward second only to that of the Holy Cities of Arabia —Mecca and Medina. From all other aspects Jaghbub is one of the most revolting spots in Libya. A few wretched palm groves and thin tamarisk scrub straggle dejectedly across the oasis-depression ; mosquitoes and sand flies swarm and the water must have been the inspiration for Epsom Salts.

In late March and April of 1941 Mitford took two patrols up into Cyrenaica to do reconnaissance work for Desforce, keeping a watch on the country south of Gebel Akhdar [1] to Msus and

[1] The Gebel Akhdar (" The Green Mountain ") hereinafter also called simply " The Gebel," is the high-lying, fertile part of Cyrenaica.

97

beyond. They had some skirmishes with the enemy, took a few prisoners and destroyed some vehicles, but early in April the Germans made their first appearance in Cyrenaica and the British withdrawal to the Egyptian frontier began.

Y1 patrol took part in the fighting outside Mechili, but escaped capture when the place fell, all save one man, Cave,[1] who was in Mechili when the Germans attacked. The following is the fine story of how he was captured, escaped, lived for six weeks with Arabs and finally reached our lines at Tobruk :

" Y1 patrol had returned from Msus to Mechili after the former had been over-run by the Germans. On arrival at Mechili the patrol was ordered to go out west again and harass the advancing enemy convoys, but unfortunately my truck had a damaged radiator, and as the Indian Ordnance workshops were at Mechili I had to stay there to get the repairs done.

" During the afternoon of April 6th the Germans began to shell us with long range. guns. At dawn on the 7th the main attack was launched with infantry supported by tanks. After three hours furious resistance Mechili fell, and I found myself a prisoner of war with 1500 other Indians, Aussies and Tommies. Here we remained for the next five days, living on one tin of ' M. and V.' and half a pint of water per man per day—perhaps.

" On the sixth day they moved us to the P.O.W. camp at Derna. During my stay there for the next seven days food was anything but plentiful, and the old Italian barracks where we were billeted were filthy. There were seven cases of typhoid and a hundred of dysentery. The only redeeming feature was that we were allowed to write one letter home ; mine arrived in England in about five weeks. The Germans treated us well but the Italians seemed to grudge us everything they did for us which was not much.

[1] Cpl. A. H. Cave, M.M., Royal Wilts Yeomanry.

" During the first few days I became friendly with eight Australians. One of them was of the same mind as myself and wanted to escape at the first opportunity. On the afternoon of Sunday 21st, feeling particularly 'browned off,' we decided to make a break for it when darkness came.

" At about seven o'clock Alfred, my Australian friend, came into the billet and told me that the guards who had been patrolling the front of the building were nowhere to be seen and this only left the machine-gun posts encircling the camp to be avoided. We had accumulated eight tins of bully and two water bottles and six Italian biscuits each, and here was the chance we had been waiting for. We said good-bye to the others and dropped off the wall into the compound which encircled the billets. It was a moonless night and nobody noticed us. We made our way along the compound wall to an old cookhouse where we noticed a gap in the wall. We got through this and, hardly daring to breathe, crawled between the machine-gun posts about ten yards away. Luckily the ground was covered with large boulders which gave some cover and after about 400 yards we found ourselves in an old stone quarry.

" The next difficulty was to get up the Derna escarpment as the road had to be avoided at all costs. The first 500 feet were fairly easy, but then we came to a precipitous cliff which took us nearly four hours to climb. At the top we found a convenient cave and sheltered there till dawn came and we could get our bearings.

" Morning found us due west of Derna and, as we had to avoid the airport at the top of the pass, we decided to make a detour inland. After a few miles we met two Arabs who gave us cigarettes and offered us a meal in their tent. But we wanted to push on, so they put us on a track which they said avoided the airfield and led to another encampment of friendly Arabs. We met two other Arabs further on who gave us a very welcome drink of tea. They advised us to leave the track and cross the Wadi Derna, but this brought us right on top of the airfield. From there we watched our own planes bombing and straffing the hangars.

" We walked all that day and the next, keeping within sight of the sea and crossing several large *wadis* on the way. In the last of these we decided to spend the night, hoping to get some shelter from the bitter night wind off the sea, and in spite of the cold did manage to get a few hours sleep. We started off before dawn but after the first few miles my sandals gave up the ghost. I had been prepared for this and had picked up an old pair of boots. They were much too small, but I found them quite wearable after I had cut out the toccaps and heels. About noon we met an Arab boy with three horses who told us there were some ' Inglizi ' in a cave not far away. He offered us a ride and we soon reached an Arab camp near Ras et Tin. They gave us a great welcome and took us to a cave nearby where to our great delight we found three other British soldiers and a Canadian. They gave us a grand meal of bully, porridge and goat's milk.

" Here we had the first good night's sleep since Derna. Our feet were badly blistered so we decided to lie up and rest for a few days. We learned that nearby there was an officer and three other men, one of whom was badly wounded. They had hired an Arab guide and intended to try and break through the enemy's lines and join our forces at Tobruk, so we moved up to their cave. Their plan was to get a boat sent along the coast from Tobruk to pick us all up, but after three days the Arab came back saying that their attempt had failed and that the officer and one of the men had been recaptured at Gazala. In the meantime two other officers who had escaped from Derna were brought in by the Arabs. At about the same time an Arab pedlar who had come from Tobruk through Acroma, told us that he had met no enemy patrols on the way. After much argument this Arab agreed to take the two officers back by the route he had come provided they wore Arab dress and paid him £30 each. They were to try and get a boat sent out for the rest of us.

32

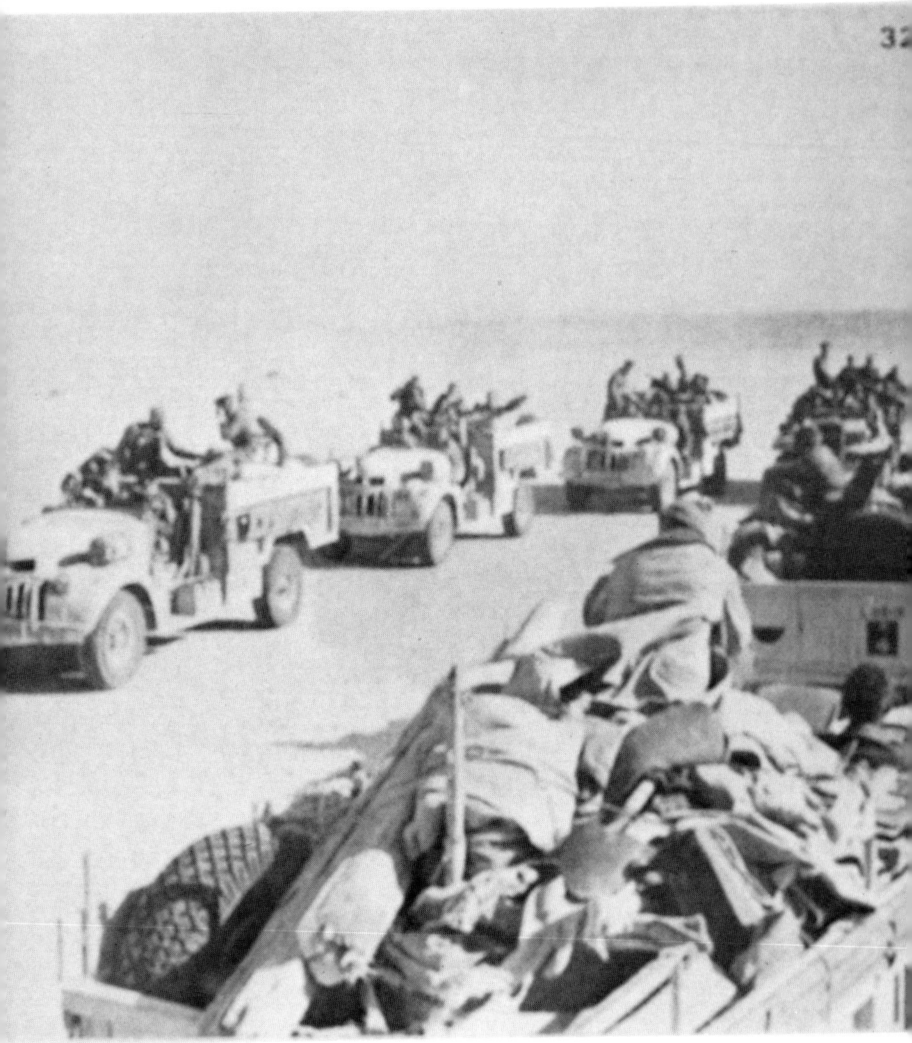

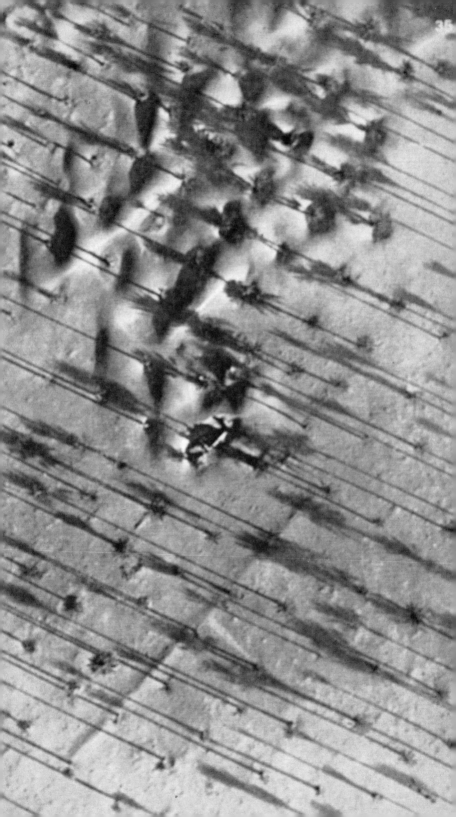

" They went off, but after 14 days no boat had arrived and food was getting scarce, so the rest of us remaining decided to break up into small parties and try to reach Tobruk. The wounded man had recovered sufficiently to go with us.

" On the 22nd May the Canadian, his friend, Alfred and I started out. By midday we were standing on the escarpment which overlooks the old Italian seaplane base at Bomba. Before we could go further we had to cross the road at the foot of the escarpment along which traffic was passing continuously. We waited till the road seemed clear and were just about to make a dash across to the nearest cover when we heard a large lorry coming. It was impossible to go either way without being seen, and I thought to myself, ' This is back to the prison camp.' We dropped flat on our faces where we were. I watched the truck coming round the corner about a hundred yards away and lumbering slowly towards us. It was an open ten-tonner with a party of Italians in the back. My heart sank lower and lower, and as it drew level with us I waited to hear shouts from the truck to say that we had been spotted, but to my amazement it simply passed by without one of the party turning his head or looking in our direction. We did not wait to see if any more lorries were coming, but got up and ran as hard as we could for the nearest cover. This time we had a good look round before we moved on. After a few miles we stopped and shared two tins of bully and drank sparingly of our water.

" By late evening we sighted the white house at Tmimi which we intended to pass after dark. As it was still too light to attempt it we stopped and had a dip in the sea. As soon as it was dark we started off following the shore, but luck was against us this time and we kept running into large waterways which ran anything up to half a mile inland. Soon we were wet and cold trying to cross them, so we decided to give it up as a bad job and wait till first light to see where we were. We shared two more tins of bully and spent the rest of the night walking up and down to keep warm.

" Daylight of May 23rd found us about two hundred yards from the white house which we had been trying to pass the night before. As there seemed to be no one about we made a dash for it and reached cover about a mile and a half beyond. We headed for the shore again and walked on untroubled till late afternoon when we sighted Gazala Point. Here we were held up by a party of Italians who were pumping water with a small engine about fifty yards from the shore. As our own supply was running short we decided to wait till dark and see if we could replenish our water-bottles. At seven o'clock the working party knocked off and went away in a lorry, except for two men who apparently lived in a tent nearby. We gave them an hour's grace and then crept up to the well. As there was no way of obtaining water without going down, I lowered myself gently down the pipe till I reached the water and then the others let down the bottles on the end of a string. The water stank pretty badly, but we took a chance and drank our fill. Later we were to regret it.

" After three more hours walking we found ourselves in the middle of a large car park, and then the water which we had drunk began to have effect on our stomachs till our legs gave out altogether and we had to stop and rest. We had to get up the escarpment which we could see in front and so round the point, and it was nearly dawn before we reached the top, much too exhausted to go on any further.

" I was roughly awakened by Alfred who told me to take a good look round. At the bottom of the escarpment was the car park we had passed the night before ; in front of us was Gazala landing ground covered with men and aircraft, and a few yards from where we were sleeping was the road on which a large lorry had appeared. There was only one thing for it, and that was to stay in the bushes and hope for the best. When the lorry had passed we buried ourselves deeper in the scrub and prepared to remain there for the rest of the day. As the sun rose we became very thirsty and by evening had drunk a full waterbottle which should have lasted two days.

We set off again at dusk and crossed the landing ground, but after walking a few miles were too exhausted to go on and had to rest for the greater part of the night. We set off again before dawn, passing several camps in the early morning light.

" By midday on the 25th we were halted by another camp, right on the coast, but could not pass it till late afternoon when the men had finished swimming. After we had got by and walked on for a bit we decided to find some cover and try to sleep for the rest of the night. We made an early start next morning, passing several German camps in the semi-darkness, but once again we were halted by another camp at midday. These continual halts had been a great strain on our water and that afternoon I shared my last drop with Alfred, although at first he refused to take any, saying that he ought to have been more careful with his own. We decided that as soon as it was dark one of us would have to try and get water from the camp. The lot fell to me, so taking off what remained of my boots, I wrapped my feet in rags so as to make no noise on the rocky ground. Leaving the other three on the shore I managed to reach one of the trucks without being seen, and had just spotted a couple of likely tins when a German popped his head round the corner and no doubt said in his own language, ' What the Hell are you doing? ' I did not wait to tell him but beat it for the shore as fast as I could with the German in full cry after me. In the dark I missed the others so could only make my way along the beach and hope that they would catch me up later on. Meanwhile the German's yells had roused the whole camp. Men were shouting and dogs barking and rifles being let off. Gradually the noise died away as I got further off, and when I was out of earshot I flopped down on the sand, absolutely dead beat. I stayed here some time, hoping the others would catch me up, but at last I gave it up and staggered off along the coast. The rags had fallen off in the mad rush and my feet were cut to ribbons on the sharp stones. To keep myself going I had to roll constantly in the sea which made me cold and wet and forced me to keep walking to get warm again. Later on I was lucky to run into an Arab camp. I woke up an Arab who gave me a piece of stale bread and filled my water bottle. Again I made the mistake of drinking too much and was doubled up with pains in the stomach for the rest of the night.

" On the 27th I was too weak to move more than a mile or two and spent the rest of the day and the following night trying to sleep ; also my water had sunk to a very low level again and my mouth was too sore to eat the remains of the bread which the Arabs had given me.

" I started early next morning but the coast was becoming more rocky, intersected with deep *wadis*. Having no boots and walking on the rocks in my bare feet slowed down my progress so much that by midday I had scarcely made four or five miles. Then ahead of me I could see an M.G. post which meant that I was held up again till nightfall. Later I learned that it was the German front line. I found a small cave among the rocks and stayed there for the rest of the day. My water had dwindled to a wee drop in the bottom of the bottle and it was all I could do to stop myself drinking it. I could feel my resistance going and began to see things, my mind wandering. It seemed as though the sea was mocking me and I wanted to get into it and swim and swim and swim. Another time I thought I would go to the outpost, only five hundred yards away, and give myself up, and I actually got up and started to walk there but realised what I was doing and persuaded myself to go back to the cave again.

" The hours dragged by and at last the sun set and it was safe for me to move again.

" All night I crawled up and down the *wadis* on my hands and knees as my feet were too badly cut to bear my weight. Sometimes I wandered up and down the *wadi* beds with the crazy idea that I might find water. I found a cactus and breaking off one of the leaves pulped it between two stones and sucked it. It tasted bitter and made my mouth and throat terribly sore, but it did ease my thirst a bit. I crawled

out of this *wadi* only to find myself on the top of another one.
Far below I could see the rollers breaking on the white sand.
Slowly I crawled to the bottom and began to walk across the
beach. Suddenly I dropped flat by sheer instinct. ; in front
of me were rows of barbed wire. I lay still but nothing
happened, so I crawled slowly up to it and still there was
nothing to be seen or heard. It did not penetrate my muddled
brain that I had reached the British front line. I crawled
through the wire and started up the other side of the *wadi*.
I had got about half-way up when I heard voices and lay
still to see if I could make out what they were saying. I tried
to think what I would do if it was the enemy, as in my present
condition it was impossible to go back or forwards. At last I
could stand it no longer : I had to find out one way or the
other so I let out a loud shout. Instantly the skyline was lined
with men and bayonets, I could hear the bolts drawn back
and click and a very un-English voice shouted, ' Come on,
come on up.' I shouted back to them to hold their fire and
scrambled to the top. Two men promptly grabbed me by the
arms and another shone a torch. ' English,' I gasped, and
the voice behind the light said, ' No English.' I was so
relieved to be safe that I sat down and nearly cried my eyes
out. As soon as I had explained who I was and where I had
come from the Indians, for it was an Indian unit, could not do
enough for me. They gave me hot tea and sugar and *chupatties*
and fetched the officer in charge. I asked if three other men
had come in but they had seen nothing of them. One of them
gave me his blankets and curled up in them I had the first
real sleep for five weeks.

" At dawn the sergeant woke me and told me that an
Australian and two other men had come in. I was so over-
joyed at seeing Alfred again that I had another good cry
feeling a hell of a lot better after it. He told me that after I
had been chased out of the German camp they stayed where
they were all that night and the next day, waiting to see if I
had been captured. The same night they started off again

and found the Arab camp where they learned that I had passed through, so they rested there for a day, arriving only a few hours after me. The captain of that sector asked us to break-fast and gave us fishcakes, bread and real butter and jam, and to finish it off a bottle of beer and a packet of Players. Later on in the day a truck arrived to take us to H.Q. in Tobruk. In the evening the four of us parted for our various units. I caught a submarine chaser going to Alexandria, where I arrived three days later. Five days after that I joined Y patrol again in Siwa and so ended my capture and my escape from Derna."

All the summer of 1941 Mitford had " A " squadron at Siwa under command of Desforce. I have not had access to all the records of that period and since I never went up from Kufra to Siwa I have no firsthand knowledge of the operations of the patrols. But stories used to find their way down to Kufra. We heard of Crichton-Stuart out on a reconnaissance of the country round Marada at the time when the Germans first appeared in Cyrenaica. By the time he turned homewards the enemy had taken Msus and were nearing Mechili, and the petrol dumps at which he had hoped to re-fuel were in German hands or had been destroyed by us. His journey ended short of Jaghbub with eighteen men in one truck and a twenty-mile walk to finish up with.

Of " Jake " Easonsmith[1] too tales began to reach us in Kufra. I first heard them from two Arabs ; they could not manage his name and thought I was rather stupid not to know it, for surely every one had heard about his exploits; the Arabs up north, they said, called him *Batl es Sahra*, the Hero of the Desert.

The main task of " A " squadron in the early summer was to keep a watch on the enemy's southern flank, working up the Wire from Jaghbub, and in the oasis itself to try with much ostentatious

---

[1] To-day, 16.11.43, I heard that Jake, who had succeeded Prendergast as O.C. L.R.D.G., was killed yesterday in Leros. Brave, wise, with an uprightness that shamed lesser men, he was, I think, the finest man we ever had in L.R.D.G.

driving to and fro to bluff the enemy reconnaissance aircraft into thinking that there was a much larger force in the oasis than the fifty odd men of G and Y patrols.

In June a proper garrison came to Jaghbub and the patrols were free to do real L.R.D.G. work again. Then began those journeys to the southern side of Gebel Akhdar which continued so successfully for the next eighteen months. There can have been few weeks during that period when some L.R.D.G. patrol, based on Siwa or Kufra or even on the Faiyum, was not out in the area between 'Agheila and Tobruk.

Jake carried out the first of these patrols. Its intention was threefold—to get an idea of the strength of the enemy reserves in the Gebel, three hundred miles behind the front line which was then at Sollum ; to discover which were the most important lines of communication in use, and to contact the Arabs of Cyrenaica and learn what amount of assistance we could expect from them. Of the three the last was perhaps the most important, for it started a partnership between the Arabs and the British which lasted till Cyrenaica was finally cleared of the Axis in December, 1942.

Part of the credit for establishing such a partnership must go to L.R.D.G., alias " Libyan Taxis Ltd.," guaranteed to transport passengers and goods on request to any point in Libya. But equal credit is due to the men whom we delivered to the enemy's back door—Haselden, Pedlar, Penman, Seagrim, Knight, Guignol, Melot, Flower, Losquier, Mackintosh, Lee Smith, Tarrant, Lewis—to mention only those whose names[1] I can remember now. From Egypt most of them—schoolmasters, cotton brokers, business men or bankers—they won the confidence of the Libyan Arabs and retained it through months of reverses and retreats.

In July Jake was up near Gambut, nearer than usual to the rear of the Axis positions at Sollum, trying to locate dumps of

---

[1] In the case of some of the exploits described in this book, where I considered it necessary for their safety, I have changed the names of those who took part in them. I ask those who find themselves treated in this way not to suppose that I have ascribed their achievements to others. If, after the war, the opportunity arises I will restore their proper names.

petrol, food and ammunition. His patrol had halted for the night and the cook was brewing up. Jake, strolling over a nearby ridge while waiting for supper, found himself looking down on to an Italian mobile workshop, spread out in a fold in the ground. It was still quite light and he waited till the matter in hand—supper —was finished, and then with three cars attacked the unsuspecting Italians. It was soon over. All the enemy save two bolted immediately. These, having surrendered, begged a moment's grace to collect their kit and, while they were fetching it, the patrol wrecked ten Diesel trucks and the workshop lorries.

At meal times on the way back to Siwa the cook, as was his usual practice, would dig a small hole for his fire, The first two or three times he got out his spade for this Ugo and Christo, panic-stricken, flung themselves on their knees and begged for mercy. It took a day or two to convince them that he was not about to dig their graves !

One day in August an Arab brought word to Siwa that a wounded British pilot was hiding near Bir Bidihi, a desert well a hundred miles inside enemy territory. A patrol went off to bring him in but at the place described there was no sign of any pilot. After searching for a time they found the mouth of a rock-cut cistern, dry after the long summer. As a last chance they shouted down this and to their surprise out scrambled an Arab, very frightened and denying all knowledge of British pilots. The patrol's hopes fell again when suddenly from the cistern mouth appeared a bald, pink head followed by the smiling face of the missing airman. " Why did you say he wasn't here ? " demanded the patrol. " Oh," said the Arab, " only yesterday he was telling me that the English soldiers never had beards, so I thought you must be Germans."

On October 14th Jake left Siwa on the last of his operations before the November offensive began. His " tasks," as the Operation Order called them, were to make a " going " recon-naissance of three patches of country across which the Eighth Army might want to move later on ; to pick up John Haselden returning from some expedition with his Arabs into the Gebel, and to drop some "doctored" Italian ammunition on any suitable desert track.

Jake had two alternative rendezvous with Haselden. He was not at the first, though hiding with some Arabs nearby were three British soldiers escaped a week before from the prison camp in Benghazi and very glad to be in safety again. So Jake went on to the second rendezvous near 'Ain Bu Sfeia. Not finding Haselden there either he hid his trucks, took three days' rations, and went off alone on foot to scour the country round. (Haselden came in to the trucks while he was away.)

Jake, in his search of the countryside, found a large enemy camp near 'Ain Bu Sfeia and, lying up for a day watching the traffic on the track which ran towards Mechili, realised that there was an abnormal amount of enemy transport on the move. This could only mean that reserves were being brought forward from the Gebel, and it was of the first importance to get more details. So he decided to arrange an ambush three or four miles beyond the camp and try to take a prisoner for interrogation.

His plan was this. With two of his three trucks placed on rising ground which commanded the track, he with the third would have a "breakdown" on the route and hold up a vehicle for help.

To begin with all went well. The ambush party was in position, an Italian lorry approaching and Jake "broken down" on the track, with his own head and the driver's inside the bonnet and the gunner lying under a tarpaulin in the back. The lorry drew near and Jake held up his hand. It stopped and he walked over to ask for help, with one hand gripping a Tommy-gun hidden not very successfully behind his back. As he stepped up to the lorry the driver realised what was up, threw open the door and grappled with him. The passenger, an officer, drew his pistol, emptied it at Jake and the struggling driver, missed all his shots and bolted up the hillside to be brought down by machine-gun fire from the trucks. The driver wrested himself free and bolted but was stopped by a quick shot from Jake.

Meanwhile the situation was developing. The lorry had in

fact been the first of a convoy of twenty which, when Jake first moved into position, had been hidden by dead ground. These had by now come up and halted and men were clambering out, some to hide under the trucks, while others, bolder, seized their rifles and opened fire. From the high ground the Lewis gun added to the confusion. But so far Jake had not got his prisoner and it was clear that he was badly outnumbered and soon would have to withdraw.

The last scene, as one of the patrol told me afterwards, was of Jake, with his pockets stuffed with Mills bombs, crying, " I must get a prisoner, I must get a prisoner," hunting down the line of lorries and bolting the Italians like rabbits from underneath them with his bombs.

In the end he got two : one died the same day, but the other gave the information we needed : Italian prisoners were never reluctant to speak, and a day later Middle East knew that the Trieste Motorized Division was moving down to Mechili.

CHAPTER EIGHT

THE AUTUMN OFFENSIVE, 1941

TOWARDS the end of October, 1941, we knew that the Eighth Army's attack on the Sollum line would begin in mid-November. There is a strange satisfaction in sharing a really big secret, and it was exciting to go with Prendergast to Main Army H.Q. at Ma'aten Bagush where in the cool, concrete dug-out among the sand hills, with the paper screens carefully let down over the maps on the walls, Thorburn and Harding Newman of the " Plans " staff told us as much as they thought it good for us to know.

L.R.D.G.'s part in the advance was to " observe enemy reactions." This meant in fact that on November 18th most of the patrols were to be sitting on the desert tracks south of the Gebel Akhdar to report on enemy reinforcements or withdrawals.

The first thing to do was to move Headquarters and the Kufra squadron to Siwa and here we profited from the Clayton-Steele reconnaissance of a year before. Untroubled by the enemy in Jalo the patrols crossed the Sand Sea by the Howard's Cairn route and were all in Siwa by November 10th. All, that is, except Holliman with S1 patrol, who was on a real L.R.D.G. job, planned before we knew about the coming offensive.

It happened as follows :

At 6 a.m. on the morning of November 7th a Lancia lorry was moving northwards on the Hon-Misurata road near Bu Ngem. In it were a handful of Italian soldiers and some Libyans. The Italians, from the garrison at Hon, were on their way to Tripoli, thence to be repatriated to Italy on compassionate grounds in view of their long service in Africa. One of them, Saladini, was a sergeant pilot in their air force who had been at Kufra in 1940 with a flight of Ghiblis, and had had the fun of bombing W patrol on their way to attack 'Ain Dua at 'Uweinat in November. When he got back to Italy he would have some fine tales to tell of how the glorious Regia Aeronautica had scattered the British desert raiders.

The morning was cold and a steady drizzle of rain was falling, but the Italians, thinking of their own sunny homes, did not worry about the weather. They could hardly have been worrying about the enemy, for they were at least 500 miles from where the nearest British could reasonably be expected to be. Life seemed pretty good to the men in the lorry.

At ten past six the Lancia was blazing by the roadside and the Italians were on top of the S1 patrol trucks at the beginning of their six-day journey back to Kufra and a P.O.W. camp.

To return to the enemy " reactions." To begin with these were few. Our advance had not gone as well as had been expected and the patrols sat watching empty roads.

Simms had some excitement, caught in one of those unfortunate incidents which happened two or three times in L.R.D.G.'s life. On November 17th, he was moving up to position on the Tariq el 'Abd when three Beaufighters roared over the horizon and opened fire on the patrol. This was one of the risks which L.R.D.G. just had to take. Naturally it was impossible to warn the R.A.F. of the position of all patrols at all times, and a pilot could hardly be blamed for assuming that a party of cars a hundred miles west of Sollum were of the enemy. Nor could we paint on the cars the standard ground-to-air recognition markings used on all vehicles up on the coast. The Beaufighters straffed Y1 patrol till their ammunition was finished and the W/T truck' ablaze, in spite of Simms's calm attempt to spread out the flapping ground recognition strips, and with fingers numbed in the cold wind to light the " flares, ground, illuminating," which were the pre-arranged signal for the R.A.F.

However, Timpson got one back on the Italian Air Force a day or two later. He was hiding up with G2 Patrol near Ma'aten Grara, watching for cross-desert traffic from Agedabia to

Tobruk, when a B.R.20, with its engine spluttering, came low over his cars and force-landed behind a rise. When Timpson, with two trucks, arrived on the scene, the Italians were busy putting up their aerial to signal for help. They might have got it from him if the rear-gunner, still inside the aircraft, had not jumped so hurriedly to his gun.

Timpson sent two prisoners back to Siwa ; the rest of the crew he buried beside the ashes of their plane.

Meanwhile most of the signals coming into Siwa said that no movement had been observed. The patrols were getting bored and begged for a job of work to do. They soon got one.

At Eighth Army things were not going too well. Our own high command had changed and Rommel was pushing his tank columns up to the frontier wire ; there was a hectic afternoon when every driver, batman and cook at Advanced Army H.Q. was being mobilised to beat off one of these thrusts. On November 24th we received a signal, on " Emergency Ops " priority, which afterwards became a household word—" Advance and attack." That was all it said, but a second message was more explicit, " Act with utmost vigour offensively against any enemy targets or communications within your reach." A free hand to carry out a tall order.

I have not space here to describe all that was done. As usual with L.R.D.G. the operations were widely spread ; Tony Hay with G1 shot up the coast road near Agedabia ; Simms destroyed a dozen or more vehicles in a car park near Sidi Saleh ; Olivey (S2) and Browne (R2) attacked traffic on the Barce-Maraua road and Lloyd Owen captured the fort at El Ezzeiat. In a small way we did what we could.

Here is David Lloyd Owen's story of the action at El Ezzeiat :

" General Cunningham's attack had been in progress for about a week and we were getting rather bored at seeing nothing pass by the crossroads at Rotunda Segnali. Before we left Siwa for this patrol I was quite sure we should have a busy time watching these tracks, all of which I felt the enemy was bound to use. However, on the 24th my impatience was relieved by a signal which came at the evening call-time, telling us to make contact with the other Yeomanry patrol and go north with them to the main Tobruk-Derna road. We had orders on arrival there to do all we could to interrupt the enemy's flow of petrol and supplies.

" At last it seemed that we were to have some fun, and though I was thrilled at the prospect of a free hand to do all the damage we could, I was at the same time a bit anxious, for the work was all so strange and unknown to me. This was my first patrol and I knew little of the country and less of the successful methods of raiding the enemy behind his lines. That night we met Y1, and Frank Simms and I arranged to attack the road simultaneously and then withdraw to make fresh plans before we went in again. We hoped that over a long stretch of road we would be able to play this sort of game for some time, and I was encouraged by Frank's reckless confidence.

" The next day we waited in cover and made all our preparations to move late in the afternoon. We knew that enemy aircraft did not usually fly later than about tea-time in that area and so we lay low all day. It was a disturbing day for many aircraft passed low over our hideout as though they had warning of our plans and were searching for us.

" After a good meal Frank moved off ahead of me and we agreed to spend the night together a little further north. We watched him go off in a cloud of dust and again I hoped that the Italian airmen would have finished for the day. We followed soon afterwards, strung out in a long line and hoping that it would not surprise any one unduly to see six vehicles moving peacefully along a track about a hundred miles behind the enemy's lines.

" The sun had set and it was turning cold when of a sudden I heard the warning cry of 'Aircraft' from my gunner. Hearing that shout so many times during the day at our hiding place I had become almost indifferent to it, but this time I knew it was serious and turned round to see a single-seater Italian fighter sweep over the last truck. It roared over our heads and we could only wait and see what it would do. I watched it swing twice round us in a wide circle and told the men to hold their fire till we were sure that it meant trouble. The third time the pilot flew a little wider and then came in straight as though to strafe us. Suddenly I thought he might think better of us if we all showed our friendliness, and so I waved up to him and in the dusk we watched him fly off waving cheerily out of his cockpit and going home satisfied to dinner.

" We moved on a bit further and slept, but did not see Frank again that night. Next morning we overtook him, made a plan for a rendezvous later in the day and parted again. We had not gone far when a single truck appeared to the west ; I knew it could not be one of Frank's, and soon through my glasses I could make out a small Ford with a lot of soldiers standing in the back. We drew closer and in the early morning light they looked cold and miserable, and one shot from my gunner behind me was enough to make them surrender.

" We were pleased to get a good vehicle and a few prisoners, but sorry for them as they were on their way to Derna on leave. One spoke English well and admitted that they did not much mind being captured as they were all keen to see Cairo.

" The interpreter said they had come from a small fort in the neighbourhood. I had not heard of this place and encouraged him to talk, and before long had all the details of the garrison and their armament and also his ready co-operation in our desire to go and attack it. ' It was only a few miles off and he sat on my truck and guided me over the best route.

" Soon we could see this small desert outpost of the Italian Empire and I hoped that by driving straight up to it we could get reasonably near before the garrison suspected

anything. As we approached I could see a man on the
roof watching us through his glasses. Our Italian friend
said they would probably surrender if we showed fight and so
I decided to attack. We made a hasty plan, but I was not
well versed in the art of attacking forts in unarmoured 30-cwt
trucks.

" We drove forward in open formation till they began to
fire by which time we were only about two hundred yards
away and it was unwise to endanger the trucks further. So
we left the drivers to guard the prisoners and rushed towards
the fort on foot. We reached some outhouses unhurt and
took cover.

" Then there ensued a short period of close range sniping
during which we killed two of the enemy and made the others
keep their heads down. It seemed that we should have to
change our plan of attack for I could see no end to this
friendly sniping ; it had done us no harm, but we numbered
only eight and could hardly hope to take the place by storm.
An idea came to me—a hope that we might bluff them into
surrender. I shouted for the Italian prisoner who crawled up
to me amidst a volley of shots from his friends. He came on
bravely and sat down with me behind a wall. I told him
that I intended to offer the garrison an armistice so that they
could come out and discuss terms of surrender because I had
strong reinforcements which would be arriving at any moment.
I stood him up and with courage unusual in an Italian he
walked towards the fort.

" For some strange reason he seemed to regard himself on
our side for he cajoled and implored the commander until he
came out to meet me. The armistice had begun and I could
not but laugh at this strange form of warfare as we shook
hands and smoked cigarettes together. We talked for about
ten minutes but the commander was quite adamant that he
would continue to fight. I said I was sorry as I had wished
to avoid more bloodshed, wondering all the time what to do
next in order to avoid an ignominious retreat. We shook

hands once again and I gave him time to get back to his position before the battle was restarted.

"We had done all we could with rifles, pistols and machine-guns and the only trump card left to us was a grenade from a discharger cup. We didn't really know how to use the thing but hoped that a well-planted shot on the tower might silence opposition from that direction. I decided to renew the attack, firing everything at once and trying to get the range with the grenade thrower. With the good fortune that comes to beginners the first grenade landed full on the tower. Such a chance was too good to miss and we rushed headlong towards the fort, shouting savage cries and firing wildly at everything. This was too much for one Yeoman, left as horseholder with the trucks, and with a shout to his Italian prisoner, 'Here, look after this car,' he sped after us to join the fun. Before we had reached the walls we were met by the garrison, seventeen strong, pouring out of the gate with their hands held high."

As so often in L.R.D.G. the disposal of the prisoners was a problem, for Lloyd Owen was still on his way to his main objective, the coast road. Finally they were dumped thirty miles south in the desert, given food and water and the general direction for a march on Rome.

The next night the patrol was on the Via Balbia near Martuba. I quote the official report of what they did :

"1700-1800 hrs.—Very heavy rain turned the *wadis* into fast flowing torrents. Made plans to take 2 vehicles with 12 men to the road that night. Left at 1800 hrs. leaving 3 vehicles with drivers and W/T operator at rear R.V. Approached to within 3 miles of road where 2 trucks were left. Walked due east to road arriving at 2100 hrs.

"2200 hrs.—One large covered wagon and one car went west. No more movement till 2400 hrs.

"2400 hrs.—Large petrol tanker with trailer fired at.

Vehicle did not stop but was undoubtedly hit as range was less than 5 yards and fire heavy.

"0045 hrs.—10-ton lorry approached. Opened fire and punctured tyres and petrol tank. Lorry stopped and two hand-grenades thrown into back. Two officers in front jumped out and were shot. One man got out of the back and was shot. Wrecked vehicle, leaving two dead officers and seven others. Cut telephone wires and withdrew to rear R.V. Moved south and lay up all day."

Next week Y 2 destroyed three 10-ton tankers on the road north of Agedabia. Five weeks later they were raiding the fort at Scemech (look on the map a hundred miles south-east of Tripoli) and setting up a new " farthest west " record for L.R.D.G. The fort was empty and all they could do was to burn it and mine the roads nearby. A high escarpment overlooks Fort Scemech from the south-east, almost impassable to cars, and Lloyd Owen spent a day and a half in pouring rain trying to find a way down. When he finally reached Scemech some Bedouin appeared and remarked in a friendly way, " So you've got down the cliff at last ; we've been watching you for the last couple of days." It was just as well the fort *was* empty.

On the same night that Y 2 patrol was at El Ezzeiat S 2 and R 2 raided the southern of the two roads through Gebel Akhdar. At dusk, with Olivey in command of the combined party, they got on to the road between Maraua and Slonta, cut the telegraph wires and turned eastwards. In a deep cutting Olivey laid an ambush and not long afterwards the first enemy lorry, its driver dead, had run off the road into the ditch. As he walked across to look at it Olivey was momentarily shocked to see a large red cross painted on the side. But then a number of Italians with rifles and automatics scrambled out over the tailboard and started shooting at him, to receive a moment later the full fire power of the two patrols.

Turning westwards for some miles Olivey arranged another ambush and by the time he drew off the road southwards some hours later had destroyed eight more lorries, leaving the roadside a shambles of petrol, oil, wine from punctured casks, wrecked trucks and dead or dying Italians.

In addition to these " beat ups " we did two " taxi service " jobs in November, 1941.

West of Cyrene in Gebel Akhdar is Beda Littoria, a small village centre of an Italian colonisation scheme. The first building on the right as you enter the village from Cyrene is a grain silo, then a row of bungalows, then standing back from the road among cypresses a larger two-storied house, dark and rather gloomy. Here in November, 1941, lived Rommel. The Eighth Army's offensive was timed for November 18th, and on the eve it had been planned to kill Rommel at Beda Littoria.

The plan came so near to success. And how different events might have been if it had succeeded. Perhaps no second withdrawal from Cyrenaica, no Tobruk and no 'Alamein, North Africa cleaned up a year earlier. Who can say ?

In October John Haselden left Alexandria by submarine and was landed near Cyrene on the Libyan coast. Haselden, killed a year later at Tobruk, was the outstanding personality of the dozen odd men who worked with the tribes in Cyrenaica behind the Axis lines. Untiring, strong, courageous, never without some new scheme for outwitting the enemy, yet with a slow and easy-going way of setting about a job which was far more successful with the Arabs than the usual European insistence on precision and punctuality which they neither like nor understand. His name and his work will not easily be forgotten in the Gebel Akhdar.

For a fortnight Haselden lived with the Arabs, exploring the routes up to Beda Littoria from the coast. On the night of November 14th he was on the beach again, signalling to H.M. submarine *Torbay* which had brought a party of Commando men from " Layforce " under Major Geoffrey Keyes. From the landing Haselden led them three nights later to Rommel's garden gate at Beda Littoria and there left them, his share in the attack done.

At midnight Keyes and the two men with him, Campbell and Terry, were at the front door loudly demanding entry in German. The sentry opened to them, but when they were inside showed fight and was overpowered. At the noise two officers appeared on the stairs and were shot down. All the lights in the house were then extinguished and silence fell. Keyes started to search the ground floor rooms. The first was empty, but from the darkness of the second came a burst of fire and Keyes fell, mortally wounded. Campbell was also hit and taken prisoner, but Terry got away.

In all this there.was no sign of Rommel. Perhaps his dossier in the Intelligence files at Middle East should have been more complete, but one does not worry much over the anniversaries of enemy generals. Rommel was at his birthday party in Rome.

The cemetery at Beda Littoria is on a hill-top a mile south of the village. In the north-east corner, far from the graves of the Italian settlers, five wooden crosses stand in a row. First four Germans, and at the end :

MAJOR GEOFFREY KEYES
V.C., M.C.
gef. 17.11.41

L.R.D.G.'s share in this adventure was a small one, to pick up Haselden at a rendezvous south of Beda Littoria and bring him back to Siwa.

The other " taxi service " job was to collect a party of David Stirling's men. The name of David Stirling will occur so often in this book that I must explain here who he is.

Stirling, now a prisoner of war in Italy or Germany, fills two hackneyed descriptions—" a born leader of men " and " does not know what fear is," and his exploits became a legend from Gabes to 'Alamein. At the beginning of the war he was, I think, in the Commandos in England, but L.R.D.G. first knew him in the Western Desert in command of the S.A.S. (Special Air Service) troops, who were later called " L Detachment," but were always

known to us as " The parashots." At that time he had trained
a small force of his own to drop by parachute from aircraft, to
march immense distances by night or day, and to specialise in
the destruction of aircraft (and of anything else for the matter
of that) on landing grounds behind the enemy's lines. In those
early days Mayne, Fraser and Lewis were his other officers, a
quartette whose initiative, courage and endurance cost the Axis
dear.

A certain amount of confusion has arisen in the public, and
also in the official,[1] mind about Commandos, S.A.S. Troops and
L.R.D.G. All three were independent units, but the S.A.S.
Troops and L.R.D.G. on a number of occasions operated very
successfully together : one squadron of the Middle East Commando was placed under command of L.R.D.G. for a short time
at Siwa in the summer of 1942.

Stirling's part in the autumn offensive of 1941 was to land
by parachute on the night of November 17th, and attempt to
destroy aircraft on the landing grounds near Gazala and Tmìmi,
and L.R.D.G. was to pick up the parashots a day later and bring
them back to Siwa.

The night of November 17th was one of the foulest of the
Libyan war. Looking north from Siwa we could see the flashes
of lightning along the coast though the torrential rain did not
reach so far south. As a result of the bad weather the R.A.F.
dropped the parashots wide of their target and when they had
landed rain, wind and mud hindered them still more. Easonsmith
had gone north from Siwa to meet them, but though he picked
up Stirling, Mayne, Lewis and twenty odd men the remainder
never came in to the rendezvous at Rotunda Segnale.

[1] The Ministry of Information pamphlet, *The Eighth Army* states (page 29) :
" The Long Range Desert Group, under the leadership of Lt.-Colonel (then Captain)
David Stirling, and the Middle East Commando carried out two remarkable raids
on Sirte and Agedabia airfields. . . ." This is incorrect : Stirling was never in
L.R.D.G. These raids were the work of his men (S.A.S. Troops, not Commandos)
who were carried to the scene of action by an L.R.D.G. patrol.

CHAPTER NINE

WHILE the battle was being fought out along the coast between the Egyptian frontier and Tobruk another operation, of which little was heard at the time and less than it deserves has been written since, was taking place in the desert two hundred miles inland. During October and November Brigadier Reid had been assembling at Jaghbub a flying column composed of the 2nd Punjab Regiment, the 6th South African Armoured Car Regiment and a few 25-pounder and ack-ack gunners. His object was to threaten Rommel's southern flank by the capture of Jalo Oasis and on November 25th the Italian garrison there surrendered to him. Now from Jaghbub to Jalo is two hundred miles as the crow flies and nearly a hundred more by the route which Reid's column had to follow. Over that length of bare, waterless desert he had to carry all his supplies and fight a battle at the end of it. The petrol problem alone was one of the greatest difficulty. We knew the country round Jalo fairly well from our reconnaissances of the previous summer and in October I took the Punjabis' C.O. from Jaghbub to within thirty miles of Jalo to see the country over which he would have to march. Up to that point the going was fairly good, but we had misjudged the extent to which the heavy armoured cars would stick in the sand north of Jalo, and in the last lap of the journey the petrol consumption was so high that Reid would have had no chance of withdrawing if his attack failed.

There were six or seven hundred Italians in Jalo but they resisted with as little spirit as their other desert garrisons in the next two years. Reid took the small oasis of Aujila one afternoon, made a skilful night march of fifteen miles to the outskirts of Jalo, and attacked the next day. By evening the defence had crumbled and Reid jumped into his car, drove up to the gate of the fort and found the seventy Italian officers of the garrison sitting calmly down to dinner. They soon made it plain to him that they regarded the tiresome business of fighting as being happily disposed of, though a mile away in the outlying hamlet of Lebba a few with stouter hearts still fought on, and were only overcome by a charge of the South Africans, dismounted from their armoured cars which they left bogged on the sandy slopes.

David Stirling's parachute raid on the landing grounds around Gazala had failed, but it had had one good result—it introduced Stirling to L.R.D.G. and out of that introduction was born a partnership which cost the Axis in Africa more than a hundred aircraft.

Steele, then commanding " A " Squadron, had gone to Jalo from Siwa with S1, S2 and T2 patrols shortly after Reid took the oasis and it was from there that the first combined L.R.D.G.-parashot raids were made.

It was an ideal partnership. We could exploit to the full what was our greatest asset—the ability to deliver a passenger anywhere behind the enemy's lines at any time he asked. And weeks of training for their airborne operations had made the parashots fine artists in getting into—and out of—places at night. They made a wager with the R.A.F. on one occasion. On such and such a night, said the parashots, we will arrive at Heliopolis, having walked the seventy miles from Kabrit, get into your hangars and write our names on your aircraft. The R.A.F. accepted the challenge, doubled their guards and prowled anxiously around the airfield, but all they caught were a few parashots on the way out after the job was done.

Early in December, Holliman left Jalo carrying Stirling, Mayne and a dozen of their men. Their objectives were the landing grounds of Sirte and Tamet, far along the coast road towards Tripoli, which the enemy were known to be using as staging points as they moved their aircraft eastwards. Late on the afternoon of the 14th two trucks drove quietly over the flat country intersected by salt marshes and low sand dunes which lies south of the Via Balbia and dropped Mayne and his party three miles from the landing ground at the north end of the Wadi Tamet, arranging a rendezvous at which to pick them up when the job was done.

By dusk the parashots were in position on the edge of the airfield and what a sight for their first attempt ! All around the edges were parked the aircraft ; at the huts on the western side the unsuspecting aircrews were finishing their evening meal ; beyond them on the coast road a little traffic was passing ; beyond the road the white sand dunes hid the sea.

For an hour or more Mayne waited and watched ; then when all seemed still the party crept up to the huts. Inside a faint light was burning and there was a murmur of voices from the few Italians not yet asleep. Quietly the door was opened and the parashots stepped inside, then a hose-spray from six Tommy guns ensured that there would be no interference from the ground staff in their work. By the time Mayne had finished and was on his way back to the rendezvous the petrol dump and twenty-four aircraft were ablaze.

Meanwhile for the last two days Stirling and Brough, with seventy pounds of explosives on their backs, had been dodging the enemy round Sirte only to find in the end that the airfield on that day was not in use.

Holliman had just time to reach Jalo again and then on Christmas Eve he was on his way back with the same party to the same task. The Italians at Tamet seemed to have learned little from their experience of a fortnight earlier and before they were aware of what was happening Mayne had planted " sticky bombs " on twenty-seven aircraft. The sticky bomb was a parashot speciality, invented, as I have heard, by Lewis, who was killed afterwards near Nofilia. It was a mixture of explosive and incendiary materials and started a fire after it had gone off. The ideal place for a sticky bomb was at the tail of the aircraft or where the wing joined the fuselage. It was always better to be sure of destroying the airframe rather than the engine, for engines could be replaced on the spot whereas an airframe had to be sent to the base to be rebuilt. The fuse for a sticky bomb was a " time pencil," an ingenious but temperamental device in which acid from a glass phial broken by squeezing ate its way through a fine wire and so released a spring. The pencils were rated to various times and the choosing of the right pencil was a matter of importance ; with too long a delay the enemy might discover what you were doing and hurry round to remove the bombs from the aircraft ; with too short an interval the first bomb would have gone off before the job was finished. Moreover, pencils do not always keep good time and on this night before Mayne had finished a bomb went off and set a C.R. 42 alight, silhouetting the parashots against its blaze. With the sentries shooting wildly, some landwards and some to repel what they seemed to imagine was attack from the sea, the parashots crawled off the landing ground and got safely away.

At two in the morning Holliman with the other half of the patrol dropped Stirling on the main road four miles west of Sirte to raid the airfield there while the patrol waited for him to return, parked by the roadside between groups of enemy vehicles. But again Stirling had no luck for he was challenged at the perimeter defences and the guards, suspecting what might happen, promptly floodlit the landing ground. So there was nothing for it but to retire and Holliman drove for ten miles westwards along the road with headlights on, letting fly at anything he could see. On a truck by the roadside an unwary Italian lit a match for his cigarette and got everything the patrol could give him ; in two lorries a few miles on the crews were sleeping in their cabs and knew nothing till the thermite bombs left by the Rhodesians awoke them, and not much then.

On raids of this kind, as on other occasions, trouble is apt to come the morning after for by then the enemy has had time to regain his wits and send out aircraft to scour the country. S1 were late in getting away, but even so they had travelled seventy miles southwards by daylight. Not long after dawn they halted for a few moments, ranging the cars for cover alongside the few straggling bushes of desert broom. Before they moved on there came the throb of engines to the northwards and two ME 110's appeared, carefully quartering the ground. But they turned half a mile short of the patrol and Holliman, blessing his luck, turned eastwards to Jalo.

While Stirling and Mayne were attacking Sirte and Tamet, Olivey had taken another party of parashots under Fraser to raid the airfield at Agedabia, where Fraser destroyed thirty-seven aircraft and got safely away.

In affairs of this sort it is always interesting to see the other side of the picture and some time later we were able to do this. In January, 1942, the Eighth Army swept forward to Agedabia and among the prisoners taken there was Corporal Pietro Nutini of the 32nd Tank Regiment. Back in the P.O.W. cage, Nutini was interrogated and described his experiences on Christmas Eve. On that night, he said, he was very surprised to see the aircraft on the airfield at Agedabia being blown up one by one. It was said that Arabs had placed time bombs in the planes and a number were arrested and threatened with hanging if they did not reveal the culprits.

He might well be surprised.

But of all these L.R.D.G.-cum-parashot operations there was nothing to surpass the adventures of T2 patrol under Morris at Marsa Brega.

On December 10th he set out from Jalo with fourteen of his own men and a dozen parashots. Their objectives were the landing ground at 'Agheila and the shallow anchorage at Marsa Brega at which the Axis was then landing a certain amount of supplies from small coastal vessels. After a day or two spent reconnoitring the salt marsh country south of 'Agheila, Morris dropped the parashots ten miles from the village to make their attack on the aircraft and went off to explore Marsa Brega. Around it the country is as flat as a pancake so any exploration had to be done on foot. All one day and half the next night Morris was ploughing his way through soft sand and salt marsh trying to find a good line of approach, but in the end he realised that

the only way to get to Mersa Brega was the way the Axis transport was reaching it at the rate of about two hundred cars a day
—by road.

The next day the parashots returned from 'Agheila; they had
found the airfield empty since the enemy, unknown to us, had
moved all their aircraft to Agedabia. At dusk the patrol drew
near to the road. There were five L.R.D.G. cars and an Italian
Lancia lorry which the parashots had collected from somewhere.
Morris watched the traffic for an hour or more and noticed that
most of it was in small convoys of about a dozen vehicles in each,
and so he decided to make up a " convoy " of his own. The road
here runs along an embankment and the Lancia baulked at the
steep slope. With a struggle they got it on to the road and fortunately none of the passing drivers stopped to give them a
helping hand.

Once on the road the convoy sorted itself out. In front was
the Lancia without lights and next behind it Morris's own truck
with headlights full on to show up the Lancia and dazzle the eyes
of oncoming drivers ; the other cars brought up the rear. In this
order they started to cover the ten miles to Marsa Brega, meeting
Axis traffic all the way ; Morris counted up to forty-seven cars,
he told me afterwards, and then lost count. The road was narrow
with little more than a foot to spare in passing, and across the
gap our drivers would shout a greeting to the oncoming trucks.

About midnight they reached the turning where a track leads
off to the anchorage. Two trucks had lagged behind and Morris
waited for them to come up. Round the buildings at the cross
roads were twenty cars or more, with their crews, German and
Italian, waiting beside them or getting a meal at the roadhouse.
A normal scene on a line of communications a hundred miles
behind the front.

Then the lagging cars came up and hell broke loose. At
twenty-five yards range, with every gun they had, the patrol
opened fire on the men and vehicles. On the outskirts the parashots hurried from truck to truck, dropping into them their sticky
bombs and dragging the bewildered drivers out of their cabs to

give them a *coup de grâce*. After a quarter of an hour of this " reinforcements seemed to be arriving," as Morris wrote afterwards, " and we moved out, my truck now leading with headlights full on, followed by the Lancia."

They still had ten miles to go before they could leave the causeway and get away southwards round the salt marshes, and behind them at Marsa Brega the enemy seemed to be organising some sort of pursuit. Garven in the last truck dealt with this. He quickly laid a few mines in the road and before they were out of earshot had counted seven explosions. By dawn they were well camouflaged twenty-five miles south of the road watching the aircraft which all that day searched the countryside without success.

But it was different next time.

T2 patrol had little rest. On Boxing Day they were off from Jalo again " to convey," as the Operation Order said, " a party of parachutists to attack MARBLE ARCH and NOFILIA landing grounds."

On the 27th Fraser and four men were dropped five miles from the Marble Arch and the next day Lewis and the remainder near Nofilia.

Let Morris tell the rest of the tale :

" 29.12.41. This day we remained in hiding.

" 30.12.41. About 18.00 hours we picked up Lt. Lewis and his party at the spot where we had left them on the 28th. He mentioned the fact that he had seen three trucks on our tracks earlier in the day, one of them being covered.

" 31.12.41. This morning we proceeded back to Marble Arch to pick up Lt. Fraser's party. During the past three days many enemy planes were sighted flying up and down the coast road. About 10.00 hours in open country we were sighted by a Messerschmidt who immediately attacked us with M.G. fire from a height of about 60 feet. We dispersed as quickly as possible. After using up all his ammunition the plane returned to the nearby aerodrome, but shortly after-

wards two Stukas and a recce plane came over, bombing
and machine-gunning from a low altitude. Incendiary
bullets were used and also cannons. By this time we had
hidden our cars and camouflaged them as well as possible,
but the planes flew low and followed our tracks. My own
truck was the first to go, catching fire. Hand grenades, belts
of ammunition and petrol then blew up, completely wrecking
the vehicle. Another truck was destroyed by a bomb shortly
afterwards. From where I was at this time I could see two
large columns of smoke from my own and the bombed truck
and after a second bomb had been dropped a third lot of
smoke was seen in the direction a truck had taken when
disappearing. Although I did not actually see the third truck
destroyed some of the men on that side of the area reported
that this happened. The vehicle unaccounted for, on which
were Cpl. Garven, Tpr. Brown and Gnr. Stutterd, may have
escaped to the south-west and if so should return. Later two
Stukas searched the area, in which there was little cover of
any description, using machine-guns and 20 mm. cannon
over a wide area. At dusk the remaining truck, T10, was
heard to move and we found it. We searched the area for
eight miles, calling loudly and flashing lights but could find
no one. Lt. Lewis was killed by machine-gun fire in the second
attack. Finally we made away to the south as ground patrols
could again be heard in the vicinity and there was no cover
for many miles in this direction. We, the remainder, which
included the four parachutists, travelled in the one surviving
truck all this night, crossing the Marada road at 05.00 hours
next morning.

    " 1.1.42. Reached Jalo at 17.00 hours."

Morris had written this when he arrived at Jalo. From Jalo
to the place where T2 had been shot up was at least 200 miles
so unless another truck had escaped destruction the chances of
seeing the patrol again seemed slight. However, we remembered
Moore's March. And so it happened. On the morning of January

9th an Arab from Augila came into Jalo. There were, he said, some " Inglizi " who had arrived on foot from the west. They were very tired and wanted food and help.

This is the story of the ten previous days as Stutterd[1] wrote it afterwards :

"About mid-morning we were halted in air formation when we were sighted by a German plane. After circling us once he opened fire and machine-gunned for twenty minutes. Luckily my truck, T6,[2] was not hit and after scattering we stopped in a shallow *wadi* and waited till the plane ran out of ammunition and left. We moved north at first, gradually working east till we sighted a salt marsh. Turning south, we ran down the marsh for about ten miles when we saw another car following us. We waited and it turned out to be T7. After another mile or so T9 also caught us up. By this time we were running south-west, skirting the marsh and ahead about three miles to the west sighted the only cover for miles so headed for it with the almost certain knowledge that we would be chased. On arrival at the cover, which proved to be only low rolling hills, we hid the cars as well as we could. Brown and I started to get the camouflage net out and our truck covered up while Garven went on look-out. Immediately he told us that there were two aircraft circling our tracks a couple of miles away. They were Stukas and wasted no time in ' giving us the works.'

" Machine-gunned, T6 burst into flames, then T7, then T9. The Stukas left after having a lash at us on the ground. Five miles away they met two other Stukas heading for us, and these drove us to cover again, if lying on the bare gravel under a bush 18 inches high is cover.

" When they had gone we got together and had a short conference, deciding that the best thing we could do would be to make for Augila, the nearest British-occupied oasis. Our

[1] Gnr. E. C. Stutterd, 2 N.Z.E.F.
[2] T6, T7, etc., here refer to individual trucks of T2 Patrol.

rations consisted of three gallons of water, salvaged by Bassett
in a four-gallon tin, one packet of nine biscuits and a tin of
emergency chocolate ration, also produced by Bassett. The
party consisted of eight N. Zedders, one Englishman and an
English parachutist.

" There was no possible hope of approaching the vehicles
as they were blazing fiercely and ammunition, bombs and
Bofors shells were exploding incessantly. So reluctantly at
12.40 we turned our steps and hopes to the east and set off.
We had travelled about half a mile in two parties of five,
carrying the water by twos for a period of twelve minutes,
when Martin on looking back saw a large aeroplane circling
very low over the trucks. We flattened to the ground and a
few minutes later the plane went off. We continued our march
for some miles and saw two more Stukas approaching. Down
again behind bushes not big enough to cover a scorpion and
spent a very unpleasant time there while the aircraft circled
around.

" About five o'clock we set off, in one party again, hoping
to cross the Marada-'Agheila road before daylight. We
travelled in spells of an hour with quarter-hour rests. At
midnight we celebrated the New Year with our first ration of
water, a quarter of a pint, and a half-hour spell, to the accom-
paniment of dropping flares and ack-ack fire in the direction
of Agheila. The R.A.F. were on the job. We marched on
until the sun rose and decided to have a break in a *wadi*.
The weather was bitterly cold and I climbed to the top of the
ridge to look for signs of the road. Three-quarters of the way
up I heard aircraft again so went to ground. Two Stukas
approached from the direction of Marada and flew north
across our tracks of the previous night. Ten minutes later
they flew south on the east side of us. These were the last
aircraft to worry us. It was impossible to sleep owing to the
cold and about 2 p.m. we moved off.

" Carrying on in spells we crossed the Marada road about
11 p.m. at night, after deploying to stalk what we took to be

a camel but proved to be a road sign which was unreadable. Travelling what we thought to be about fifteen miles we holed up for a rest in the sun. The weather was still very cold and sleep was out of the question. My great-coat had by this time been cut up for moccasins, because our sandals had given up the ghost the first night. Only the collar and the pockets and a small part of the front being left, I noticed the difference. However, it put me on a level with every one else.

" Between the Marada road and our halting place that morning some of the boys sampled the desert snails. I made a half-hearted suck at one in the shell which turned out to be more obstinate than my hunger and so I desisted. In the mid-afternoon we decided to get going again. Here White, the parachutist, left us. He had had the long march to the landing ground at Nofilia and back and his feet were almost raw. He said he would go towards Marada and try to seize a truck and get home that way. Actually we thought he meant to give himself up so as not to hinder the rest of the party. We gave him some water and did not see him again. We pushed on all through the night. Our halts were more frequent now and we were getting very tired. Bassett about this time found us a piece of chewing gum each. This did not prove very successful and after a short time it turned to powder in my mouth. Tobacco was also finished : a good job too really, as it only tended to increase our thirst.

" At dawn the next morning we sighted a fire which seemed to be about seven or eight miles away. We reasoned that where there was fire there were Arabs and where there were Arabs there was water and perhaps food. By this time our water ration had been reduced to three-eighths of a pint per day. After a short conference we decided to head for the light of the fire which we took to be at Ma'aten Barbar, a spring on the southern side of a salt marsh, but after marching several hours towards this place it appeared to be no nearer. Five of the party lay down to rest and Garven, Martin, Brown

and I set out to locate the fire. We marched for an hour or
so and came to some very moist ground in the marsh. Our
thirst by this time was getting very bad and we dug a small
well, hoping for water. Brown carried on towards the fire,
saying that he would fire a shot if he found anything. After
a while we struck water at about three feet, but it was far
too salt to drink. We baled it out for a while with a tin hat,
trying to clear it up, but it was no good. Then I thought I
heard a shot and we headed for the sound. After an hour's
walking we found Brown with four Arabs and it was not long
before we were gargling the small drop of water they had
with them and eating a few dates. One of the Arabs told us
there was a spring three kilometres away and we were all
impatience to get to it, so he offered to show us the way.
The three kilometres turned out to be about six miles, but
on arrival the Arabs who were camped there could not do
enough for us. We had been there about an hour when the
rest of the party arrived.

" We spent the night there under one or two Arab blankets
which, however, were useless to keep out the cold, and most
of us sat around a large fire all night. In the morning we
walked on another mile to the spring and proceeded to soak
our insides with very brackish water. From here Garven and
Brown moved on about three miles to a knoll to watch for
any of our patrols which might be about, having seen two
vehicles the day before, identified later by the Arabs as
British. The remainder of the party followed at midday with
a full can of water. This proved to be too heavy for us in our
weakened condition and we had another drink, reducing the
water and now carrying it in relays of four for six minutes
each.

" We moved off about 3.30 and at dark, the cold being
so intense, gathering a little scrub we boiled some water and
made chocolate from the emergency ration. This seemed to
put new life into all of us for that night we estimated that we
walked forty miles. About 6.30 in the morning we were very

tired and dug holes in the sand to try and rest out of the wind. But the cold was still against us and we had to tramp on. We were making fairly slow progress now, being very tired. The weather also was very threatening. About 3.30 it began to rain, and judging our distance from Augila to be about twenty-five miles, we decided to drink as much as we could, leave the water and make all speed for the oasis. We moved off but after a couple of hours had to stop for a rest : sleep was overpowering.

" Bassett, who throughout the trip had been wearing boots, was having trouble with his legs, which were aching terribly. At about 3.45 a.m. we were ' all in ' and decided to dig a hole in the sand and try to rest, though Brown and Martin determined to go on as it was so cold. We were at that time following tracks which exactly coincided with our compass bearing. At about 7.30 a.m. we got ready to move but after a short spell Bassett said he would stop and have some rest while we pushed on. A dust storm was blowing up and after an hour it got so violent that we had to lie down and take turns at sheltering each other. We stayed put for about two hours and then pushed on into a very strong head wind. At 3 p.m. we saw in the distance a row of posts and on getting there found it to be the Italian track from Agedabia to Jalo. We travelled another couple of hours and dug a large hole and stayed there all night. It was freezing cold and we were most uncomfortable.

" The next morning spirits were getting fairly low. Thirst was troubling us badly and our feet were getting almost unbearably sore. Our marching spells were cut to a fraction and every one was getting very tired. About 11 a.m. we sighted a *wadi* to the left of the road and as the sun was the warmest we had felt it for the whole journey we got down for a two hours' sleep. After five minutes travelling, on moving off again, I saw what I thought were palm trees but hesitated to say anything about it. Our eyes were sore and by this time we were seeing things. However, they became so distinct that

I mentioned it and we decided that they *were* palm trees. We headed off the road for the oasis which was about five miles away at that stage. We could only go about half a mile at a time though here Sanders decided to have a go at it—non-stop. We made the place, which proved to be Augila, at dusk, and Garven, Walsh, Fair and I found an empty Arab garden and a hut which we appropriated for the night. We lit a good fire, boiled some turnips and onions and had a glorious drink out of the well. After the most comfortable night since December 30th (it was now January 8th) we cooked more turnips and onions, made some date tea and set off for the fort. On the way we met two Arab policemen who took charge of us and led us to their barracks. Too much praise cannot be given to those Arabs for the way they treated us. On arrival we found Brown, Martin and Sanders. Bassett had come in to another part of the oasis about the same time as we did. The night after he left us he had spent inside a 44-gallon drum !

" At about 10.30 Major Steele arrived from Jalo and our troubles were over. Never have I enjoyed the sound of a motor more than the one that took us back to Jalo and safety."

In the second volume of *Scott's Last Expedition*, the official account of his explorations in the Antarctic before the Great War, there is a photograph of Wilson, Bowers and Cherry Garrard taken a few minutes after they had arrived back from their winter journey to Cape Crozier. Cherry Garrard wrote a book about it afterwards—*The Worst Journey in the World*. It was twenty years since I had read Scott's book but I had never forgotten the look in the eyes of those three men in the photograph.

I saw the T2 men the day after they reached Jalo. I remembered where I had seen that look before.

Thus the T2 men got back to Jalo but " circumstances over which they had no control " prevented them from picking up Fraser who was waiting at the rendezvous south of Nofilia.

He stayed for three days in vain and then started home. For a week the small party of five moved eastwards, walking by night, often up to their knees in salt marsh, and hiding by day. Soon water became a problem for they had little with them at the outset and the pools were too salt to drink. A home-made condenser produced a little—two water-bottles with a piece of rubber tube between and a fire of desert scrub under one of them—but it took two hours boiling to fill a bottle. Then they got tired of walking and started to hold up cars. Two Italian trucks provided some food and rusty water from the radiators and a German car carried them for twenty-five miles and then, turning off the road for a halt, was bogged beyond extraction. So they walked on again and after eight days reached the British lines.

While all these operations were going on Group H.Q. was still at Siwa, but it soon became clear that we were getting too far behind the front line. Benghazi had been captured for the second time and the Eighth Army was pushing Rommel back towards Agheila. So by January 10 the whole L.R.D.G. had moved to Jalo.

Jalo is just the opposite of the conventional idea of a Saharan oasis. Here are no babbling rills, no luscious fruits, no mysterious village with labyrinthine streets from whose windows dark-eyed beauties look lovingly down on to the passing sheikhs. A month in Jalo would be a very good astringent for those novelists who specialise in oasis scenery. (Actually it would be quite the reverse, for the water, which is almost undrinkable, is charged with Epsom or some other equally revolting salts.)

To the east is the Sand Sea, to the north an area of scrub and brackish wells, to the west an uninteresting gravel plain and to the south the vast Serir of Kalansho (a name whose origin I have never been able to trace) which must be one of the few places in the world where one could drive a car for 200 miles on a given bearing without ever being compelled by the nature of the country to deviate by half a degree from one's course. A hole in the desert with a few thousand palms and two mud-built villages comprises the oasis. Every day the sand blows ; the houses in El Ergh are gradually being overwhelmed by it and round their miserable gardens the Arabs build ineffective fences of palm fronds to keep the sand off their meagre crops. If you want drinkable water you must go out to Bettafal, twenty miles away. Jalo is not a pleasant spot.

It is an interesting speculation—a suitable problem for a Staff College study circle—what might have been achieved by our having in Jalo a force of all arms, say, ten times the size of L.R.D.G., together with fighter aircraft, at certain periods of the war in Libya—during, for example, Rommel's advance from Agheila in 1942 or his retreat from 'Alamein. Generals are properly cautious about their flanks and their lines of communications and from Jalo to the coast road at Agedabia is only about 150 miles. The difficulties of supplying such a force at Jalo, either from the Nile by way of Kufra or through Jaghbub, would have been very great and might have proved unsurmountable, but it would have been a very sharp thorn in the enemy's side.

To me personally Jalo was full of interest. For in the past Jalo had been a great place and it was the Majabra who made it so.

The Majabra are an Arab tribe, with a mixture of Sudanese blood to judge by the dark faces of some of them, and are, or were, the most enterprising merchant caravaneers of the Eastern Sahara. They held a position rather like the merchant adventurers of Elizabethan England, for they were the great promoters of desert trade. All round the fringes of the desert you find the Majabra—in Jalo, in Benghazi, along the coast towns to Alexandria, in Kerdaseh below the Pyramids, in Khartoum, in El Fasher and in the towns of the French Sudan. And between these scattered tribesmen trade flows. A Majbri in Cairo will give you a draft on his agent in Fort Lamy and it will be honoured. We had not been long in Kufra in the summer of 1941 before the merchants there sent off a caravan of three hundred camels across the terrible Sand Sea route through Abu Mungar to Egypt to bring the merchandise which the oasis had lacked for so long.

Until the Italians, with their totalitarian economy, closed the frontiers, entrepôt trade had made Jalo, like Petra and Palmyra two thousand years earlier, a " caravan city " of importance in Saharan trade.

But for most of us, drinking the nasty water, shivering in unheated rooms and plodding around in the soft sand, it was an unattractive place. " Doc " Lawson struggled with the filth and flies the Italians had left behind them ; the periodical recce aircraft occasionally came low enough for us to blaze off at it and the patrols came and went. Our task was to harass the enemy as far as possible behind his front line which then was between Agedabia and Agheila. So Timpson with G2 beat up the Hon-Misurata road again ; Easonsmith struggled across the north-eastern corner of the Harug and mined the Hon-Zella track—and got well strafed by two Savoias and a Ghibli while doing it—and Hunter took a party of parashots to attack Buerat el Hsun.

It was while we were at Jalo that the Heavy Section—as we called the Supply and Transport Section—really came into its own. Many L.R.D.G. officers had done a turn with the Heavy Section : I, the first, for one trip only, Holliman, Croucher, Morris, Sutherland, but it was Philip Arnold who really made it what it was. Philip had all the qualifications. Half-French, half-English, naturally perfect in both tongues and a good Arabic speaker too, there was little he did not know about getting trucks across the Middle Eastern deserts. He had worked for a firm in Aden, had sold cars in Abyssinia, served in the Foreign Legion in Syria, fought in some strange amphibious battles in the Somaliland campaign and in the summer of 1942 came to us. His last peacetime job was with an American mining company which was successfully extracting gold from the barren hills between Mecca and Medina. Philip ran their transport for them and once a month took the gold right across Arabia to be shipped from the Persian Gulf ports. It was a bad day for L.R.D.G., and for many other people too, when he ran his Jeep on to a land mine on the outskirts of Hon.

Perhaps we rather took our " Q " problems for granted. We were always the best-fed unit in the Middle East ; we were never really short of essential supplies ; the mail used to turn up, often soaked in petrol or dieseline, but it arrived, and we seldom considered how all this happened. That it did was due to Prendergast's thoughtful planning, to the Heavy Section, and even more to " Shorty," the Prince of Quartermasters, and Bevan, his S.Q.M.S. " Shorty " was Barrett, New Zealander, nearing forty, a lawyer in peace time, in the first party of 2 N.Z.E.F. to reach Egypt, a foundation member of L.R.D.G., who left us to go through the fighting in Greece with his own " Div. Cav." and then returned to be Quartermaster in the autumn of 1941 and in February, 1943, just to keep himself from idleness, took on the job of Adjutant as well.

The responsibilities of the L.R.D.G. Quartermaster were heavy and it was distance that gave them weight. The Quartermaster of an ordinary unit in the Western Desert drew his rations daily, sending his own transport back to the nearest D.I.D.,[1] and it was unlikely that he would have to go more than twenty or thirty miles for most of the things he needed. Where he thought in days Shorty had to think in weeks or months. Where he had to go thirty miles Shorty had to go three hundred. In Jalo we drew our supplies from railhead at Misheifa, a week's turn-round for the Heavy Section. From Siwa we sent to Matruh ; from Zella and Hon we had to go to the Marble Arch or Tamet ; at Kufra the R.A.S.C. brought us food and petrol from Wadi Halfa, but for anything else we had to send to Cairo, distant a thousand miles. Week in and week out small parties of the Heavy Section, a few three-tonners or two or three Macks, used to set off on journeys which were adventures in themselves. Before the war to reach Kufra from Cairo through the Gilf would have been a major expedition ; in the summer of 1942 Clark, with three 3-tonners, did the trip in four days and nobody thought much of it.

Prendergast would ring up the Q.M. store. " Shorty. The

[1] Detail Issue Depot.

brothers Y " (Y1 and Y2 patrols), " go out on Thursday. A month's rations and petrol for 1100 miles. And three Heavy Section 3-tonners under Mitchell go with them for the first four hundred miles with petrol for their return journey. Will you fix it ? "

Or else :

" Shorty. ' A ' Squadron leave for Oliver's Dump next week. When Zella falls they'll go in there but they'll want a week's food and water while they're waiting at Oliver's. And we must build up a dump of 500 gallons of water and 4000 of petrol for the patrols attacking Hon and Sebha when they come back that way. Have you got that new lot of a thousand Jerricans ? "

Or :

" Shorty. The Rhodesians are going down to Tibesti on the 17th. The French'll feed them when they get there but they'll need all their other stuff for, say, two months."

And then there were all the other things we needed. *Chapplies* (Indian North-West Frontier sandals) as well as boots. Special petrol and oil for the Wacos. Theodolites for the navigators. Breda 20 mm. ammo. Vickers .5. Breda 12.7. Bofors 37 mm. Bofors 47 mm. Ammo. for the tank (we had a tank once !) 4.5 How. ammo. 25-pdr. ammo. (we had one of each of these guns for a time), incendiary, tracer, armour-piercing, explosive, Mills bombs, landmines, gelignite, sticky bombs, detonators, time pencils, fuse, Indian rations when the Indian L.R.S. was with us, Arab headdresses, smoke generators, camouflage nets, telescopes for the road watch, paint, sheepskin coats, sun-glasses, 44-gallon drums for storing petrol, Jerricans, water cans, tents. and always enough extra up the Q.M.'s sleeve to enable him to be a " universal aunt " to all the strange units who had business in the desert behind the enemy's lines—Commandos, British and Arab ; Parashots ; lost travellers ; " Escape scheme " promoters ; stranded airmen ; escaped prisoners—all at times needing petrol, rations, clothing and half a hundred other things.

Shorty was unrivalled in his ability to extract what we needed from reluctant supply officers : if he had persuaded the

Navy to give him two minesweepers for use in the Sand Sea I would not have been surprised. Perhaps, like all good quartermasters, his methods of acquiring things were not always orthodox, but unlike many of them he never forgot, what should be written in all their hearts, that it is more blessed to give than to receive.

By mid-January Rommel's counter-offensive at 'Agheila was gaining ground and by the end of the month our position in Jalo began to look uncomfortable. We asked Eighth Army's advice, and on the 26th they told us to get out. It was heartbreaking to have to trail all the way back to Jaghbub and Siwa again, so we put off the evil day as long as possible by moving out of Jalo to Ghetmir, fifteen miles to the north-east. Here there was good water, good cover and a good position if we were attacked, but after waiting there for a week it was clear that we had no alternative but to move on. While we sat at Ghetmir, Timpson with his patrol remained to scorch the earth in Jalo, and by the time he had finished there was little left that would be of use to the enemy. From Ghetmir we could hear his explosions and see the clouds of smoke that hung over the oasis.

Rommel's advance was too swift for us at one point. At Jalo we had to get our petrol from Msus and on the 24th January Richard Carr, then Adjutant, had left with a party to get a supply. As luck would have it there was no spare wireless to go with him and we could not warn him of the speed of the German advance. Msus was in German hands by the time he got there and the whole of his party was captured. All that day they waited under guard and in the late afternoon started off for Benghazi, Carr in a staff car with three Germans and his men in a lorry behind. They had not gone far along the Sceleidima road when two armoured cars, I think of the 11th Hussars, opened fire on the small convoy. The men in the lorry fell upon their one guard, overpowered him and made a dash for it, and seven of them got safely away to the armoured cars.

Two or three of the men who failed to get away were right out of luck, for only a week or two earlier they had been saved from a different sort of fate when they were picked up, lost in the desert north-west of Aujila, by the small patrol which Prendergast kept out there as a screen for Jalo.

A good many men in the Eighth Army must owe their lives to L.R.D.G., but for every lost man found by us how many are still in the desert, now only a skeleton with a few rags of clothing round it and an empty waterbottle beside, and, maybe, with its teeth fastened in the dry stem of some desert shrub?

For a heedless, unthinking man it was terribly easy to become lost in the desert where, whichever way you look, the landscape seems the same. You drive over a ridge which hides your camp or the last known landmark, follow a track which you think will lead to your destination, do not bother to remember on which cheek the wind blew or where the sun's shadow fell when you started, hurry on imagining that that cairn ahead, that bush, that low rise is a feature which you can recognise and in a few miles are thoroughly lost. Then is the time to force yourself to make no move at all for half an hour, till you have had time to sit down and reason out the situation and not, so strong is the temptation, push on because you feel so sure that just beyond that next ridge there is the place you seek.

Such a case was Driver X of the Y Motor Brigade, found by Olivey one hot May day in 1942 near Hatiet Etla and heading for Jalo, though he asked Olivey if he was on the right road for Matruh. He had one gallon of petrol left in his tank and had just drunk his radiator water, so his expectation of life at that moment was about twenty-four hours. Though X, a careful man, felt he had been the victim of foul play. He had left his unit to go back to draw water, turned his car and parked it facing the direction in which he must return, gone off to get authority for his water issue, and returned to the car and driven off. While he was away, X reckoned, some enemy had faced his car about to the wrong direction and hence his disaster.

Five months later, Holliman, going from 'Alamein to Siwa to guide home the garrison of Jaghbub, halted for a meal above the cliffs at Qattara Spring. A thousand feet below him in the

Depression was a small party of men lost during the retreat from Sollum. Holliman signalled to them and one man started to ascend the cliffs. For an hour he climbed steadily, at last arriving within sight of the Patrol. But one glance at the bearded Rhodesians was enough for him : these, he felt, must be Germans or some worse, new enemy, and in five minutes with a broken nose and foot he was down with his companions again. A Rhodesian descending reassured them and later they were delivered safely to Cairo.

S Patrol was apt to get landed with tiresome convoy tasks. In December, 1941, Reid, who had just taken Jalo, was in desperate need of petrol and Holliman had to guide a convoy there. He picked them up, a very raw collection of men just arrived from England, at Jaghbub and passed through the Wire that afternoon. The Wire, starting on the coast and running southwards as far as the Sand Sea near Jaghbub, 200 miles long, 6 feet high and 30 feet across, had been put up by Graziani at a cost of more than a quarter of a million pounds to stop gun-running from Egypt into Libya. It had been there since 1931 but the convoy, with memories of trench warfare in France, were sure that they were passing into No Man's Land. New to desert driving, they got stuck wherever possible. When stuck they sat and waited for the " Desert Patrol " to dig them out, meanwhile washing their clothes in petrol as they had been told to conserve their water ration at any cost.

CHAPTER TEN

SIWA AGAIN

By February 1st we were back in Siwa, disappointed and sick at heart, trying to explain to the Siwans the value of the Eighth Army's withdrawal to the " previously prepared positions " between Bir Hakim and Gazala and little thinking that in four months we should be leaving Siwa for 'Alamein.

But in spite of this and of the heat and flies and of the malaria which caught so many later on, life in Siwa had its compensations. For Siwa, so unlike Jalo, is all that one expects an oasis to be.

It was in 1935 that I first saw it. We had come up from 'Uweinat, four of us in three Fords—Ronnie McEuen, Mike Mason, Rupert Harding-Newman and I—along the west side of the Gilf to Wadi er Riquba and northwards through the Sand Sea. In much of the Sea the dunes conform to a type and after a few days digging and pushing you learn how to tackle them, but there is a ten-mile belt south of Siwa where they run all anyhow and the arrangement of the soft and hard sand patches does not follow the rules.

April 5th that year was hot and all day we had struggled through these fringing dunes. Towards sunset we mounted the last of them and below us was the long east-west trough in which Siwa lies, an alternation of salt lake and salt marsh with the villages on their hill-tops and the great palm groves between.

The dates are the best in Egypt, perhaps the best in North Africa, and as far away as Tripoli the Arabs say, " Ya tamr Siwa ; ya laban Gargaresh." [1] But best of all, when you come back from a May fortnight on patrol in Libya, are the pools—the Island Pool, the Sheikh's Pool, Figure of Eight, Cleopatra's, Bubbly Pool—with the warm artesian water, clear and sparkling, pouring up from a twenty-foot deep spring.

[1] " Oh for the dates of Siwa and the curds of Gargaresh ! "

For a chairborne soldier as I was then life at Siwa was peaceful though there was plenty of work to do. " Siwa Bill," the enemy recce aircraft, used to come over at a great height about every third day and once there was a moment of excitement when it dropped a stick of bombs, a near miss on Ashdown's Ordnance workshops.

" Plugs " Ashdown for eighteen months, and later Mallinder, was our O.M.E. (Ordnance Mechanical Engineer). In the first months of L.R.D.G.'s life, when it was based on Cairo, the bigger repair jobs could be done in the workshops at Abbassia. But when we moved to Kufra this was no longer possible and Bagnold got Middle East to give him a Light Repair Squadron, R.A.O.C., known more familiarly after its master as the " Pluggeries." In L.R.D.G. work, driving over all types of country, the wear and tear on vehicles was very heavy. The limelight which fell on the patrols did not reach the " Pluggeries," but in their unending and unromantic job of keeping the cars on the desert they had a large share in our successes. They had few idle moments. When they had the repairs for two patrols in hand a third would come in from the desert with the inevitable crop of broken springs, leaking radiators, severed U-bolts, loose steering and oil-drinking engines to change, followed by a message from Prendergast that X patrol must be ready for the road by Tuesday night.

From Siwa during the weeks that followed the patrols went in to Cairo by turns for leave and a refit. From the Western Desert the ordinary unit retired as a whole to the Delta after a period in the field, but it was an accepted principle of L.R.D.G. operations that some of the patrols were always at work.

In Cairo we behaved, I suppose, no worse if no better than any other unit. There were, of course, " incidents," some of which ended in the Military Police barracks at Bab el Hadid. It was Y patrol, I think, who insisted on sand-channelling their way down the length of Sharia Suleiman Pasha to the fury of the police and the dislocation of the traffic. X will remember the incident of the bath and the lift shaft, and Z the night when he removed the bits from a row of cab horses and then retired to shout " Gharry, Gharry " from the pavement. Our reputation, never low, was high at the time and the red and blue L.R.D.G. shoulder patches were always good for a few free drinks. More than once we found men of other units wearing our badges, which was flattering perhaps but not always desirable, as on the occasion when two men so adorned brought us into disrepute by stealing his accordion from a blind musician in the orchestra of some shady " dive." The town Egyptians, an unlovable folk, made a walk through the streets of Cairo an unpleasant obstacle race. I have often wished that I could go through them placarded with two sandwich boards announcing that I did not want to buy a fly whisk, a stick, sun glasses, fountain pens, cigarettes, hair combs, dirty postcards, razor blades, hand-kerchiefs, or to hire a guide or have my shoes cleaned or accept any of the dozen other services so offensively offered.

It was on reconnaissance work that most of our time was spent in those busy months at Siwa in the spring of 1942.

And they were busy months. Siwa was then the " Clapham Junction " of all the behind-the-line traffic and there was a lot of it on the move. I wondered if the enemy had any idea how much there was; if he did have an observer in Siwa—and when the Army came back in the autumn some of the Siwans were arrested as enemy agents—he made little use of the information.

Day in, day out, the patrols came and went. To the road watch at the Marble Arch ; to the other road watches in the Gebel Akhdar ; taking Stirling and Mayne to Benghazi or Fraser to Barce ; Timpson dropping a couple of Arabs to spy out the garrison of Jalo ; Olivey carrying another pair to Agedabia ; one patrol taking Pedlar and Knight to the western part of the Gebel ; another Penman and his Arabs to the Obeidat country ; Eason-smith off for a recce of Soluch and Sceleidima ; Crisp bringing in an aircrew force-landed after a raid on Benghazi ; Melot and Seagrim with their wireless sets leaving for Wadi Gattara ; Lazarus off to survey the desert south of Jalo and the Heavy Section on its unending journeys to Matruh.

And from the verandah of the Rest House where Group H.Q. lived one might at times have been looking down from the control tower of an airport—at Bombays bringing parties of parashots and their stores ; Lysanders with staff officers from Eighth Army ; a Hudson to evacuate a sick man ; a Wellington to pick up a crew we had rescued, and the Waco on its constant errands.

We had many visitors at Siwa during that spring. Some, such as the Army Commander and the Air Officer Commanding, we were honoured to receive. Some, such as the Engineer in Chief, we were glad to " lush up " in the hope of favours to come, in his case a bigger and better landing ground, which we got, though it was finished just in time for the enemy to make use of it during the retreat to 'Alamein. Others we suffered less gladly and among these were the Official War Correspondent and his Boy Friend.

We had received a message about them the day before. They would come by air and were clearly in the " every facility " class. We were asked to provide a car and to give them lunch. There was a hint at the taking of photographs of great strategic importance.

At the appointed time the adjutant was on the landing ground with car and driver. We had suffered in the previous months from the indiscretions of Press and Wireless and the adjutant murmured a quiet, formal protest against taking pictures of our arms and vehicles. This roused the Boy Friend, a young and exquisite but by no means junior officer who was bear-leading the O.W.C. The O.W.C., he explained, was allowed to photograph *anything*. They went off in the car and it was at once apparent that there was no question of strategic photographs ; all the O.W.C. wanted was a pleasant day in the country and some good pictures of Siwa at the taxpayers' expense.

We were at that time feeling a bit sore on the subject of aircraft. The two Wacos were both unserviceable in Cairo. The R.A.F. had bent the propeller of one in landing after a test flight at Heliopolis, and their ground staff had taken the other to pieces and then said they were sorry but they could not put it together

again for three months. A rough calculation showed that it must
have cost about £50 in petrol alone for the Lysander which
brought the O.W.C. and his B.F. to visit us. We were not
amused.

The pair reappeared late for lunch and sweating, for the day
was hot and the car, strangely enough, had broken down some
distance away. After welcoming them, somebody asked with
interest if their visit was helping along the war effort. For a
moment conversation faltered.

Pressmen were always anxious for copy about L.R.D.G.
" The Highwaymen of the Sahara " or " Desert Raiders play
their Part " looked well in a headline. Our view was that the
less said about our activities the better, and with the help of the
Censorship at Middle East we usually won our point. But there
were some unfortunate lapses. For example, the XI Bn. of the
Trieste Motorised Division, writing on May 25, 1942, to its
Company Commanders—" The B.B.C stated that a new motor-
ised section had been formed and given special tasks to perform.
The distinguishing badge to be worn by members consisted of a
scorpion." On such occasions we envied the studied reticence of
Russian communiqués.

It was during those months when we were at Siwa that the
Italians in Cyrenaica reaped the fruits of their early brutalities.

In 1911 Italy on some trivial pretext went to war with the
Turkish Empire, then in its dotage, and seized Libya. In 1914
the Arabs revolted and the invaders lost all but a few coast towns.
During the 1920's the Italians were reconquering Tripolitania
and the Fezzan, and this completed they turned to Cyrenaica
where the Arabs under Omar el Mukhtar, Saleh el Ateiwish, the
Seif en Nasr family and half a dozen other leaders resisted them
year after year.

The nomads were the backbone of the Arab resistance, and
Graziani, " the Butcher," realised that to crush the Arab rebellion he must crush them. By rounding up the bedouin he would
prevent them from harbouring Omar el Mukhtar's followers and
supplying them with arms, food and recruits.

The nomad Arab hates a crowd. Crowds of people mean to him crowds of animals and crowds of animals mean not enough grazing to go round. And the Arab, an individualist and a lover of freedom which is not found in cities, likes some elbow room and space to breathe. So he pitches the few tents of his clan apart, unseen in a fold in the ground, and when you pass through Cyrenaica by road you hardly see an Arab and wonder where the two hundred thousand of them can be.

Between Agedabia and Benghazi Graziani made concentration camps and into them he crowded 80,000 of the nomads in neat rows of close-pitched tents. Outside the animals sought in vain for grazing ; inside the Arabs sickened and died. How many died may never be known, but the figures ran to thousands of men and more than three-quarters of a million animals.

In the end the " Butcher's " plan worked. Resistance in the Gebel was over by 1929 and in 1931 Kufra fell. But Graziani reaped where he had sown, for he left a legacy of hatred among the Arabs which proved to be a very potent force in our aid.

A few of the Italians realised the position. Here is the opinion, written in August, 1941, of one candid official who was instantly removed from his post and sent home :

" We were surrounded by a sullenly hostile population. Rare were the families who did not lament the death of a parent executed by us or killed in fighting against us. We were living in the midst of a people who considered that they had been harmed when they were dispossessed of their lands and of other resources for the benefit of our " Demographic colonisation " ; people who had been forced to give up, even before the war, their traditional trade and exchange of goods with Egypt ; people who resented the innumerable restrictions, orders and regulations which raised unsurmountable difficulties and imposed unnecessary hardships upon them.

" Traditional ethnic groups have been broken up or

destroyed. The chiefs who could have governed them for us are no more. The native officials we were using had little or no qualifications. They were normally employed because of their family connections and sometimes for worse reasons."

The British Government made a promise to the Arabs of Cyrenaica. In January, 1942, the Foreign Secretary said in the House of Commons : " His Majesty's Government is determined that, at the end of the war, the Senussi in Cyrenaica will in no circumstances again fall under Italian domination."

Whether we shall keep our promise, in the spirit as well as the letter, remains to be seen ; at the moment we seem to be in a fair way to do so. But it was the Arabs' hatred of the Italians far more than their love of the unknown British thát put them so wholeheartedly on our side.

Their services to us were not spectacular. They did not rise in arms against our enemies—in the first months of the war they had no arms to rise with—and in any case we never wanted them to do this. In Egypt with the help and encouragement of Sayed Idris es Senussi, four battalions of what was known as the Libyan Arab Force were raised from amongst those Arabs who had fled from Italian oppression. But it was the Arabs inside Cyrenaica, the Obeidat of Wadi Derna, the 'Abid towards Barce and the Bra'asa south of Cirene, who served us so well and who, above all, never lost hope. And they had good reason to lose it. In February, 1941, we took Benghazi ; by April we were back at the Egyptian frontier. In December we took it again ; by June we were back at 'Alamein. There was not much to give the Arabs confidence that Britain would be victorious.

And each time the Italians reoccupied the country they put the screw on. (Not the Germans ; they were too clever for that, letting the Italians do their dirty work. The prestige of the Germans was high among the Arabs who regarded them as " men " by comparison with the Italian " dogs.") They brought Tripolitanians into Cyrenaica to police the country ; they exiled the Arab leaders to Tripoli or Sicily ; they sent General Piatti, one of the best-hated men in Libya, to Barce as a Special Commissioner to hold the country down ; many Arabs they shot or hanged for aiding the British.[1]

There were, of course, some cases on the other side and a few British were betrayed. But for every one given up a hundred were helped. Baled-out airmen ; Commandos landing from submarines ; escaped prisoners ; G(R) men in the Wadi Derna ; Robert Baird's agents and ourselves most of all. Cave's story I have already told. Carr, the navigator of Y1 patrol, missing after Simms' attack on the coast road near Sidi Saleh in December, 1941, lived for some weeks with Arabs till our advancing forces picked him up. Duncalfe and McNobola, two Guardsmen who became separated from the rest of their patrol during the Barce raid in the following September, stayed for three months in the Gebel, fed and sheltered by the Arabs, till they were able to rejoin the Eighth Army as it swept through Cyrenaica in November. At the road watch near the Marble Arch some of those who saw the patrols must have realised who they were and what they were doing, but the secret was always kept. All the summer of 1941, often in the same autumn, most of all in the spring of 1942 the patrols were coming and going in Libya, but there were very few instances of their having been betrayed.

What sort of a life was it, living for weeks on end in the Gebel, with good friends, but wondering always whether to-day was the day when you would run into an enemy patrol and if not shot as a spy be carried off to an Italian prison camp ?

In April and May of 1942 Knight was up in the Bra'asa

[1] There is so much misunderstanding about the Senussi that it may be useful to explain here just who they are. The Senussi are not a tribe but the members of a Moslem religious sect which demands a fairly strict adherence to the Moslem code. The founder of the sect, Sayed Mohammed Ibn Ali es Senussi, settled in Cyrenaica at the beginning of the last century. Finding the Moslems there divided into a large number of religious sects, he united them by evolving the Senussi code which was a sort of common denominator to which they could all adhere and at the same time a return to a purer form of Moslem observance. Senussi influence spread rapidly over North-east Africa and by the end of the century had attained to considerable temporal as well as to spiritual power. The present head of the sect, Sayed Idris es Senussi, grandson of the founder, has been a firm friend of Great Britain throughout the war. Probably 85 per cent of the Arabs of Cyrenaica recognise him as their spiritual leader though in Tripolitania he has fewer followers.

country, doing a road watch and collecting information about enemy movements. Here is some of his diary :

"*April* 26.—At about 21.00 hours Hunter of L.R.D.G. dropped us at the mouth of the Wadi Retem. Found a suitable side *wadi* and dumped our stuff. L.R.D.G. went off and we settled in for the night.

"April 27.—Ahmed Bu Seif went off early to contact Suleiman Bin Salem. Ahmed is of the X tribe and knows the country. Rest of day sorting out kit and preparing to move north.

"*April* 28.—Ahmed returned bringing Suleiman with him. Had a council of war and got the latest news. Suleiman advised us to move out of the *wadi* we were in to one farther north. The one he wanted us to go to was where Pedlar had had his wireless set and was much more off the beaten track. He also told us that the Italian Carabinieri officer at Slonta had called in all the sheikhs and told them that it was no use their denying the presence of British in the district as he had definite information that they were there. The Italian said that big rewards would be given to any one who gave him information. Suleiman also said that it would be very difficult to hide up in the Cueifat area at the moment as Piatti had ordered that all the tribes were to move up there from the Baltet ez Zalagh. Wirelessed this back (to Cairo). Hired a camel and some donkeys from nearby Arabs and moved our stuff up to the Wadi Maiyit.

"*April* 29.—Suleiman did not turn up till after dark. Before he came Penman hired some camels from elsewhere and moved off. When Suleiman arrived with the camels he said he had had to go to the officer at Slonta where he had been cross-examined and told that reports had been received that he was helping the British. However, he had persuaded him that the reports were false and had managed to slip away.

"*April* 30.—About 17.00 hours we packed up and the seven Commandos and I moved up to the South Road, leaving

Longman and the two wireless sets behind. I decided that as the Slonta-Maraua area was said to be full of Arabs the wireless set and especially the charging motor would attract too much attention. Arrived at the Wadi Cueifat without mishap.

" *May* 1.—Suleiman led us to what he said was the best place in the district, about a mile east of where we had camped the previous trip. He left us there to go and find out the latest news.

" *May* 2.—Suleiman turned up late, full of alarming reports that he was suspected of harbouring the British but that with great difficulty he had persuaded some other sheikhs to vouch for him and so had got off going to Barce to see General Piatti himself.

" *May* 3.—At dawn Z and I went up to the South Road to start the road watch. Our plan was that two men should go up at dawn and be relieved at sunset as movement at any other time was too risky.

" *May* 4.—At 17.00 Ahmed, one of Suleiman's men, and I started for the North Road, carrying three days' rations. We found it very heavy going and it took us seven hours walking.

" *May* 5.—Ahmed led us to a good spot between Qasr Bu Megdem and Wadi Shahrise, about a couple of miles west of the Wadi Cuf. We made our camp on a hillside overlooking three strips of the main road from where we could see an Italian roadhouse. On the way up, when we were within a mile or so of our destination, we came round a bend in the path and ran straight into a pack of native dogs which promptly set up a most terrific din, barking and yelping, and a man came out of some tents nearby and asked us who we were and what we were doing. I slipped on ahead a bit and Ahmed explained that we were just looking for some sheep and we passed on. Later in the day, while I was on the road watch, Ahmed went to get some water and again met this Arab whom he recognised as an old friend. The man asked him if by any chance I was an English officer. Ahmed admitted that I was and took the man completely into his confidence. He sent word that he would expect me to supper that night ; I went along and he proved most useful and friendly. When we first arrived at the road there was no sign of any traffic so we had a rest. About dawn the first cars started to pass and at 11.00 hours thirty-three Italian armoured cars came up and parked round the roadhouse. Some moved off the road into the small *wadis* at the side and all camouflaged themselves very carefully with branches of trees. I assumed from this that they were expecting an air attack as the drivers stood about in groups and kept gazing up into the sky. The chaps manning the A.F.V.s were dressed in blue dungarees and wore black berets with a bunch of cock's plumes on the right side so it looked as if they belonged to some Bersaglieri unit.

" *May* 6.—Continued the watch on the North Road but nothing of any interest passed. Just the usual procession of trucks, lorries and staff cars.

" *May* 7.—Kept the watch all that day but decided to move back to the South Road that evening and send up the Commandos to take my place."

Such is a picture of their work in the Gebel in those months in 1942. And Knight's party was only one of many. Melot and Seagrim spent six weeks in the Wadi Gattara which cuts through the escarpment twenty miles east of Benghazi. They lay up in caves all day and at night, like animals of the jungle, came out for exercise and air, to put up their wireless masts and signal the day's news to Cairo. To their hiding place Arab agents came and went. Some into Benghazi to watch the port ; others to the airfields at Berka and Benina ; others to count the traffic on the Gebel roads.

One night in May, 1942, in an Italian mess in Benghazi the officers were talking freely ; perhaps their N.A.A.F.I. had had a ship in and there was something to drink for a change. They were discussing the coming attack at Gazala and Bir Hakim

which was due to start on May 27. They were careless, of course,
little suspecting that their Arab mess waiter had a brother and
that the brother was in Melot's pay. No more than they would
suspect that the foreman of the Arab stevedores in the port was
a friend of Melot's too.

Penman worked in the east, in the Obeidat country round
Derna and the Martuba By-Pass. He must hold the record, I
think, for time spent in the Gebel, for Lloyd Owen took him up
in May and it was not till August that Hunter brought him and
his party back to Kufra, for after we had been forced to leave
Siwa and the passes out of the Qattara Depression were closed
there was no other way.

Before he came back one of his Arabs turned traitor and
informed the Italian civil official in Derna who set out to search.
But the risk to Penman was small for the Italian's guides were in
his pay and each day he had advance information of where they
would take him on the morrow, and so he had no more trouble
than the inconvenience of moving out of the Italian's way.

After a few days of this the Italian returned to Derna,
informing his chief, General Piatti at Barce, that the reports were
false and that there were no British in his district. Piatti, angry
and unconvinced, ordered him out again so his subordinate, tired
by this time of trailing aimlessly round the hills, moved out a
short distance from Derna, waited a few days and then returned
to send in a second negative report.

On May 15th Gurdon with G2 patrol left Siwa to take
David Stirling and a party of his men to Benghazi for the second
time since our withdrawal from Jalo.

How well the patrols had got to know that run. Out of the
Siwa depression, through the minefield at the foot of the scarp,
up past the gloomy notice board which announced " You are
now entering a malarial area," across the R.F.C. landing ground
of the last war, along the Sollum track for eighty miles, through
the Wire at Weshkha, and then the long run across the desert to
the southern slopes of the Gebel, keeping south of the rough

country round Medawwar Hassan, going gingerly across the Tariq el 'Abd to avoid the thermos bombs, skirting round to the east of Msus and then up towards the Wadi Gattara and the escarpment which overlooks the Benghazi plain.

A paragraph in Gurdon's Operation Instruction shows how completely we had the " freedom of the desert " at that time.

" INFORMATION.
(b) Own troops.
    " The following patrols will be operating in the area between SIWA and REGIMA :
        " 1. S2 with 4 Chevs. and 1 Ford, returning from HAGFET GALGAF.
        " 2. R1 with 5 Chevs, at Lat. 31° 45′ 30″.
            Long. 21° 52′ 00″.
        " 3. Indian 1 ⎫ with 5 Chevs. each, in the area bounded
            Indian 2 ⎭ by Lat. 31° 30′ on the north and Long. 20° 30′ on the west.
        " 4. Commandos with 5 3-tonners, making a dump in MEDAWWAR HASSAN.
        " 5. T1 with 4 Chevs. leaving SIWA 16/5 to relieve R1 on 19/5."

S2 was bringing some Commandos back from the Gebel ; R1 was at the Marble Arch road watch and T1 leaving to take over from them ; the Commandos' Heavy Section was making a dump of petrol for future operations and the two Indian patrols,[1] newly arrived from Syria, were out on a training run to " see the country."

Having reached the escarpment Gurdon's party split up. In his official report the story sounds simple enough :

    " 21.5.42. At 17.30 hrs. Major Stirling in the staff car accompanied by two Chevrolet trucks moved off."

    [1] The Indian Long Range Squadron, consisting of Squadron H.Q. and four patrols and commanded by Major S. V. McCoy, had been formed in Syria in the winter of 1941-2. The squadron operated under command of L.R.D.G. from Siwa in the summer of 1942 and from Kufra and Hon in the following autumn and winter.

(The Chevs. were taking explosives to plant under the BARCE-BENGHAZI railway.)

" The road BARCE-BENGHAZI was reached after 14 miles at 22.45 hrs. and Major Stirling continued in the direction of REGIMA with his party.

" 23.5.42. Major Stirling returned to the R.V. at 06.00 hrs. and stated that he wished to move off that evening. The party moved off at 14.30 hrs. and drove all night."

And so to Siwa.

Now to fill in the gaps.

There were six in Stirling's party : himself, Maclean, Randolph Churchill, and three others including Seekings and Cooper who had a part in all Stirling's wildest exploits.

Just before midnight they left the rendezvous and drove northwards to the road which leads down to Regima from El Abiar, and here the trouble began. Stirling's car was a Ford, a staff car of the type which he always used in the pre-Jeep days, with the body cut down to the level of the doors and looking in the distance or the dark rather like a German Volkswagen. Coming across country from Siwa the track rods had been bent on some bump and as a result the front wheels were not truly parallel. In the desert this did not matter much but once on the smooth tarmac the tyres, askew, produced a high-pitched scream. There was no time to do anything about it so, screaming, they drove on towards Benghazi.

Near Benina was the road-block, a fairly old friend by this time. Stirling slowed at the bar as the sentry came forward into the glare of the headlights and inside the car, below the level of the body, the safety catches on five Tommy-guns slid back. Not to be used here, of course, but just in case . . . if the sentry did something tiresome.

However, the sentry was a good Italian, and when Maclean, the linguist of the party, answered " Staff officers " to his challenge he raised the bar and let them through.

With the tyres still squeaking Stirling drove on. By making a circle round Benghazi and coming in along the Tocra road from the north he could avoid much of the town and arrive more easily at the harbour for he was after ships this time, not aircraft, his usual game.

On the causeway outside the Derna Gate a car met them and passed by, then stopped, turned hurriedly and came back. This looked bad ; the sentry at Benina must have suspected something after all and done some rapid telephoning. So squeaking louder than ever and with the car behind seemingly in pursuit Stirling drove headlong into the town. Gaining a little on the pursuers, he turned quickly into a side alley and stopped ; the car behind dashed past and on down the main road.

In the alleyway the car's crew waited anxiously but all was quiet ; it seemed as if they had dodged their pursuers successfully. Then all over the city the air raid sirens started to wail. There was no sound of aircraft and no bombs falling ; moreover it had been arranged with Middle East that Benghazi should not be raided that night, and they assumed that this must indicate some special form of alarm against British ground forces. If this were so all the roads would be held and the best thing to do seemed to be to put a time bomb in the car and try to get away on foot. They could hardly hope, if the hunt was up, in the same squeaking car to drive out of the town and through the road-blocks. So they started to walk out, creeping along the dark and narrow streets.

Before long an Italian policeman appeared who gave Maclean his opinion that the air raid was a false alarm and said that he, at any rate, was going home to bed. By now the sirens had stopped and all was quiet : it seemed that they might make an attempt on the harbour after all. In a few moments they were back at the abandoned Ford again, wondering if the half-hour time-pencil would last out another five minutes, for these fuses tend to be temperamental and disregard the smaller divisions of time. Someone groped in the back of the car, pulled out the pencil and detonator and threw them round the corner. The town was still quiet so they started to get on with the job.

Stirling had brought with him from Cairo two collapsible rubber boats and a supply of heavy explosive charges for use against enemy shipping in the harbour. He hoped to get down to the water's edge, inflate the boats and paddle out to the ships. A steamer or two sunk alongside the moles, or better still in the fairway, would cause the enemy a lot of trouble.

Stirling, Maclean and Cooper started off for the waterside carrying a boat and the charges. A barbed wire fence surrounded the harbour but they found a convenient hole and scrambled through. Inside a sentry challenged. " Militari," Maclean answered, and asked him the way to the hotel, for the " luggage " they were carrying needed some explanation. The sentry knew of no hotel ; the British bombing had wrecked those which existed formerly so Maclean thanked him and passed on.

Down at the water's edge they began to pump up the boat but that night they seemed to be dogged by squeaks and the pump screeched with each stroke. From a ship moored not far out a sentry challenged. " Militari," shouted Maclean, and continued pumping. Again the guard on the ship challenged. By this time Maclean was beginning to get rather tired of Italian sentries. " Will you stop challenging me ? " he called. " I've already told you twice who I am," and went on with the pump.

But the rubber boat refused to be inflated. On the long journey across the desert from Siwa it had been rubbed against the car and punctured so Maclean went back to the car for the other boat. With this he started back to the harbour but to save time and a scramble through the wire entered at the main gate. Here were five or six sentries who gave no trouble, but down by the waterside there appeared another who was more inquisitive and would not leave them in peace.

By now Maclean's patience with Italian sentries was exhausted. He returned to the main gate and demanded to see the N.C.O. in charge of the guard. From a dimly-lit shack came a sleepy Italian corporal, pulling on his trousers. Maclean turned on him sharply.

" This," he said, " is simply disgraceful. Half a dozen times you have let us through this gate, carrying all this stuff. It might be bombs. How do you know we are not British ? You should have asked for our identity papers."

The corporal was anxious and apologetic. He would certainly reprimand the sentries who were no doubt reluctant to bother such important officers as Maclean and his party.

" Well," answered Maclean, " don't let this sort of thing occur again. We are now going to collect our kit from inside the wire and leave." And did so.

Back at the car where the driver was hammering at the bent track rods it was beginning to get light and it was evident that there was no time to get clear of the town before dawn. So a hiding place for the day had to be found. First they found a garage which looked suitable but the door was too narrow to get the car inside. Nearby was a second garage large enough, and by good luck it had above it a flat which seemed to be deserted. Creeping up the stairs they found it empty and here spent the day, lying for the most of the time on the floor to keep below the level of the blown-in windows. On the opposite side of the road there was much coming and going at a German headquarter office of some sort, and at the back the flat shared a courtyard with an Arab family who could be heard talking on the other side of the partition wall.

Till evening they were undisturbed. Then at dusk were heard footsteps on the stairs, slow and unsteady. They neared the top and the party gathered themselves for a fight. Churchill, with a week's beard and a week since his last wash; looked out —into the face of a drunken Italian sailor, intent on loot or rape. In a moment the man was at the foot of the steps, running for his life.

After dark Stirling decided to make another attempt on the shipping in the harbour but a blazing oil tanker lit up the fore-shore like day, though none of the sentries of whom Maclean enquired seemed to know how it had been set afire. Then there was nothing to do but leave Benghazi, so they drove out by the

Berka road, through the road-block at Benina and back to Gurdon waiting on the escarpment.

I write this in Tripoli on May 21st, 1943, with a wish that, I am afraid, is never likely to be realised. It is that one day Mussolini may have this chapter read to him and learn that a year ago to-night the son of England's Prime Minister spent thirty hours in his Cyrenaican capital.

The orders which L.R.D.G. had received from Eighth Army at that time were rather contradictory. For we were told to keep the road watches going at the Marble Arch and on the Msus-Mechili track and on the North and South Roads in the Gebel, and at the same time "interrupt enemy supplies along the Tripoli-Benghazi road."

Now a road watch needs peace and quiet. You cannot have a patrol sitting day in, day out, counting traffic if it is going to be disturbed by searching aircraft or ground patrols sent out as the result of a "beat-up" on road transport a few miles away. And although the Tripoli-Benghazi road looks long enough on the map there are only a limited number of areas at which approach—and get-away—from the south is suitable. When their M.T. is shot up at Kilo X to-night, the enemy's immediate reaction is to send out ground forces and aircraft to comb the country round Kilo X. So we needed some means of attacking traffic without the enemy knowing where the attack had taken place. The problem reduced itself, in fact, to planting unseen bombs in trucks at X which would go off fifty miles away at Y or Z.

The Siwa Brains Trust—every one in Siwa—was turned on to the problem. There were various schools of thought. The Easonsmith school, for instance, would have a man sitting on one side of the road holding a cord the far end of which was tied to the top of a telegraph post on the other. In the middle of the cord, over the road, would be an explosive charge with magnets attached. As the car passed the man would lower the cord and an ingenious quick-release device would drop the charge on to the top of the cab. Here it would stick and go off with a time fuse some miles later, blow the top off the driver's head and send the lorry into the ditch.

Then there was the cow-catcher school whereby the truck itself picked up from a hole in the road a bomb, with hooks attached, which having tangled itself up in the axles or radius rods exploded later and blew the bottom out of the truck.

In the end the Timpson plan seemed to have the best chance of success. By this the enemy lorry was slowed up at a bogus road-block while a man, leaping from behind in the roadside ditch, ran after it and lobbed a bomb into the back. Even here there were many difficulties as there might be passengers in the back of the truck or the tarpaulin cover might be fastened down.

G1 patrol spent some nights on the road leading into Siwa, throwing bags of sand into passing vehicles, and after much practice the scheme seemed worth a trial.

A special type of bomb was needed, one which would both damage the lorry and if possible kill the driver and at the same time set it afire. After many experiments, in which all the derelict vehicles in and around Siwa were destroyed, an approved bomb was produced. This was packed in an Italian haversack of which a supply had been procured from Salvage. The idea was that if the haversack were noticed in the truck Antonio would merely think that Giuseppe had left his shaving kit behind.

So on May 8th, Timpson left with four 44-gallon drums to make a road block, two poles to place across the drums, a couple of red hurricane lamps and two notices in German which read " Achtung, Strassenbau," the German equivalent for " Road Up." A night watchman with a brazier of coke was ruled out as being incompatible with a Libyan summer.

Going north of Jalo and across the Marada-'Agheila road, Timpson was fifty miles west of the Marble Arch on May 14th, far enough away, we hoped, from the patrol at the road watch.

A large heap of road metal seemed to be an obvious excuse for a road-block and here the empty drums were placed, the

notices set up and the metal shovelled across the road to narrow
down the gap.

But things did not turn out according to plan. The first cars
to arrive, apparently suspicious, hurried past the drums. So the
gap was made narrower but still they had no luck. With only
one car approaching the bomb thrower would crouch behind the
barrel, but when there were two the lights of the second showed
him up as he dodged the first. So the throwers retired to the
ditch but then found it difficult to catch up the truck.

By 2 a.m. Timpson realised that this plan would not work.
So he decided to try a new one of chasing the enemy vehicles in
his own truck with Fraser sitting on the bonnet, bomb in hand,
ready to throw it into the overtaken lorry.

The first chase ended at his own road block where he found
two gesticulating Italians with a broken down lorry and another
on tow. To take the Italians prisoner or destroy the lorry would
give the game away so Timpson assumed the character of a
German officer, explained that he was in a great hurry, and
promised to send out help from Sirte, driving off among cries of
" Grazie, Kamarade."

He had no more luck that night and a burst tyre on the main
road at dawn put an end to operations.

So Timpson abandoned bomb throwing and retired sixty
miles south into the hills to consider matters. On the way he
had a fight with some ground troops in which Guardsman
Matthews was killed.

A few days later he attacked a Road House[1] near Sultan.

" At 7 p.m. we set off for the road. The going was bad,
particularly the last four miles, and we did not reach it till
10.00. We swarmed up a telegraph pole and cut the wires, and
laid some mines in the road. Driving on with the headlights
on we came to the Road House and passing by slowly opened
up on men and vehicles. The blaze of fire was tremendous,

[1] These Road Houses (Casa Cantieri) are placed every 20 km. or so along the
coast road. They serve as a halting place for convoys, base for road-gangs, etc.

the first three trucks firing with one Breda 12.7.(tracer, incendiary, A.P. and H.E.), 2 Vickers .303, 3 Vickers " K," 1 twin Browning, 1 single Browning and a Lewis. In fact there was too much fire for the rear trucks were blinded by the light of those ahead and the multi-coloured ricochet of the tracer. Six large trucks were parked by the roadside and into these we poured ammunition. We halted after half a mile and cut the telephone wires again. As we drove back to the rendezvous we heard a tremendous explosion, evidently a vehicle going over the mines."

The delayed-bomb plan seemed to be a failure so we reverted to the old, straightforward " beat-up" and Wilder took both T patrols to attack the Agedabia-Benghazi road. This was an old hunting ground where the patrols had shot up traffic during the autumn offensive, difficult country to operate in because the plain across which the road runs is as flat as a pancake and the nearest cover is in the low escarpment twenty miles to the east.

At dusk Wilder left the shelter of the scarp and, crawling slowly across the flat ploughland, was on the road by midnight. Near Magrùn, at a road block, the sentry shouted to him to stop but Wilder, preferring to fight on ground of his own choosing, drove through the zigzag while the guard did nothing to stop him. A few miles farther south he saw he was being followed by enemy trucks. Drawing off the road, with lights out, he waited till two cars carrying troops drew level. For months past, from abandoned British vehicles, crashed aircraft and elsewhere, the patrols had been collecting extra weapons, Vickers K's and Brownings, and their fire power was immense, ideal for an occasion like this. A long burst from all the guns killed or wounded twenty of the enemy and set the vehicles ablaze. A short way down the road was a car park from which the drivers had fled in terror, and here, with bombs and incendiaries, all the trucks were destroyed.

For two days Wilder lay up in cover in the escarpment and

on the second evening, on the way back to the road, encountered
an armed patrol which was probably searching for him. In the
fight which followed the New Zealanders killed two Italians and
brought the remaining five back as prisoners to Siwa.

In relation to the efforts which L.R.D.G. expended in men,
vehicles, petrol, ammunition and food, the direct losses inflicted
on the enemy in these raids may seem small. But we knew from
prisoners and from captured documents that in addition to the
casualties—and these were at least five to one in our favour—
the nuisance value was very great. The scale of the attacks, here
to-day and fifty miles away to-morrow, made mostly at night
when accurate observation was impossible, was greatly exaggerated, especially by the fearful Italians. At times all traffic after
dark was stopped. Transport drivers, many of them from semi-
civilian contractors, were terrified, not knowing when their turn
would come. Troops, armoured cars and aircraft had to be
diverted from their proper use to convoy protection work. Thus
the enemy, in an Intelligence summary of April, 1942, wrote :

" The L.R.D.G. plays an extremely important part in the
enemy sabotage organisation. The selection and training of
the men, the strength, speed and camouflage of the vehicles
for the country in which they have to operate have enabled
the Group to carry out very effective work, particularly in the
destruction of Axis aircraft on the landing grounds at Agedabia
and Tamet."

Early in June, Gurdon took Stirling and Mayne to Benghazi
again. On the way up the parashots' one car had been blown up
on a thermos bomb on the Tariq el 'Abd and so from the usual
rendezvous on the top of the escarpment they went forward to
Benghazi in a borrowed G patrol truck.

On the night of the 12th Stirling got into the hangars at
Benina airfield. It was dark and the guards were unsuspecting
and the small party crept from hangar to hangar with their load
of bombs. By the time they had finished they had placed time

bombs on five machines and on fourteen crates containing aircraft engines. The three hangars were burnt out when the bombs
went off later.

In the last hangar which they dealt with a crack of light was
showing from under a door in the side wall. Quietly they crept up
to it and Stirling, with a Mills grenade in one hand, gently
opened the door. It was the guard room, a small place with
bunks in tiers round the walls and the men off duty asleep in
them. At a table in the middle of the room sat an officer, reading.
As the door opened he glanced up from his book, expecting one
of his men with a report. Stirling lobbed the grenade gently
across the floor and slammed the door shut. Cooper was
behind him, looking over his shoulder : afterwards he told me
that it was a long time before he began to forget the expression
on the German officer's face.

While Stirling was at Benina Mayne had gone to the airfield
at Berka. But here all went wrong. At Middle East someone
had made a muddle, had forgotten, or not been told, that the
parashots would be at Berka that night, and had laid on a raid
by the R.A.F. So when Mayne got to the edge of the landing
ground he found that the bombing and parachute flares made
his task impossible. In the end he destroyed one aircraft but his
party were seen as they moved off and all the next day troops
searched the plain east of Berka across which they were trying
to make their way to the rendezvous with Gurdon above the
escarpment.

It was a burning hot summer day and soon they were all
suffering terribly from thirst. At midday one man was hiding
in the thin shade of some tamarisk bushes, halfway across the
plain. All around were Italians listlessly combing the scrub, some
on foot, some with bicycles. Suddenly round the tamarisk bush
came a soldier, pushing his machine. It looked like the end of
the war as far as the parashot was concerned, but the Italian
had left his rifle behind and was unarmed. The other dared not
risk the sound of a shot. For a moment they gazed at each other,
weighing up their chances. Then the Italian tried persuasion :

" Campo, campo," he said. " Agua, mangeria."

" B—— off," from the parashot.

" No, no. Campo, campo," repeated the Italian.

" All right, if you must have it," said the parashot, and strangled him.

On the 14th Stirling and Mayne rejoined Gurdon and two days later started for Benghazi again. This time their objective was the harbour and they drove past Benina where the hangars were still smouldering. West of the aerodrome was the road-block but this time in the place of easy-going Italians there were Germans on guard, alert after the events of two nights before.

The bar was across the road and as Stirling stopped the car the German N.C.O. came out into the headlights, demanding identity cards and passwords. But this had been foreseen and one of the parashot party spoke German. He began to spin a tale to the sergeant. They were just out of the front line, had been driving day and night from Gazala ; surely he wasn't going to keep them hanging about now on the outskirts of Benghazi when they wanted to hurry on and get a bath and a drink. And more in that strain.

The N.C.O. began to waver and in the glare of the lights, as Stirling told me later, he could see the man's face struggling with a decision. His expression showed that he was almost sure that the party was bogus but if he forced the issue he would have about five seconds more to live. He thought better of it, lifted the barrier and Stirling drove through.

But one thing after another delayed and hindered them and they had to turn back before reaching the port. All the latter part of the night they were bumping back over the plain towards the escarpment the top of which they reached at dawn. There for some trivial reason the truck halted for a moment, the engine running quietly. In the comparative silence someone in the back heard the sharp click of a time pencil going off, and immediately afterwards another. At his wild shout of warning each man leapt from the car and ran for his life. When they were about thirty yards away the whole load of bombs went off and the truck simply disintegrated but by a miracle no one was hurt.

While the parashots had been away G patrol carried fifty pounds of ammonal and buried it under the Barce-Benghazi railway. They could not wait to watch the result but next day the sentry at the rendezvous reported a heavy explosion and clouds of smoke rising from the direction of the line.

Four days later the party was back in Siwa again.

It was about this time Almasy first showed up.

Though the Axis could not produce a counterpart to Bagnold, for Bagnold was unique, they had an *ersatz* Bagnold in Almasy. We had realised this as soon as L.R.D.G. was formed and kept an eye open for him, for there are ways and means of finding out where people are and what they are doing, even in Hungary in 1940, but in those early days Almasy did not seem likely to give us trouble.

A year passed without further news. Then from a sign here and there, from a letter foolishly preserved by a German soldier, from a careless word in a prisoner of war cage and from those other sources of information which the Censor would strike out if I set them down, we realised that Almasy was on the move.

" Who," you ask, " is this Almasy ? "

Ladislaus Edouard de Almasy, Count (?) of Szombathely, Hungary. Motorist. Aviator. Traveller. Explorer (of a sort). Author. Linguist. Spy (?). Educated in England. Speaking many languages perfectly. A friend (or so we once thought) of the English. A friend (but for different reasons) of the Egyptians.

I had last seen Almasy in the Mess of the Western Arab Corps at El Fasher in the Sudan in March, 1935. While he and I sat and argued about the position of a " lost " oasis, Mike Mason was drawing a caricature of Almasy's sharp alert profile on the back of an envelope.

He first appeared in the Libyan Desert in 1929 accompanying the Prince of Lichtenstein on a journey from East Africa to Egypt by car. From then until the outbreak of the Nazi war Almasy was often travelling in Libya, usually at somebody else's expense. He had a real passion for the desert and much of it he knew extremely well. He had been to 'Uweinat with Robert Clayton and Penderel in 1932 ; to Kufra a year later ; to 'Uweinat with Frobenius, the German archæologist, in the autumn of that year, and to the north-western Sudan with a party of Hungarians in the spring of 1935.

He had some discoveries to his credit of which the most important was the fine group of prehistoric rock paintings found at 'Ain Dua in 'Uweinat in 1933. An Italian archæologist by name Caporiacco, and later the German Frobenius, tried to steal the credit for the discovery which was justly due to Almasy, and for some months an acrimonious correspondence trailed its way through the columns of German and Italian scientific magazines. I think all the governments interested in the Libyan Desert— British, Egyptian, Italian—wondered if Almasy was a spy working for the other side. The Italian officials in Kufra were careless and when the French captured the oasis they found in the archives, foolishly unburnt, enough evidence to put Almasy into a concentration camp if not up against a wall. But even so I doubt if he was really an agent in the Italians' pay and in any case they did not trust him for on his return to Cairo after his expedition in 1933 they managed, by an ingenious trick which the Kufra papers describe, to steal a copy of his maps and his report.

Matters looked worse for Almasy in 1938 when he was taking von Esch for trips into the desert between Sollum and Alexandria and paying special attention to the rain water cisterns which, except for the wells close to the sea, are the only source of water in that barren area. That von Esch was a German spy no one doubted, though as a nephew of General von Schleicher who had been murdered by the Nazis he might have been expected to be no friend of their regime.

So we were rather sore when, in the spring of 1942, we realised that Almasy, turning on the British and Egyptians who had befriended him, had thrown in his lot with the Huns. Though to do him justice in the years before the war he had never made any bones about his admiration for Totalitarianism.

In the winter and spring of that year we had little to go on. It was known that Almasy was in Libya, attached to the Afrika Korps, but not exactly what he was doing.

Then early one morning in June the Arab watchman on the landing ground at Kharga saw a car approaching as he stirred himself from sleep. The car stopped and an officer leaned out, speaking to him Arabic : he wanted to know just where the road to Asyut left the oasis. The Arab showed him and the car drove off. It was a British type of car and no doubt, thought the watchman, the officer was British. These mad foreigners were always roaming about the desert and a few of them spoke Arabic. He turned his thoughts to breakfast.

The next morning at about the same time the same car passed him returning from Asyut and drove off westwards into the desert. " Well," thought the watchman, " that's a bit odd. I may as well tell the Mudir." So he told the Mudir who forwarded a report through the " usual channels " which finally reached someone in Cairo who wondered if there really *had* been a British car in Kharga at that time on that day and took the trouble to find out.

Then more things began to happen and two and two looked like adding up to four. First, there were indications, through what were known as " reliable sources," that Almasy might be getting more active. Second, a S.D.F. officer on his way from Wadi Halfa to Kufra passed three cars near Wadi Sura on the west side of the Gilf. They waved and he waved back but later, when he mentioned the meeting in Kufra, there was some doubt as to who they had been, for no other S.D.F. party was known to be out at that place and time. Thirdly, there was the dog. It was a tiresome dog and it barked at night so that the neighbours in the Cairo suburb complained, first to the owners and then to the police. The police investigated the complaint and were not quite satisfied about the identity of the owners. They made further inquiries and to cut a long story short Herren Reichert and

Vollhardt, German spies, found themselves in a prison camp. There they talked, quite a lot.

But we heard of all this too long after the event. Some clever fellow in Cairo thought he knew more about catching Almasy than L.R.D.G., the only people who had both the organisation to do the job and the personal knowledge of Almasy and what he was likely to do and where he was likely to go.

Gradually the story came out. The " Sonderkommando Almasy " was based on Jalo in the spring of 1942, organised in six small patrols rather on the lines of L.R.D.G. In June Almasy with two or three cars had sneaked down past Kufra, through the Gilf and across the desert to Kharga and on to Asyut where he dropped Reichert and Vollhardt. While they went on to Cairo Almasy returned safely to Jalo. Though Reichert and Vollhardt achieved nothing it was a good effort, a 900-mile run through enemy country and worthy of Almasy's desert craft.

The only place where cars can get through the Gilf north of Wadi Firaq is at the Gap (El Aqaba) where a winding sandy *wadi*, in places only ten yards wide, leads up from the western plain to the top of the plateau. Clayton had first noticed the place in 1931, but Almasy and Penderel, a year later, had been the first to go through. It was both common sense and in keeping with Almasy's character, proud of his own discoveries, to use this route, and as soon as the news reached us we sent out a party from Kufra to mine the narrow passage and later put a watching post there. But it was too late ; the fresh car tracks showed that he had passed through to the east and returned.

That, I think, was the end of him. Perhaps he kept a road watch on the Matruh-Alexandria road, but I doubt it. There were never any reports of raids against our lines of communications or airfields which sounded as if they were the work of the Axis' L.R.D.G. When Jalo was taken there were no signs of Almasy there. There were more in Hon when we got there ; indications of a " Sonderkommando Dora " which appeared to be a similar organisation, a few German sun compasses and other special kit, but it seems that he achieved little though he had good opportunities.

In October, 1941, Ballantyne with T1 patrol was doing a job near Benghazi, looking for places at which the escarpment south of Regima could be crossed. On the way back he picked up a party of Germans who were out in a couple of trucks collecting spare parts from derelict British vehicles. As they were only fifty miles from Benghazi and the front line was then at Sollum the Huns were extremely surprised when the New Zealanders rounded them up.

On the journey back to Siwa the German officer became talkative and by that time he had seen a good deal of the way L.R.D.G. worked. " You know," he said to Ballantyne, " we Germans couldn't do this sort of thing—out five hundred miles from our base for days or weeks on end. We like to go about in a crowd." [1]

He may or may not have been right : anyhow Almasy failed.

[1] Six months after writing this I read in Alan Moorehead's book, *The End in Africa* : " It appeared to me as I travelled among the prisoners, especially the Germans, that they lacked the power of individual thought and action. They had been trained as a team, for years the best fighting team in the world. They had never been trained to fight in small groups or by themselves. . . . And so they leaned heavily on the machine and trusted it. They never tried out the odd exciting things we did—things like the Long Range Desert Group. . . . They liked to do things *en masse*."

CHAPTER ELEVEN

SIWA, 'ALAMEIN, FAIYUM

On May 27th, 1942, Rommel attacked the Gazala line, forestalling by a few days an advance by the Eighth Army and in the month which followed came some of the bitterest fighting of the Libyan war—" Knightsbridge," " The Cauldron," Acroma, Bir Hakim. Three days after it started things seemed so much in our favour that we never dreamed that in a month we should be leaving Siwa, where part or all of L.R.D.G. had been based since the spring of 1941, and which we had left with such high hopes in January en route for Jalo.

But the fall of Tobruk and the withdrawal from Sollum left us no choice. The Matruh road was cut on June 27th and if we did not hurry we would barely get away through Qara.

Having to leave Siwa was a serious blow, for it was an ideal base. Covered by the forces at Jaghbub, with good water, good quarters, a good road to the coast, too far for enemy raiders to worry us, it had all the advantages. However, we still had Kufra and it was clear that in future all the forward raiding would have to be done from there.

The move itself was a pretty problem. When a normal unit of the size of the L.R.D.G. has to move the C.O. can probably give verbal orders to his officers, or at least written ones, for they should all be within a few miles at the most. Prendergast's problem was to fit in the following moves :

S2 at the Marble Arch road watch to go to Kufra, for by the time they had handed over to the relieving patrol Siwa would be in enemy hands.
Y1 en route to the Marble Arch road watch.
R1 to leave Siwa to take over from Y1.

T2 and R2 to go straight to Kufra across the Sand Sea,
   not an ideal June journey.
" A " Sqn. H.Q. to Kufra, going via Cairo for supplies.
All the rest of the patrols and Group H.Q. to 'Alamein via
   Qara.

We left little or nothing of use to the Axis in Siwa and the
Rear Party got away on June 28th preceded by a few hours by
an aircraft carrying a man whose appendix Dick Lawson had
cut out the night before.

At Gerawla on the coast road we met and joined that amazing
stream of traffic, the retreat to 'Alamein. For two days we drove
in the stream and then five miles east of 'Alamein pulled out of
it into the sand dunes, to wait and hope that we need go no
farther east.

We camped among the scrub and low dunes of silver sand.
On one side lay the sea and half a mile away on the other the
main road, running along a ridge of low hills. For four or five
days we stayed there and whenever you looked out to the south,
day or night, morning or evening, you saw the same sight—a long
line of transport, head to tail, orderly, moving slowly back to
Alexandria. How many trucks passed in those days I have no
idea, perhaps fifty thousand, perhaps a hundred thousand ; a
whole army was on the move. And then you realised what the
Eighth Army owed to the Desert Air Force for scarcely one Axis
aircraft came over to strafe this perfect target. What havoc they
could have caused, for example, on the causeway below 'Amiriya
as I saw it one morning, with a tank transporter on its side across
the embankment and a double line of traffic waiting an hour till
the block was cleared.

The Official History, when it is published, will no doubt
estimate how critical was the position in Egypt at that time. The
Palestine-bound trains were crammed ; the Sudan Agency
besieged for visas ; at G.H.Q. the air was filled with the smoke
of burning documents—Ash Wednesday they called it ; the
Egyptians, with Nahas Pasha and all his family dining unalarmed

at the Continental, remained remarkably calm. At Army H.Q.,
which I visited frequently during that time, the " Ops " people
showed an unshaken confidence ; one day they were preparing
to move to Daba the following morning from their position south
of 'Amiriya on the Cairo road.

From 'Alamein we moved on to the sea shore outside Alexandria, waited there for a week hoping that we need go back no
farther and then moved to the Faiyum. Here on a bare ridge near
Kom Aushim, where the Mena road enters the cultivation, we
spent the rest of the summer of 1942.

It was hot and the sand blew and we had little cover, but on
the whole it was a suitable spot. To have gone to Cairo or to
Mena would have been a great mistake. There there were
thousands of other troops, black-outs, inspections by Area staffs
and endless nuisances. And strategically the Faiyum was a
convenient place, for now having lost the good base at Siwa we
had to find another back door to the country behind the Axis
lines.

The 'Alamein line, from the cliffs of the Qattara Depression
to the sea, was soon closed. " A " squadron at Kufra could still
get up to the Gebel Akhdar from there, but the patrols coming
from the east would have to go through the Depression or, when
that route was denied to us, past Bahariya to 'Ain Dalla and
across the Sand Sea. But the enemy were strangely slow to block
the passes on the west side of the Qattara Depression. The Italians
were in Siwa a few days after we left but there they remained,
apparently not daring to move out to the east. And from the
beginning of July till the middle of August the patrols were
passing through the Depression on their way from the Faiyum
to the Gebel or to targets between 'Alamein and Sidi Barrani.

The battle line at 'Alamein had hardly been stabilised when
on July 1st Hunter and Timpson were off to No Man's Land.
Hunter somehow got through the southern end of the 'Alamein
positions but Timpson had no luck. Wire, minefields, and being
soundly shelled by our own troops forced him to take the long
route round through the Depression.

It is strange that the true character of this great hole in
Egypt, which so conveniently guarded our southern flank at
'Alamein, was unknown till the last war. When the Light Car
Patrols were operating in the Western Desert Dr. Ball, then
Director of Desert Surveys in Cairo, used to lend the officers
aneroid barometers and get them to, record the height readings
along their route. One day a man brought in to the Survey Office
the sketch map of his last patrol with the aneroid readings he had
taken. When Ball worked them out they showed figures a
hundred feet or more below sea level and Ball thought that the
man had mis-read the instrument or that it had been out of
order. But he remembered the incident and after the war sent
one of his surveyors (G. F. Walpole) to make a more accurate
survey. When his work was finished there was added to the map
of Egypt this huge basin, 150 miles long and half as broad and
at its deepest point 450 feet below the Mediterranean.

There is, on paper, a fascinating project of Ball's for opening
a canal from the sea to the Depression and dropping the Mediterranean over the 1000-foot cliffs to produce an immense supply of
hydro-electric power. Evaporation in the Depression would be
so great that the sea could be poured in for hundreds of years
before it filled up. At the moment an unindustrial Egypt has no
need for so much electric power but the plan may be put into
force some day.

There can be few more horrible places in the world than this
at midday in July. To the north the unscaleable cliffs shimmer
in the heat haze ; to the south are the tongues of sand dunes, the
outliers of the Sand Sea. In the basin the heat is stifling, no hill
gives shade, no tree breaks the monotony of the salt marshes.
Drive your truck two yards from the beaten track and it will
be sunk to its axles in the quicksands. And, in July, 1942,
there might well be a couple of Stukas in the distance, slowly
circling the tracks of the last patrol which had gone through.
Then it was best to cross at night if you could see the way,
or at midday when the heat haze would reduce the visibility to
nothing.

The old caravan masters had found a way across, a narrow strip of harder ground with a rivulet of salt cutting across it ; El Qaneitra they called it—the Little Bridge. But there was a limit to the amount of traffic it would stand and that limit had been passed. At the end of June, when we evacuated Siwa, Holliman had stayed behind to bring away the garrison of Jaghbub, a mixed party of Free French, Indians and British. By the time he got to Qara the enemy were pushing fast along the coast and he had to take the Qaneitra route or stay behind. There were 250 vehicles in that party and how they got across the Depression is a mystery. A good many did not and their carcasses still line the route. But Holliman got the garrison to Cairo in the end.   He had signalled " Qaneitra completely wrecked for further traffic " which did not look hopeful for our new operations.

However, we used alternative routes, along the telegraph line to Qattara Spring and then following the cliffs to the pass at Qara or a bypass round the Qaneitra to the south. And after some weeks at Qaneitra dried up enough for light cars to get across it.

When the Eighth Army went back to 'Alamein it was expected and hoped that in a very short time we should again be advancing westwards. It looked as if the enemy had over-reached himself on his rapid push into Egypt and that we might catch him on the rebound.

The share of the parashots and L.R.D.G. in this anticipated advance was to do everything possible to upset the enemy's communications behind the 'Alamein line and to destroy aircraft on his forward landing grounds. So from the beginning of July till mid-August patrols were going out across the Qattara Depression to Stirling's base at Bir el Quseir and from there northwards to " pinprick " the enemy anywhere between Sidi Barrani and 'Alamein. The parashots had changed their organisation a lot since we had last done a job with them ; they had got their own transport and were working out very effective new tactics for the use of heavily armed Jeeps. But they still relied on L.R.D.G. to some extent for signals and navigation and also occasionally for supplies.

While Timpson was blowing up the water pipeline west of Matruh, Hunter had gone to the landing grounds round Fuka with a party of French parashots, for Stirling had a Free French section in his force. They had two targets, L.G.'s 16 and 68. Hunter dropped the French on the edge of No. 16, waiting in support while they did their attack. In an hour they returned successful. Meanwhile the Italian guards on the other landing ground, either because they thought they were being attacked or to keep up their courage, were letting off all their guns and the night was lit up with Breda and M.G. fire.

Not proposing to run slap into this shooting, Hunter skirted round the landing ground and in the dispersal area found three or four aircraft which he destroyed. A few yards farther on he had trouble. In the darkness the cars were following each other closely to keep in touch, when suddenly the first fell headlong into a deep and unseen hole and the second, close behind, crashed into it and wrecked the engine. The next ten minutes were hectic ; in the hole, cursing and sweating, Y patrol were trying to get the front, undamaged truck out ; all around the Italians were firing furiously and ineffectively. In the end it was done and Hunter got away with the loss of one truck only, but two days later he was caught near Qattara Spring by three Messerschmidts and another car was set on fire and burnt out. Tyres of some of the other cars had been punctured in the attack and Miller Kerr and two other men, with the ammunition going off inside the blazing truck, jacked up the wheels and took three spares from it.

A week later Wilder and Gurdon reached Bir el Quseir with their patrols. On the 8th July Gurdon was on the coast road near Fuka destroying parked transport, fuel tankers and tents. Three days later, going up for a second attack, he was caught late in the evening by three Macchis and severely shot up. Gurdon, mortally wounded but conscious and giving orders till the end, died before he could be taken back to the parashots' doctor fifty miles away ; Murray his driver, badly hit in arm and legs, reached Cairo after a five-day journey through the Qattara Depression and recovered from his wounds.

Stirling, with his new Jeeps, had evolved a fresh technique for destroying aircraft. Having got on to the landing ground to be attacked, the Jeeps formed up in a hollow three-sided square. In each car was a crew of three, one driver and two gunners firing twin-mounted Vickers guns outwards from the square. In this phalanx Stirling, leading, would drive slowly round the airfield pouring out a volume of tracer, explosive and incendiary which would destroy or damage any aircraft within range and send the guards hurrying into their slit trenches.

After a night or two of practising this formation Wilder and the parashots went up to raid the landing grounds near Ma'aten Bagush. By dawn they had destroyed fifteen aircraft and Wilder had captured four surprised and sleepy Germans whom he had almost run over by the side of the track.

The next morning the Germans reacted, sending out aircraft which soon found the patrol and were followed by a strong ground force. In the confused fighting which followed, Sanders, the T patrol gunner, knocked out four enemy trucks. The enemy's attack appeared to be directed by a Fiesler Storch which kept circling slowly round the battlefield and occasionally landing to confer with its ground troops. In the end it did this once too often when two New Zealanders appeared over a ridge with Tommy guns, held up the crew, and burnt the plane.

All these operations needed supplies and in the middle of July Stirling signalled us for 1500 gallons of petrol, 5000 rounds of ammunition and 300 Mills bombs, oil, rations, etc. To get this load from the Faiyum and across the Depression would have been a big enough job in peace time ; this was war and the enemy were waking up. By this time they must have realised where these attacks were coming from, and though oddly enough they had not closed the Qattara passes their aircraft were over the Depression every day and patrolling the road which runs north-east from Qara.

But the Heavy Section rose to the occasion and Arnold, with S1 patrol as escort, set off with four three-tonners carrying Stirling's needs. Lazarus worked out a new route across the Depression south of the Qaneitra Crossing, delivered the load to Stirling and was back in the Faiyum a week after he had left.

By the end of July it was clear that the closing of the passes was imminent. Enemy armoured car patrols were moving down south from the coast and Lloyd Owen, returning from the Tobruk area, learned from the Arabs in Qara that enemy aircraft had bombed the village shortly before his arrival.

Meanwhile, far off in the Gebel Akhdar, some of the behind-the-line Intelligence men were running short of supplies so on August 8th Hunter set off for their old hiding place on the escarpment above Benghazi. From the Faiyum to Benghazi is 700 miles, and from Benghazi Hunter might have to go back to Kufra. This was too far even for an L.R.D.G. patrol, so Sweeting, who had taken over G2 after Gurdon had been killed, went with Hunter carrying extra petrol. I took three cars as far as Qara with a load of supplies for the natives there. They were cut off from both Siwa and the coast and were beginning to run short of food. Also I wanted to make a plan with Sheikh Hamza, an old friend of L.R.D.G., to let us know if the passes had been closed by the enemy. We arranged to send over an aircraft periodically and as long as they were open Sheikh Hamza would spread out on the flat roof of his house a large white sheet with a black triangle on it. When the passes were held he would show nothing.

We left the Faiyum early one morning and as we halted for a moment before turning off the Cairo road on to the desert Lloyd Owen with Y1 came over the hill. We waited to get his news and while we stood there talking Arnold with the Heavy Section caught us up, and it struck me how this chance meeting by the roadside was typical of the long rangeness of L.R.D.G. Lloyd Owen had left Kufra ten days before, gone up to the coast road between Tobruk and Sollum in an unsuccessful attempt to find in that bare waste enough cover to hide him while he did a road watch, and then come on to the Faiyum. Since Kufra he had travelled 1100 miles. Hunter was off to Benghazi and Arnold was setting out with supplies for " A " squadron at Kufra, a week's journey which would take him down the Nile Valley to Asyut, across the plateau to Kharga, and from there a run of 600 miles through the Gilf Kebir. Before we parted the Waco roared over our heads taking Prendergast back from Cairo to the Faiyum.

As far as Mushroom Rock we were on the old track to 'Ain Dalla and the Sand Sea but beyond was new country to me. And except for a few patches of acacias it was as bare as the back of your hand. So to dodge aircraft we travelled before dawn or else at midday when the shimmering heat-haze made the visibility almost nil. In the early half-light a Y patrol truck crashed into the one in front of it and wrecked the radiator and the front of the engine. While we waited to change their guns and gear on to one of my three trucks, I walked up the low hill beside us. On the top was a heap of potsherds, fragments from the water jars of some Roman caravan from Siwa to Bahariya. We towed the damaged car into cover to pick up on our way back. Near the hiding place were the remains of a Beaufighter, blown into a thousand pieces, which had crashed after some sortie months before. I wondered who in two thousand years would next find the remains of two empires.

It was scorchingly hot as we crawled across the Depression, bumping over the slabs of rock salt and the endless giant sand ripples. In the late afternoon I did my business with Sheikh Hamza and left Hunter to go on from Qara. I wanted to get to the east of the Depression before the next dawn which meant going by the Qaneitra Crossing for the route we had come by would be impossible in the dark. For the first forty miles from Qara the tracks are plain enough but it was dark before we got to the Qaneitra and on the slab rock which skirts the salt marsh the tracks were invisible. For an hour we searched with torches for the narrow gap leading between the quicksands, found it in the end and by first light were well away towards the east.

Sheikh Hamza put out no signals for the aircraft which flew over Qara a few days later and so we used that route no more. Stirling also withdrew his force which was needed for the coming operations in Cyrenaica ; the last of his men were brought out by two Bombays of 216 Squadron which landed after dark down a flare path on a dry mud-pan near Bir el Quseir.

CHAPTER TWELVE

'TULIP,' 'DAFFODIL,' 'SNOWDROP,' 'HYACINTH'

WHEN the Army is planning an operation it does not announce its objective to all the world, or even to its own men. So if you found your way into the G (Plans) room at Middle East and rolled up the blank-paper curtains which hid the maps pinned to the wall you would not find on them the legend " Plan for proposed operation at 'Alamein. October 23rd, 1942," but merely Operation—" Rosemary " or whatever name had caught the fancy of the Plans staff when the scheme was born.

Hence " Tulip," " Daffodil," " Snowdrop," " Hyacinth," in all of which L.R.D.G. had a share.

The purpose of all four was the same, to disrupt the enemy's lines of supply. Rommel, with the front line steady at 'Alamein, was bringing all his supplies through Tobruk or Benghazi. It was known that he was about to attack ; if he could be held and then caught on the rebound short of supplies it might be the finish of him. The Navy and the R.A.F. were hitting hard at his Mediterranean convoys and serious damage done to the two ports might tip the scales. So in late August, when the plans were made, hopes were high.

" Daffodil " stood for Tobruk—a simultaneous attack from land and sea, designed to capture the coast defence guns and destroy as much as possible of the harbour installations, particularly the large, unbombable petrol storage tanks. For if the enemy were unable to land petrol in bulk from tankers the difficulties of their fuel supplies would be enormously increased.

" Snowdrop " was for Benghazi, a simpler plan in which Stirling, who commanded the force, would try to sink shipping in the harbour and then wreck all else he could. Lazarus with S2 was to guide the advance party up from Kufra and then, joined by Olivey with S1 from the Faiyum, attack the aerodrome at Benina.

" Tulip " plan was also simple, the taking of Jalo by the
Sudan Defence Force from Kufra to provide a base to which
Stirling could return and from which he could make further raids
against Rommel's lines of communications in the Gebel. Hunter's
patrol and Talbot's were to go with the S.D.F.

" Hyacinth " was a purely L.R.D.G. show. T1 and G1
under Easonsmith would go from the Faiyum by our old " underground " route to 'Ain Dalla, across the Sand Sea to Big Cairn,
out of the sands at Garet Khod and then north-west across the
open desert to Barce to raid the airfield there.

Such were the general plans. And there seemed a good
chance of success. The enemy garrisons were believed to be
small and composed of low category troops. Surprise was essential and the danger here was the passage through the bottleneck
at Jalo, the twenty-mile gap between the oasis and the edge of
the Sand Sea. If the force were seen here the cat would be out
of the bag and beyond recapture.

I was in Palestine on a week's leave when the patrols left
the Faiyum but came back a few days before D Day—September
13th. Prendergast went to Alexandria where the operation was
to be run by a combined staff of the all-highest—C.-in-C.
Mediterranean, A.O.C. and D.M.O., Middle East—and I stayed
at the Faiyum to deal with the signals coming in to Group H.Q.
Tim Heywood had had a big share in the Signals planning and
from H.Q. we could communicate with all the patrols and with
Alexandria, Cairo and Kufra.

Up to D Day all seemed to be going well. Lloyd Owen and
Lazarus had got through the Jalo gap unseen ; the Italians there
must be as sleepy and feckless as we were entitled to expect.
Jake had not been so lucky ; one does not get across the Sand
Sea for nothing. But two broken steering arms, three burnt-out
clutches and a broken nose were the least of his troubles—at any
rate he had spares for the first two. On the morning of the third
day in the Sea a Jeep in which Timpson and Wann were driving
swept up the blind side of a razor-back dune, crashed over the
crest, threw the two men out and rolled over them. Timpson

lost some of his front teeth and cracked his skull but Wann hurt his spine badly and was paralysed from the waist downwards.

After some hectic wirelessing a Hudson took off from Kufra for Big Cairn to collect the injured. Now the bigness of Big Cairn is strictly relative. It is about five feet high and stands on a low gravel ridge. Coming westwards out of many miles of pure sand, it seems a fine landmark in a country where there are no stones as big as eggs, but to a pilot at the end of a 200-mile flight from Kufra it is as nothing and the Hudson failed to find it. More signalling and Tony Browne left Kufra in a Blenheim and found the cairn. But a Blenheim is not designed for stretcher cases and it seemed impossible to get Wann inside. Lawson was experimenting with a specimen patient strapped to a sand channel when the Hudson made a second attempt and this time succeeded. With just enough petrol for the flight it took Timpson and Wann back to Cairo direct, while the patrols pushed on.

Faiyum to Barce and back to Kufra was beyond the range of the patrols so at Howard's Cairn Arnold and the Heavy Section were waiting with fifteen hundred gallons of petrol. Jake hurried on and made up lost time, and at Group H.Q. we waited for D Day.

Early on D+1 came the first news, from Tobruk. David Lloyd Owen has written for me what follows, the whole story of his adventure.

" That evening I went to G.H.Q. and in the ' Ops ' Room John Haselden was waiting for me. Spread out on a table before him was a large-scale map of Tobruk. As my glance fell on it he grinned and chuckled as he would often do when he was lit up with the thought of some trickery. He was delighted with the whole project which he was bursting to explain to me. He had been the originator and indeed the inspiration of the whole plan, whose chances of success lay in complete surprise and a very great measure of luck.

" John's mind was always open to hitting the enemy hard where he would least expect it and the plan of the raid on

Tobruk was a bold exposition of this idea. He had convinced the ' Ops ' people that he was capable of taking a striking force overland to Tobruk by way of Kufra to capture a small cove near the harbour and thus allow reinforcements from destroyers and special landing craft to exploit this initial bridgehead. He would then lead the whole force in organised and wholesale wrecking of the harbour installations, and finally evacuate by sea both his own force and the British prisoners of war whom he planned to release from the cages in Tobruk.

" The troops available for his own force were mostly Commandos, with detachments of Sappers, Signallers and some coast defence gunners. The latter were chosen as they were to storm the guns which they had manned through-out the siege of the previous year. My patrol was to guide the force to Tobruk and play other small parts in the gamble. The total of officers and men under his command was a little less than a hundred and with them he hoped to ensure a safe landing for the Navy.

" On August 24th we left the Faiyum with six patrol cars and seven 3-tonners for the rest of the party. Before us lay a journey of nearly a thousand miles, and this only to Kufra, the base where we would make our final plans. The journey was uneventful but trying to many of those to whom long days of travelling in the August heat were a new ordeal. Some suffered from the sun and in the evenings there were many who were unable to carry out the routine tasks which made the next day's work so much easier. They were not equipped or organised for moving across stretches of burning desert and my impatience with them was often unsympathetic and unjustified.

" However, on August 31st, we reached Kufra and had a few days of final preparation before we were to leave on September 6th. My men were still quite ignorant of their final objective and rumours and speculations were crazy and rife. We spent those hot and pleasant days cleaning our guns and every round of ammunition. I knew the urgency of our task and something of my enthusiasm went to the men, though I had told them no more than that we were on to a first-rate job at last. They were amused when I suggested that each gun should take one more box of ammunition than usual and when I issued extra compasses and maps for use in case we lost our cars and had to walk home.

" On September 4th John arrived by air from Cairo and I told him that it would be better in the interests of security to tell the men the object of the raid rather than to let the many rumours continue. He agreed and the next day we got the whole party together under the palm trees for him to explain his plan.

" I shall never forget that keen, bright look on every face as John unfolded a large map of Tobruk in front of them and they began to murmur to each other in speculation as he, in his genial, vague way, explained the risks he demanded and convinced them of the sincerity of his confidence. Till that time few of us had had the chance of knowing John well, but from that moment every one had the utmost confidence in his leadership and the party loved him to a man. John was not a born soldier but he was an honest, simple man with a courage which was only equalled by his.charm.

" The next day we left Kufra. The party which had come from Cairo was by now considerably better acquainted with the desert and their outlook was one of supreme confidence in their ability to arrive unseen at Tobruk and successfully to hold.the cove until the arrival of the Navy.

" As I knew the country well, John left to me the choice of the route and the command of the party till we reached Tobruk. I chose a route which would bring us up through the bottleneck between Jalo and the Sand Sea during darkness. This was the only place where there was any real danger of our being seen by enemy ground or air reconnaissance. We had learned that from Jalo the Italians would normally send out a patrolling aircraft at dawn and again at dusk and so we decided to give them no chance. We drove all night with few interruptions and were safely through by first light. I knew of good cover at Hatiet Etla, about ninety miles south of Tobruk, and we turned north-east from the corner of the Sand Sea to arrive there on September 10th. John had insisted that we leave plenty of time to cover possible breakdowns and so we had three days to wait till the raid on the evening of the 13th.

" Again we spent our time cleaning guns and equipment and going through every detail of the plan day after day. Those few days were well spent and every man left the hiding place with a thorough knowledge of what he was to do.

" At last on the morning of the 13th we moved north to another area of cover about forty miles south of Tobruk where we were to wait again before moving off in the late afternoon. By this time the original plan had been altered in detail but the principle of the scheme was the same. John's force, now in only three 3-tonners, was to drive boldly down the main road and to take a chance on their being held up for identification which was not likely so far from the front. The plan worked, for they passed into Tobruk with only a careless wave of the hand to a few bystanders.

" When they were inside the R.A.F. were to send over a force of seventy bombers to drop heavy bombs from 9.30 till about 2.30 in the morning. The havoc and confusion caused by this raid was designed to keep the enemy below ground and to drown any suspicion of a separate operation. Having taken the coast defence guns which covered the cove, John was to man these and silence any other guns which tried to interfere. Then at a given signal the landing craft were to come in with reinforcements to enable him to complete the capture of the town by dawn. He would then have the whole of the next day in which to destroy the harbour installations.

" While John was carrying out his part of the plan I had a completely separate job to do and one which promised a lively night for my patrol of twenty men and five cars. I was to enter the perimeter two hours after him, fighting my way in if need be. Then leaving Sgt. Hutchins with two trucks to cover our retreat we were to go on and wreck the radio direction finding station. Having done this we would return to the perimeter and hold it for the rest of the night against all comers. At dawn we would re-enter the perimeter and try to destroy the aircraft on both the landing grounds. After we had done this we would come out again at the eastern gate and hold it for the rest of the day till we received a signal to go in again, this time to try to release the British prisoners from the cages and send them down to the shore where the Navy could take off about four thousand. When all this was over we were to escape from Tobruk and go back to Kufra.

" All this reads now as a very big task for a very small force, but we were relying entirely on our own confessed ability to surprise the enemy at every turn. John would hardly countenance any suggestion that the Navy might fail to land or that he would not seize his objectives. His very nature did not leave room for the possibility of defeat and we all went in with the same savage desire to forestall any attempt at organised resistance.

" So on the evening of the 13th the force moved once again towards Tobruk. We were all rather quiet and at the occasional halts conversation was a little forced. With clouds of dust rising high in the air from the ploughed-up desert which had been the scene of so much bitter fighting we stalked up between masses of derelict vehicles to the neighbourhood of El Duda. At last on the far horizon we saw small dots and clouds of dust and I knew that John must leave us there and go on brazenly to the main Axis road. I stopped my truck and backed it below the horizon where I stood with John. We waited a few moments and the evening was growing cold. Then he turned and wished us all the best of luck. As his force drove past they waved a good-bye and we felt that these men had a cold courage which filled us with admiration, and then all of a sudden we began to feel kindly towards those who had bored us a bit on the way up. For a few minutes we stood and watched them go, feeling bare and huge on this naked, scrubby waste of dusty earth.

" I had decided to move a little way forward and then to have a good meal which might be our last for twenty-four hours. So we mounted the trucks and as I got into my seat I saw an enemy patrol moving parallel to John's small force. We could still see his cars winding across the desert with huge clouds of dust billowing out behind them. The setting sun was low in the west and we had that advantage when I gave the order to drive fast in open formation towards the enemy. They must have seen us coming, for I watched them stop and could see men walking about the cars. We still had some way to go and I was standing behind my gun, half turning to see that the others were following, and the radiator in front seemed very large and vulnerable as I wondered when we would hear that first crack of bullets. But as we drew near they seemed little interested in us till we closed in on them with a wild, savage cry from my gunner. I have never before seen such abject terror on men's faces as they stood there, a desolate party of surrendering enemy. It must have been a maddening shock for them to have been caught so far behind their own defence line at 'Alamein. Some fell to the ground in tears and screamed about their homes and families.

" I had no time to bother with these Italians and after setting my navigator to interrogate them I tried with the wireless operator to contact John as we had arranged. The cook excelled himself that night and we sat round the fire and talked happily of our first success. But I was worried, for I could get no sound from John, and I remember tripping over the stays of the aerial in the dark as I kept walking anxiously between the fire and the harassed wireless operator. But we could not wait much longer and after a final warming tot of rum we were ready to move on and into Tobruk. There was no moon that night and we drove in line ahead with the headlights on. I reckoned we had only about fifteen miles to go and should be at the perimeter soon after 10.00. But the going was bad and the escarpment at Sidi Resegh delayed us while we removed boulders and almost built a road down the slope. At the bottom we halted and heard the first sorties of the bombers roaring overhead and then the rumble of bombs over the next horizon. We could see, too, a few lights dotted about on the plain ahead and steering by the stars we aimed to drive between them. In front my lights were bright and the going was a little better when quite suddenly I saw ahead what seemed to be a concrete pillbox. We heard men shout and my first instinct was to drive straight by before they had time to fire. I shouted to the driver to ' step on it ' and we went on safely past. But I had heard our other trucks open up with their guns and I knew they were all too close to be healthy. I drove on for half a mile and then got out and shone a torch round to try to attract the others. Timorously I shouted to them and seemed to split the silence as my cracking voice echoed through the cold night. Soon, not far away, though it seemed across an ocean, I heard an answering cry from Sgt. Hutchins, and after more shouting and flashing of torches they joined us. But the truck behind me was missing and worst of all it was the wireless truck. While we were considering what to do the crew loomed up out of the darkness. All they could say was that the car had been hit and they had been unable to start it.

" We had either to recover the car or destroy it for on it was a lot of valuable equipment and the codes and ciphers. I took ten men with Tommy guns and rifles and moved towards where we though it must be. I fired a Verey pistol which seemed to light up the heavens themselves and silhouette me as a Colossus towering over the flattened bodies of the men. We moved on and again I lit up the sky and ahead we saw a shape. A sort of futile laughter broke out when we saw it was a derelict, horse-drawn water cart. After firing a few more Verey lights among the uninterested enemy we at last saw the truck and a few yards to the right of it the pillbox.

There was no time to waste and I decided to attack the post and destroy the car with an incendiary candle. Hutchins took on the post and after some sporadic firing he shouted that it was silenced. Then I heard the truck start. It drove on a short way and then stopped to change the back tyres which had been punctured. Safely away again, we saw lights flickering behind us and heard the noise of engines, but had no time to investigate.

" It was getting late and I began to wonder if I should be through the perimeter in time to take the R.D.F. station by midnight. So we drove on hastily, giving little heed to hummocks and slit trenches. In front I could see great flashes lighting up the sky as the R.A.F. dropped their 4000-lb. bombs. At last we reached the Axis road which was rough with a rippled surface and turned right to join the main road. We drove past tented camps and dispersed vehicles and guessed that they were there to avoid the pounding that Tobruk used to get each night from the R.A.F. The Axis road seemed endless but at last we joined the main road where I expected to find a check post. Turning the lights out, we drove on, hindered only by the sudden appearance of steam rollers and barrels across the road.

" I stopped to have a word with the navigator and could see a few yards ahead of me some defences and a ditch. There was no sound and I hoped that this was the perimeter, deserted. So I walked along it, plaintively shouting ' Rosalia ' which I knew to be the enemy's password. But it was not the main perimeter. All this delayed me and I looked at my watch to find it was after 1.0 and realised that I had no chance of getting inside by the time arranged. So we decided to attack the R.D.F. station at dawn on our way to the landing grounds and meanwhile to stay at the entrance to the perimeter for the rest of the night. Our immediate concern was to get into touch with John and, all through the night the operators were calling him but without success.

" By now the noise of battle was increasing, and we could see searchlights playing across the sky and hear the roar of the coast guns and bombs mingled with the sound of distant transport. The noise grew louder still and we could see gunfire coming from the sea while the searchlights came down and swept the water. The gunfire was incessant and we tried to distinguish the calibre of bomb and gun as we stood listening.

" Perhaps fear is only great when the danger is personal. I walked round the men that night and found the majority asleep over their guns and the others talking of the magnificence of the varied tracer shells and flares. They were not worried by the fact that we had the enemy all around us, who, though they were still quiet, might at any moment awaken across our only line of retreat."

" But they could not sleep long for we had to stir ourselves and deal with some vehicles coming noisily along the road. I grabbed a few men with Tommy guns and ran up the embankment on to the tarmac. I got there first and stood illuminated in the headlights of the car but a few bursts from the others brought it to a standstill. I was very relieved, for my gun had jammed. The crew were Germans and we made them help us turn their car over and roll it down the embankment. One of them, an officer, could speak a little English and he explained that the chaos in Tobruk was too much for him and he had come out to escape it.

" I looked at my watch and realised that it would soon be dawn. The situation now seemed to be very different. I could still see the searchlights and the gunfire from the sea. This could not be right, as by this time the Navy should have landed and opposition have been overcome. I still had no news of John and no idea what had happened. I was faced with the alternatives of remaining and carrying on with my plan without knowing if the landing had been successful, or of withdrawing to a suitable spot where we could put up the aerial to communicate with Group H.Q. and find out what they knew. I decided that if we went at all we must go while it was still not quite light, and reluctantly but with a disappointed relief we retraced our steps of the previous night. We moved fast in the increasing daylight and watched the enemy sentries pacing idly in the cold grey dawn and others lighting fires for their early cup of tea.

" We were cold and tired when we stopped on Sidi Resegh airfield and tried again to communicate with John and with our own H.Q. Our breakfast was hurried as we watched the horizon for pursuers and the aircraft passing to the north. I was disconsolate and unhappy at the thought of leaving John and played with the idea of returning to avenge our failure. But the sun was rising higher and we had to move again farther away to lie up in safety. So we drove fast for twenty miles, only stopping once when we saw a German aircraft flying at about fifty feet across our path. The dust was thick and those behind did not see me halt and we watched the plane fly between our truck and the next behind. It did not suspect us and we wasted no time to let it reconsider its assumption.

" Once in good cover we had to contact John if we possibly could. With both operators hard at it I soon received word from H.Q. that there had been no news of John all night and that the Navy had failed to land and suffered considerable loss. Then I was almost glad as I knew my decision had been right and that we had not left John when we could still have done more. All that day we called in vain and the operators found it hard to suffer my impatience. We lay there tired till dusk and then knew that the raid had failed and that we had lost that grim game of chance which we had entered so confidently."

Exactly what happened in Tobruk that night is not known, but it appears that Haselden's force entered successfully, captured the coast defence guns round the cove east of the main harbour but lost them again in the subsequent fighting with a garrison which was stronger than had been supposed. In this fighting Haselden is believed to have been killed. The sea-borne part of the raiding force, which had come from Alexandria in M.T.B.s, succeeded no better. Only two of the M.T.B.s managed to land their troops ; four of these craft were lost and also two of the destroyers which were to make a landing on the west side of the main harbour.

Early on the morning of the 14th we realised that the Tobruk raid was unlikely to succeed. Soon afterwards a signal came in from Lazarus with "Snowdrop." The two S patrols had been led into impassable country in the dark by a stupid Arab guide and when dawn came it was too late for them to attempt the attack on Benina airfield.

Three hours later Lazarus signalled again.

"Since previous signal S1[1] completely gutted. S2 badly shot up. Both by aircraft. No casualties. Still no news Stirling."

Stirling had, in fact, fared no better than Haselden. His force had approached Benghazi from the south-east but on the outskirts of the suburb of Berka had met strong enemy positions and had no alternative but to withdraw. All the next day they were attacked by aircraft in the Wadi Gamra, forty miles south-east of Benghazi, and lost a lot of cars. In the succeeding days they made their way back to Kufra, some joining up with the Sudan Defence Force withdrawing from Jalo.

At Jalo things were not much better. The S.D.F. had left Kufra on September 11th. By the 14th they had reached the advanced base, "Middle Lift Wadi," where Edmundson and our rear party had lain up during the reconnaissance of the Sirte desert fifteen months before. On the late afternoon of the next day the column drove out of the cover of the wadi on to the bare gravel desert which stretches northwards to Jalo. So far they had not been spotted but if they were caught by aircraft here the attack would be over before it had started. But by nightfall all was well. Fifteen miles from Jalo they halted while Carr, the

[1] S1 and S2 here refer to the individual trucks of S patrol, not to the patrols themselves.

Y2 navigator, took a set of star sights to check the position. Then on to the western edge of the palms, still apparently unseen.

Three columns started off on foot in the dark, each led by an L.R.D.G. guide. All went well to within a hundred yards of the village and fort, but there Italian sentries challenged and it was clear that they had not been taken unawares.

Confused fighting went on till dawn. The S.D.F. got into the north fort but were driven out again and at first light our forces had to withdraw. For the next four days they held the western edge of the oasis, shelling and being shelled by the enemy. They had no supporting aircraft and had a bad time from the air.

The short siege of Jalo had its lighter side. Arabs crawled from palm to palm between the shell bursts to sell the attackers eggs and chickens, and one optimist presented a claim for a palm tree damaged by gunfire. With all the enthusiasm of a true surveyor John Willie Wright, dodging the bomb bursts, strove to complete the map of the oasis which he had begun to draw at Kufra, using the R.A.F. photographs of a year before.

During the early hours of the 20th, just before a second attack was due to start, Middle East gave orders for the operation to be broken off and for the force to return to Kufra.

It is easy to write wisely after the event, but as soon as we knew that the attack on Jalo was not to coincide with those on Benghazi and Tobruk, we felt that it had little chance of success. In Cairo we had stressed the need for simultaneous action, and up to the last moment had been told that this would take place. The need for it was obvious enough. The enemy would know immediately that the attacks on Benghazi and Tobruk had been made by ground forces. They would know that the Qattara Depression routes were closed to us ; even if they knew of the Garet Khod route, which I doubt, they would realise that the one past Jalo was one of the only two left open. Obviously they would warn the Jalo garrison of the possibility of an attack, either by Stirling on his way back from Benghazi or by other forces from Kufra. And this is just what happened. The fact that a hundred odd vehicles got through the Jalo gap unseen shows that the Italians were asleep at that time ; the reception the S.D.F. got a few days later shows that by then they had woken up.

But for us the worst of all was the lack of news from Eason-smith and " Hyacinth " of whom we had last heard on the evening of the 13th, just before he was going in to attack. On the 14th we heard nothing. On the 15th nothing, on the 16th nothing. In their tarpaulin shelters at the Faiyum the sweating signalmen fingered their frequency dials, sickened with our endless inquiries, " Heard anything of ' B ' Squadron ? " The best we could hope for was that all his wirelesses had broken down ; at the worst both patrols were wiped out or " in the bag."

Then at 11.10 on the 17th Olivey spoke up. "Jake and twelve men found. Doctor with one truck and six wounded may now be at L.G. 125. From there heads for Kufra. Get aircraft to search. Details later."

And later the details.

> " Doc. left Barce area with 30 cwt. night 14th for Kufra via L.G. 125. Navigator Davis. Tell Lloyd Owen hurry L.G. 125 try pick up tracks also R.A.F. if poss. Doc. will skirt Sand Sea to Kufra probably non-stop. Several serious wounds."

Translated, this meant that Lawson in one car with nine men of whom six were wounded had left Barce three days before on his 700-mile journey to Kufra and might now be anywhere along that route. An interesting problem of the needle-haystack type —except for the wounded.

Lloyd Owen, back from Tobruk, was lying up at Hatiet Etla seventy miles from L.G. 125, and at the first signal we had started him off. At the second we asked the R.A.F. at Kufra to search the edge of the Sand Sea northwards from Zighen. If the Doctor had been going non-stop he should be well south of Jalo by then.

Before the R.A.F. could start from Kufra, Lloyd Owen had got to L.G. 125. On the evening of the 17th he signalled :

" Arrived L.G. 125. Lawson here. Plane urgently needed for wounded. State E.T.A. and landing requirements."

We knew there were some Bombays at Kufra and had warned the R.A.F. of what was on. They were ready in a few hours.

" E.T.A. L.G. 125 1100 G.M.T. rpt. 1100 G.M.T. 18/9," their signal said.

But to Expect to Arrive at L.G. 125 was not to get there, and whatever Stevenson might say, travelling hopefully was no use to us. From Kufra it was 450 miles over desert as barren and featureless as any in Libya, and that is saying a mouthful.

Sitting at the Faiyum waiting for a signal the afternoon seemed unending. Time went backwards rather than stood still. Again and again I went over the journey in my mind's eye. The first hundred miles stretch would not be so bad. With fair visibility one would see the high peak of Gara Thalma, a hundred miles north of Kufra, the first landmark we used on the Kufra-Siwa flight. After Thalma it would be a navigator's hell, mile upon mile of *serir*, flat gravel plain, with nothing to take a drift sight against and no landmark the size of an egg to recognise. Then the northern edge of the Sand Sea, a useful check on latitude but no help with longitude or drift. Then undulating stony desert for another 40 miles.

Nearing the L.G. it would be better, as about ten miles south of it is a huge sand dune—Mont Thérèse, named after the wife of someone in Reid's force which took Jalo from Jaghbub in November, 1941. And on the L.G. itself, which " A " Squadron from Siwa had discovered for the R.A.F. a year before, the burnt-out Blenheims and broken Hurricanes of the autumn operations would show up from the air. But roughly it was like finding a cricket field in Inverness-shire from Croydon, with one check, if visibility was good, on the way.

The afternoon dragged on. At two o'clock (11.00 G.M.T.) there was nothing from Lloyd Owen. At three we were anxious.

At four almost in despair. Then at 4.30, " Aircraft left at 12.45 carrying Doctor and wounded."

At 6 p.m. the next day they were in Cairo, forty-nine hours after Lloyd Owen had found them. A fine bit of work by 216 Squadron R.A.F.

It was all in the Two-Sixteen tradition. The squadron had been flying over the Libyan Desert ever since I could remember ; they started, I think, in the Great War. In our desert expeditions of the 'thirties they did us many a good turn, with Penderel (killed in England a week before I wrote this chapter) flying their Valencias and bringing us beer to 'Uweinat or tyres to Kharga. Penderel was an air ace of the last war with, I think, twenty-three Huns to his credit. Afterwards, in Egypt, he had caught horizon fever like the rest of us and used his skill and opportunities to push the first line of landing grounds down past the Gilf to 'Uweinat. In 1933 with Clayton he had been by car across to Kufra.

The tradition carried on to the Nazi War. The Valencias gave place to Bombays and the Bombays to Hudsons but Two-Sixteen Squadron remained masters of the desert sky, taking Stirling and his parashots to Jalo, ferrying supplies for the French when they attacked Kufra, evacuating our wounded, bringing us stores to Siwa and all this but a fraction of their everyday work for Middle East.

Weeks afterwards, from Jake's official reports, from tales told in the New Zealand Hospital, from Lawson's diary and from Findlay when he returned to us in October after living for a month in the Gebel, I got the whole story of the Barce raid, the best " beat up " L.R.D.G. ever did.

The accidents in the Sand Sea had delayed them and they had no time to spare. From Big Cairn they hurried across the fast going of the *serir*, then had a day's pushing through the centre of the horseshoe of sand where Steele had first found a way in 1940. On September 10th, the patrols, so far unseen, came out of the northern edge of the Sea. The dunes here end abruptly in a straight east-west line, as if tidied up by a giant's broom. At their foot runs the old caravan route from Jalo to Siwa, the route of the Majabra traders, scores of camel tracks meandering across the soft gravel. Then 200 miles over country we knew so well, at first bare and plantless, then, with the beginning of vegetation, the low sweet-scented desert shrub the smell of whose wood makes the evening fire worth all the suffering of the day's heat. Then rolling " downs " with taller bushes, then the foothills of the Gebel, with warped pines which remind you of southern Greece and a few birds and Arab shepherds with their flocks.

On the morning of the 13th Jake pushed on with Penman and two of his Arabs and dropped them a few miles south of Barce. Here the Arabs would contact their own tribesmen, learn what they could of the garrison, and meet the patrols coming up for the attack that evening at Sidi Selim. On the way back to the patrols Jake met a private car going northwards. It was an anxious moment but a friendly salute disarmed the driver's suspicions and he drove on.

Fifteen miles south of Barce the party halted for the afternoon. Jake explained his plans in detail, guns were cleaned, belts filled, grenades primed and after a meal they set off.

It was a dark, moonless night when they hit the Gerdes el 'Abid track, cut the telephone wires and turned northwards. At the police post at Sidi Raui a soldier came out into the road and challenged. Jake switched on his lights and the man, dazzled, was soon disarmed and put on a truck. This was Hamed, a cheerful Tripolitanian, who spent some months as a scullion in our cookhouse till he was delivered to his home near Tripoli in March of the next year.

There was movement in the police post and Jake, as if seeking help for Hamed, called " Ta'ala henna. Ta'ala henna ! " (" Come here. Come here ! ") This produced an Italian officer who ran out blinded into the car lights and was shot down. Excited noises from the building showed that the garrison was getting away over the back garden wall and our men, prowling in, found nothing but a dozen horses.

In this sudden halt at Sidi Raui two trucks collided and had to be abandoned. At Sidi Selim, five miles farther on, Penman was waiting but his Arabs had not returned ; in any case they had hardly been given enough time.

At Sidi Selim the Doctor was left behind as a rear rallying point and with him the T patrol wireless truck to keep a wireless watch for Stirling at Benghazi. The others pushed on to the main road and turned westwards.

Five miles out of Barce at the top of the escarpment were two Italian-light tanks, parked one on each side of the road. The lights of the cars deceived them and till they were level they could not tell friend from foe. L.R.D.G. gave them all they had got and had no more trouble from the tanks.

At the cross roads outside Barce Jake stopped and sent each party off on their job ; Penman with one car remained behind to deal with any pursuers.

Wilder with T1 patrol had the biggest task, to raid the airfield which air photographs taken a few days earlier had shown to be in full use. Skirting round the outskirts of the town he came to the landing ground, beside the road which leads to Maddalena. At the entrance Wilder stopped, jumped off his truck, opened the gate and drove in. Some Italians appeared running and were shot down. Then the New Zealanders had some luck ; a big petrol tanker caught fire and lit up the whole town. Back at Sidi Selim the glare in the sky told the Doctor that things had started well.

Moving on, Wilder found himself among the Mess buildings, threw some grenades into the windows and turned on to the landing ground.

He now had five trucks, a Jeep and four 30 cwts., for one was damaged at Sidi Raui and the wireless truck was listening for Stirling. In single file he led the patrol round the airfield firing incendiary at each machine in turn. In the last truck Craw, with a load of short-delay-action bombs, dealt with any aircraft which did not catch fire.

Meanwhile the Italians were firing wildly in all directions

but without any result whatever ; towards the end they got a mortar going from near the Mess but had no better luck.

After about an hour of this Wilder had visited in turn thirty-two aircraft, of which twenty were definitely alight and the rest damaged. When his ammunition was running short he left without a man having been hit.

A long, straight road runs from the airfield through Barce town to the railway station. By this time the Italians had been able to pull themselves together and at the far end of the road were two tanks firing down it, their shots luckily all going high. There was no time to turn and no way round, for the tanks blocked the road, so Wilder in the leading Chevrolet stood on the accelerator and charged. Crashing into one tank he pushed it aside and cannoned into the other. This cleared the road but wrecked his truck. The crew scrambling to their feet thrust grenades under the tank tracks, someone (Dobson, I think it was) tried to drop one down the turret but found it shut.

The Jeep following into this shambles picked up the Chevrolet crew and dashed on down the road. At the station turn the driver, blinded by the tracer which Wilder was firing, hit the kerb and overturned. When they had picked themselves up Wilder was found pinned down by the Jeep, soaked in petrol and unconscious. The next truck behind righted the Jeep, picked him up and got out of the town. But Craw and his crew in the last car had been cut off and were not seen again.

Meanwhile the Guards under Sergeant Dennis, who had taken command of the patrol in Timpson's absence, were dealing with the other end of the town. His job was to attack the barracks and keep busy any troops who might interfere with Wilder. The hospital lies between the barracks and the town and here two armed sentries stepped out and challenged. Dennis rolled a four-second grenade between them and turned them from sentries into patients.

Farther on he came to the barracks where two more sentries shared the same fate. A man fired from the roof and got all the patrol's gunfire in return. Then Dennis and his party hurried through the barrack buildings, throwing grenades into doors and windows and into the slit trenches from which the Italians were shooting wildly. Ammunition finished, he withdrew, meeting two tanks on the way with whom he played hide and seek for a time in the hospital grounds. In the darkness one truck under Findlay became separated from the rest. In October he rejoined us at Kufra—but that is another story.

While all this was going on Jake was playing a lone hand. Having seen the patrols off to their tasks at the entrance to the town he drove in in his Jeep. On the east were some buildings which looked like officers' quarters, small detached bungalows standing in a courtyard, and from one of these light showed through the window cracks. Stumbling around the flower beds Jake sought in vain for an entrance for his Mills bombs. In disgust he threw one on to the flat roof, which at least put the lights out and the fear of God into the occupants, and retired in search of other targets. These came in the form of two tanks parked in a small square. He opened fire with two twin Vickers K's which disconcerted the tank crews and made them slow in pursuit. Having parked his Jeep in an alleyway he started on a tour of the town. In what seemed in the dark to be some sort of market place, a building with arcades and pillars, he ran into a party of Italians and for a time chased them around the columns, bowling Mills bombs among their legs. The Italians soon tired of this, so Jake recovered the Jeep and moved on till he found an M.T. park with a dozen unattended vehicles in it and here with grenades and Tommy-gun fire he and Gutteridge, his driver, wrecked all the cars.

By now the night was nearly over and it was time to collect our forces and withdraw. The tanks which had been guarding the escarpment had vanished and by 4 a.m. the party was re-united at Sidi Selim, with three Jeeps and seven 30-cwts. of the total of twelve vehicles which had gone in the night before.

The next thing was to collect the trucks abandoned at Sidi Raui and towing chains were got ready.

But during the night the Italians there had made a plan.

South of Sidi Selim the track runs through a narrow valley and as the patrols passed through this in the half light of dawn a heavy fire burst on them from the roadsides. For a moment things were very unpleasant ; two men were wounded in the leg, a bullet took off Penman's little finger, and another punctured the Doctor's car. In front of him Dennis halted, turned his truck back, and covered them while they changed the tyre. In the end they got through the ambush, picked up the trucks at Sidi Raui and drove on.

A few miles farther on they stopped to get the damaged trucks going under their own power, for it would be impossible to tow them across country. The Tripolitanian Arab troops appeared again and started to interfere. Jake went off in his Jeep, out-flanked them and drove them off. By the time he got back the trucks had been mended and the party started on. But after a few miles the G patrol wireless truck stripped a rear axle pinion and stood immovable on a bare hill top.

It is a commonplace that the dissipations of the night before bring the headaches of the morning after. As Morris had found at Nofilia, Hunter at Fuka and many patrols at other times, the comparison was applicable to L.R.D.G. To-day it was the same. At that moment, before the disabled truck could be dragged under cover, the fighters arrived.

First two C.R. 42's, then a recce plane, then six more fighters. From eleven o'clock till-dusk they made a day of it, bombing and machine-gunning the trucks and men, ill hidden in the low scrub. Two more men were wounded, one of them, Wilder, with bullets through both legs. In the heat of the attack Lawson worked at getting the wounded away to a safe spot, cheerful and inspiring. But one of them, Parker, was lying up in the truck shot in the stomach and took some time to move. So Lawson stayed with him, shifting from side to side as the aircraft swooped down and sheltering Parker with his own body. Happily for the wounded in the days to follow he escaped unhurt.

By evening there remained one 30-cwt. and two Jeeps to take thirty-three men back to Kufra. The last blow of the day was the hardest of all. Jake, an old hand at this sort of game, had had all rations and water unloaded from the trucks in the intervals of the strafing. At dusk when the attacks seemed over, most of the rations were reloaded on to one of the two surviving Chevrolets. Then as the light was fading two more fighters returned, spotted the truck and set it ablaze.

However, they had a last string to their bow for Jake on the way up before the raid had left at an old hiding-place of ours near Bir Gerrari, sixty miles south-east of Barce, a 30-cwt. truck with a load of petrol and hard rations.

At nightfall on the 14th this was the position : The Doctor leaving for Bir Gerrari and Kufra in a Jeep and a 30-cwt. with six wounded men, a driver, a fitter and a navigator—Davis— and what a responsibility was his, to guide his party for 700 miles with no other instruments than two compasses, one magnetic and one sun : two walking parties setting off for the same destination and with them one Jeep carrying what rations and water remained.

For the first few hours the going was so bad that the cars could make no headway and the Doctor and the walkers level pegged. Then Lawson had to abandon his Jeep ; a bullet high up in the petrol tank had made a hole which leaked too freely. In the 30-cwt. he pushed on ahead. Soon the walkers' Jeep seized up ; in the darkness a rock had punctured the sump and all the oil run out. Two hours' work repaired this and the party struggled on. Towards dawn at a roll call one man was missing. Dennis went back to the last halt where he had been seen, calling in the darkness, but no reply came ; the missing man, exhausted, must have stopped for a moment and fallen asleep.

All the next day the walkers pushed on, periodically flattening to the ground as searching aircraft passed and re-passed overhead. At dark a distant fire showed in a valley bottom ; an Arab encampment where they bought and cooked a lamb and got milk to drink.

On the 16th they found water, more than they could have dared to hope so far south of the coast in mid-September. Before

dawn on the 17th cars were heard passing nearby and knowing
that they must almost certainly belong to L.R.D.G. Jake fired
Verey lights, but they did not stop. Dispirited, they walked on.
An hour later at the top of a rise their troubles were over—below
them in a hollow were Olivey and his Rhodesians having breakfast.

That night they reached the car left at Bir Gerrari where a
note from Lawson showed that he had taken some water and
passed on. But of the second walking party, separated from the
others in the darkness of the first night, there was no sign.

For the next three days Jake and Olivey combed the area.
First, some Arabs reported that the missing men had passed their
way, staying two days for rest and food. Following their tracks a
note was found, saying that two men were behind wounded and
eight pushing on to Bir Gerrari. On the 19th the eight were
found, split into three and five, and nearly at the truck. But of
the wounded men there was no trace, and on the 21st the search
was abandoned and the survivors headed south following the
Doctor.

At L.G. 125 they found Lazarus with two Guardsmen of
Dennis's party who had walked out of Barce and with the good
news that the R.A.F. had evacuated the wounded. As they left
for Kufra two aircraft appeared and bombed the airfield but the
patrols, halted anxiously two miles away, escaped unseen.

Two days later they were through the Sand Sea and at
Howard's Cairn where Arnold was waiting with food and petrol
and on the 25th reached Kufra, roughly 2000 miles from the
Faiyum by the route they had followed, just in time for a retalia-
tion raid by the Luftwaffe.

That was the end of " Hyacinth." It had cost the Axis some
thirty aircraft and perhaps the same number of casualties in
Barce. It cost L.R.D.G. six wounded, all of whom recovered,
ten prisoners of war and fourteen vehicles. Two D.S.O.s, one
M.C. and three M.M.s went to weigh down our side of the
scales.

CHAPTER THIRTEEN

THE ROAD WATCH

As YOU DRIVE westwards along the coast road from Agheila with the sun at your back, you see ahead, blurred in the heat haze, a white speck on the horizon appearing and disappearing with the undulations in the road. On the right, behind the white dunes of silver sand, is the Mediterranean ; on the left the nondescript semi-desert of Sirtica. Later the speck turns itself into a tall narrow arch, straddling the Via Balbia, the Arco Philænorum to the Italians but to all the British Army the " Marble Arch." A couple of hundred yards to the south-west is an Ara Philænorum, an altar to the Philæni, rebuilt by the Italians on the traditional site, and carved with a long quotation from Sallust's *Jugurthine War* which tells this story.

In the fifth century B.C. Carthage and Cyrene were rivals for the domination of the North African coast. Constant war raged between them, draining the strength and resources of both, and finally they decided to put an end to the strife and fix their common frontier once and for all.

It was to be done thus. On a given day from each city a pair of runners were to set out and where they met the new frontier would be established. The runners from Cyrene are unknown but the Carthaginians were two brothers called Philæni who out-ran the Cyreneians so successfully that they met them far east of halfway between the two towns. The Cyreneians, fearful of retribution for their laziness when they got home, accused the Carthaginians of having started before the appointed time and proposed a new method of settling the boundary. The Carthaginians agreeing, the Cyreneians gave them the choice of being buried alive there, at the point where they claimed the boundary should be, or of allowing the Cyreneians to continue farther westwards to a point where they in turn should suffer the same fate. The Philæni chose to sacrifice themselves for Carthage and were buried alive at that place, where afterwards an altar was built to their memory.

Here two thousand years later Mussolini, while adding to his desert empire, built an arch over the road, adorned with suitable reliefs of himself, and with inscriptions to preserve his memory :

"BENITUS MUSSOLINI
SUMMUS REI PUBLICAE MODERATOR IDEMQUE FASCISTARUM
DUX."

And inside the arch quotations from his speeches :

> " Il popolo Italiano ha creato col suo sangue l'impero, lo fecondera col suo lavoro e lo difendera contro chiunque con le sue armi."

which all sounded a· bit thin in December, 1942.

If slogans could win wars the Italian victory over us would have been a quick one. From one end of Libya to the other—on forts, barracks, colonists' houses—were plastered in wearisome repetition : " Credere, Obedire, Combattere."—" Il Duce ha sempre ragione."—" Duce vinceremo."—" Noi tireremo diritto."

Hundreds of thousands of British troops have passed under the Marble Arch and stopped to wonder at it. Probably not one in a hundred thousand turned his eyes to the southwards at a point about five miles to the east. If he had troubled to do so he would have looked on to a flattish, gravel plain, a mile or so wide, covered with sparse scrub, and beyond, dancing in the mirage, a low escarpment with one or two narrow *wadis* opening out of it. An uninteresting view.

But this spot also deserves a monument, the inscription on which would read :

" HERE
L.R.D.G. KEPT THE
ROAD WATCH."

It was always known as the " Road Watch." In Siwa in the spring of 1942 or in Kufra in the autumn of the same year a patrol commander, asked what his next job was to be, would answer you with little enthusiasm, " I'm on the Road Watch." I think the idea in the first instance was Prendergast's—to send a patrol up near enough to the coast road to take a census of all the traffic that passed along it. Here for a trial week in September of 1941, for four and a half months with scarcely a break in the spring and summer of 1942, and for seven weeks in the autumn, day in and day out, for twenty-four hours a day, four hundred miles behind the enemy's line, L.R.D.G. made a census of every-thing that passed along the road.

I have described the place as seen from the·north. Coming from the south one crossed an area of good going—undulating gravel desert—then bumped over the sand hummocks of the Wadi Scemmer and up on to the low plateau of Dor Lanuf from which the sea and the Marble Arch were in sight, then wound down one of the wadis which cut through the plateau to camp near the mouth where it ran out on to the plain. The plain itself was bare, but there was a little scrub in the wadi bed, enough to hide the cars when camouflage nets were well used.

This was the drill. Before dawn two men started off from camp towards the road. Within four or five hundred yards of it they stopped, found what cover they could—a fold in the ground or a low bush—and there settled down for the day. Once down they had to stay there till nightfall ; unless the traffic was very light they could not stand up or move about. With them they had high-power field-glasses, notebooks and up-to-date photographs of enemy M.T. and A.F.V.s. Taking it by turns one wrote to the other's dictation, noting tanks, guns, lorries, oil tankers, armoured cars, tractors, stores, troops and sometimes sadder sights as the record for June 10th, 1942, shows :

" Westbound. Estimated 500 P.O.W., Free French and R.T.R."

and the same number for some days afterwards, for these were the fruits of the fighting on the Gazala-Bir Hakim line.

It was a weary task. Bitterly cold in winter ; blowing dust in your face in spring ; blistering heat in summer ; from dawn at five to dusk at seven was a long, long day. As one watcher said cynically : " You look at your watch at 11 and look again four hours later and it's 11.15."

There was never much traffic at night but at dusk the two men would move down closer to the road, to within fifty yards or less, and try to judge by sound and outline the types of vehicles which passed.

Back in camp the rest of the patrol were killing boredom—a sentry on the hill, some men asleep, some reading or playing bridge. Before dawn next day the relieving pair of watchers would set out from the camp, passing the returning men unseen in the dark, to take over at the appointed time. At the camp after dark the wireless masts would go up and if tanks had gone by moving eastwards a signal would come to Group H.Q. at Siwa or Kufra and soon afterwards, perhaps when the tanks were nearing Agedabia, Ciphers at Middle East would be de-coding :

> " Flash from Tripoli road watch. Eastbound March 18. Tanks 6 Mark 3 and 1 Mark 4. Armoured cars German 4-wheeled 7. Italian Autoblinda 5."

And so it went on, day after day, for the normal spell of ten days, or maybe more if the relieving patrol was late. Then at nightfall the incoming patrol would be waiting at Two Cairns, the rendezvous, the change over would be completed and the watch would go on. And when the outgoing patrol was clear of the area and able to signal at leisure a full report would go back to Cairo with the totals of all the classes of traffic seen in the ten-day period.

Consider what this meant to our Intelligence. There is only one road from Tripoli to Cyrenaica and everything that went along it we saw. Admittedly we missed the supplies landed at

Benghazi (though not always),[1] but it so happened that the Axis brought nearly all their tanks and reinforcements to Tripoli. Tanks were the things that the Intelligence people always worried about. Give them accurate numbers and types and they were happy. But they welcomed other details too. They would suspect, for instance, from other sources of information that the Littorio Division was leaving Italy. A few days or weeks later L.R.D.G. would report many fresh, unsunburned troops in clean uniforms moving eastwards with new transport, including perhaps field-cookers—which reinforcements or reliefs do not take with them. Fairly good confirmation of earlier suspicions.

The watch was not always dull. There was one occasion when a party of school children in a bus drew up and started a game of rounders nearby and a second when two sportsmen from a staff car halted to shoot desert hares. And another when a German battery turned suddenly off the road and camped with its vehicles well dispersed around the watchers. It arrived at midday and the two men, Brown and Parkes I think they were, crouched for six hours under their khaki-coloured sheepskin coats speculating on life in a prison camp in Italy until at dusk they were able to move away unseen. Once a unit halted for firing practice, setting up their targets straight in line for the watchers. Then there was nothing to do but to get up and walk unconcernedly away, hoping to be taken for a wandering Arab.

One day in May Holliman thought that the secret was out at last. He and his companion were writing busily behind a bush which they had uprooted and dragged forward nearer to the road when an Arab suddenly sat down beside them, picked up their waterbottle and took a drink. " Yes. Inglizi," he said, " but don't be afraid," and true to his word never gave them away.

We were always expecting that one day the disaster would come, that the whole patrol would be captured and the secret lost. But it was not really strange that this never happened when you consider how easily the enemy could have done (and perhaps

[1] See page 152.

did do) the same thing on the road between Alexandria and Matruh.

In camp in the wadi they had fewer thrills but more annoyances. Arabs would wander by grazing their flocks ; aircraft came hedge-hopping over the wadi banks ; with weeks of occupation the ground grew foul and flies swarmed, for though they buried all their food tins for cleanliness and concealment, jackals dug them up at night. Once an inquisitive Arab witnessed the change over at Two Cairns and knowing then too much, was collected and brought protesting back to Siwa.

It took three patrols to keep the watch going ; one on the job, one going out and one returning, for the distance from Siwa by the route between 'Agheila and Marada was six hundred miles. In May, 1942, the enemy must have had some suspicions of the routes we were using into the Sirte Desert, for Croucher, returning to Siwa, found a party putting up a double-apron wire along the Marada-'Agheila road. After that the patrols had to go south of Marada, a hundred miles longer, but safer till the Italians started mining our old car tracks and S1 patrol had a car blown up and wrecked.

Remembering T2 patrol's walk back to Jalo,[1] and against the day when disaster should befall we made a chain of dumps between the Marble Arch and Jaghbub, small depots at 25 mile intervals with water, map, compass, shoes and hard rations which might enable a party who had lost their cars to reach home.

For four months in the spring of 1942 the watch went on. Then when Tobruk fell and Rommel could use that port as well as Benghazi the importance of Tripoli decreased and the watch was discontinued. In October Middle East asked for it to be resumed again and we guessed that something was in the air. Spicer with Y1 went up from Kufra to restart it and from October 30th to November 8th saw little of importance. But by November 10th, when Talbot had taken over, the westbound traffic was showing the effects of Montgomery's victory at

See Chapter 9.

'Alamein, and we began to have some inkling of Rommel's intentions when lorry loads of civilians with their furniture showed that the Italian settlers were being evacuated from Cyrenaica.

The salt marches at 'Agheila make one of the best defensive positions on the Libyan coast, difficult to force in a direct attack and not easy to turn from the southern flank. The Germans had stood on this line in January, 1942, and the question of the moment was whether they would do so again. At Middle East H.Q. Intelligence weighed the probabilities ; at home Our Military Correspondent expounded the strategical pros and cons ; fifty miles behind the front line R2 patrol sat and counted two to three thousand vehicles a day going westwards and practically nothing moving east. Their last signal left the answer in little doubt :

" November 8 to 14. Westbound. Motor cycles 528 and sidecar 18. Cars 1264. 15-cwt. 407. 30-cwt. 607. 3-ton 2316 and trailer 474. 5-ton 2697 and trailer 899. 10-ton 125 and trailer 117. Tractors 3. Transporters 2. Troop carriers 13. Tankers 23 and trailer 3. Tanks light 8. Armoured cars 24. Guns 68 mostly light A/T. Miscellaneous 400. Troops estimated 42,500—repeat 42,500."

Though the Axis evidently did not mean to make a prolonged stand at 'Agheila there were yet many troops about and by November 15th the area had become too hot for Talbot and he had to move. Sweeting with G2 relieving him re-established the watch forty miles farther west but even here it was difficult enough for he was amongst the rear units of Rommel's forces.

Middle East were now insistent that the watch must be kept going at all costs in order to give them information of the enemy's intentions, so it was decided to double-bank the patrols on the job and Tinker (T2) and Timpson (G1) left Kufra on November 20th to do this.

As I have explained, our old route between Marada and

'Agheila was no longer open and for some time past we had been sending the patrols through the Marada-Zella gap. But though they seem never to have known about the road watch the enemy were by now well aware that we were using this route and had put down minefields across the old tracks and were sending out patrols from Zella and Marada. On November 25th one of Tinker's trucks ran over a mine north-east of Zella and Burke had his leg broken. He was brought back to Tazerbo and the little Waco earned its keep again when Barker went out from Kufra and collected him there.

This was one of those events which remained a lurking horror all through the existence of L.R.D.G. Bad casualties behind the enemy's lines, hundreds of miles from proper medical treatment, were just one of the risks which had to be taken. Fortunately they did not happen very often though in November, 1941, Simpson of S1 patrol travelled 700 miles from Buerat el Hsun to Kufra with a severe wound in the shoulder and Murray had much the same sort of journey from Fuka to the Faiyum in July, 1942.

The medical organisation of L.R.D.G. consisted of an M.O. at Group H.Q. and a medical orderly with each patrol. Accommodation for sick varied from place to place, from quite a good hospital at Kufra to the lee side of a palm tree for a case of pleurisy when we spent a week waiting at Ghetmir outside Jalo in January, 1942. Some of the orderlies were of the R.A.M.C., others willing learners taught by the M.O. They worked under difficulties for it is not easy to treat a patient who is moving a hundred miles a day in a bumping truck. But they were resourceful and did not lack the power to improvise : the use of a grease gun for an enema might find a place in the pages of the *Lancet* !

The Doctor too had to be ready to improvise. To Siwa one night there came a message from Olivey who was taking two Libyan Arab Force men to the outskirts of Agedabia whence they would walk into the town to learn the strength of the enemy garrison. " Arab corporal " signalled Olivey, " has temp. 100

pulse 90 symptoms appendicitis from 1400 hours advise treatment." I took this to Lawson and we answered " Keep in semi-
sitting position knees slightly raised small drinks of water or weak
tea with sugar only water bottle filled hot water to right side no
repeat no aperient Dovers for pain morphia if bad if condition
deteriorates send Jaghbub in two trucks." Whatever was wrong
with the corporal Dick Lawson's radio-therapy was successful.
He was better next day and Olivey went on to do the job.

Timpson, like Tinker, also ran into trouble and his success
in maintaining the road watch in spite of all the difficulties he
encountered was one of the outstanding achievements of L.R.D.G.

He had left Kufra on November 20th. Five days later, in the
Marada-Zella gap, he met an enemy patrol of double his own
strength and with vehicles which included armoured cars. As
his orders were to keep the watch going at all costs Timpson
wished to avoid a scrap but the Italians knew their ground well
and manœuvred skilfully, forcing him to fight. For an hour or
more the skirmish continued, with Timpson making every effort
to disengage himself and the enemy moving to block his escape.
In the end he extricated three cars of his original seven ; the rest
of the patrol, as we heard later, was captured and taken into
Zella.

Timpson had now lost more than half his force and much of
his rations ; he had not enough petrol to get back to Kufra ;
the weather was foul with cloud and rain making navigation
most difficult, but none of this deterred him and three days later
he was nearing the coast road west of the Marble Arch. On
November 30th he had got the watch going, on a hilltop four
hundred yards from the road.

The whole area was rapidly filling up with Axis troops, the
rear units of Rommel's front at 'Agheila, and it was impossible
to follow the usual plan of camping in a wadi a mile or two south
of the road. So Timpson placed his camp twenty miles inland
and every evening at dusk the Jeep brought up the relieving
watchers, dropped them a mile or two from the road and waited

to pick up the outgoing pair who left the road at midnight, guided to the car by the flashing of a torch and the occasional running of the engine.

Coming up to the rendezvous one evening a figure appeared over a ridge and ran towards the car, shouting and gesticulating. Timpson halted, but as the man drew near realised that he was an Italian officer, apparently lost and seeking a lift, so started the Jeep and moved slowly away, calling out advice in German to the Italian who pursued him, roaring angrily, till he was too exhausted to go on.

Thus they carried on till December 10th when the Jeep failed to pick up the two watchers coming off duty who were never seen again. All next day a search was made for them but they had probably walked in the dark into the midst of an enemy camp and been captured.

The 13th was the last and most hazardous day of all. Of it Timpson wrote afterwards :

"*December* 13th. Road watch from Wadi Ahmed. (This was, as far as we knew, the one possible point in the vicinity unoccupied by enemy camps.) Position in thorn bush 200 yards from the road. Starting at dawn enemy formed camp all around us, except between our position and the road, though there was another camp on the far side. They were well disciplined and quite cheerful though a bit rattled when a British night fighter strafed the area by moonlight at 8 p.m. They apparently fed well : macaroni and goulash for lunch !

"I decided to leave at 8.15 p.m. in order to stop the next party, if possible, from coming to the same area, which I knew was their intention. The moon was up but it was raining. I think the enemy must have spotted us getting out of the bush, but they did not challenge until we were passing some vehicles as we walked up the wadi, which was shallow and open near the road. After their sentry had shouted ' Passorio ' twice and. I had replied with an ineffective ' Freund ' he fired one shot.

We walked on slowly : he fired twice more and we walked a bit faster. Then he started firing hard and was joined by others and the chase began, with a number of them after us, running and shooting. We were much hampered by our heavy coats and kit.

"However, we finally eluded them though Welsh and I got separated. We both lay low while they searched all around. I could see their figures silhouetted against the sky as they hunted for us, but after half an hour they gave it up and I heard the leader of the first search party say to the second party, which had come up later, ' I think they were only food thieves.'

" I passed close by another camp, then went back to the wadi at a point where we had first joined it the previous night and waited for Welsh for three-quarters of an hour, calling him by name, for I had the compass. Then after failing to find him I made my way to the Jeep. The relief party had heard the shooting and luckily had not gone down to the road, but awaited my return.

" Welsh, after waiting for me in the wadi for an hour, went on, thinking I had been hit when they opened up with an automatic, for I had stumbled and fallen twice in the deep water of the wadi. After that he had many adventures, walking into four camps and being shot at in three of them and getting away with much courage and resourcefulness. He reached the R.V. at 4 a.m., but after three hours of giving the usual signals I had decided to leave at 3 a.m. in order to tell the remainder of the patrol to move to join Indian 1 patrol " (who had been sent up from Kufra to help Timpson in his difficulties) " in case the enemy found Welsh or some of his kit and chased us the next day. At the same time I had received a signal from H.Q. saying that Lazarus with S1 patrol had already established their road watch " (west of Buerat el Hsun) " and I felt justified in suspending my watch, at least temporarily, till Welsh was found.

" *December 14th.*—I returned to the R.V. in the Jeep at

dawn and finally found Welsh. He had actually walked to within two miles of our camp, twenty miles from the R.V., after a very strenuous night. For this reason I took some time to find him as I searched the R.V. area first, finally picking up his footmarks which showed clearly after a rainy night. He had hurried back fast to warn the camp of what had happened, for he thought the enemy had got me, and was much concerned in trying to remember the figures of the vehicles we had counted the previous day."

Tinker was out of the running and Timpson in difficulties, but the watch must go on. So Lazarus with S1 set out from Kufra but before he had gone far Rommel's intention to abandon the 'Agheila position was beyond doubt and it would therefore be just as useful if the watch was kept much farther west. So Lazarus went west through Henry's Gap, north past Fogha and for the first time in L.R.D.G. history across the terrible basalt country of the Harug, over the Hon-Zella road, south of Bu Ngem and finally to the coast road north of Gheddahia. This was a good effort. Lazarus was 800 miles from his base ; he knew he must rely on us to send out petrol to him before he could get home, and he was right in the enemy's line of retreat. In his own bald report :

"The watch began 17.00 hours 13 December. During the evening of 14 December a section of S.A.S. shot up the road and camps in the near vicinity of the road watch." (We could never persuade Middle East that "beat ups" by David Stirling's chaps and a careful traffic census by us were incompatible.) "The watch on day 15/16 was made at RS2910. The country here is very open with little cover and convoys were frequently pulling off the road so this place was not used again. The Wadi Gheddas was cultivated for the greater part of its length and there were many Arabs about who frequently approached the watchers. Money, tea and sugar ensured friendly relations. The activity of S.A.S. along the road brought out many enemy aircraft which carried out intensive searches for four days along the Wadi Zerzer and the country surrounding our forward base."

But the watch must go on. So Tinker left Kufra again. On the 20th December he took over from Lazarus and that was the last we heard of him for a week until on the 28th came a signal from a troop of the Heavy Section at Tagrifet : " Tinker met here with four trucks. Have given him enough petrol to reach Zella."

This was the story of the week.

Having made a rear base thirty miles south-west of Gheddahia, Tinker went north with nine men to take over from Lazarus. They met and Lazarus started home. But by this time the area was filling up ; enemy camps were being formed all along the road and also some miles to the south of it and a new watch site had to be found. While they were preparing to do this Tinker's party was discovered. They were hidden in a small tributary to the main wadi when a German armoured car patrol crossed their fresh tracks.

The Huns started to beat the wadi as one beats a copse for rabbits, firing into the bushes and throwing grenades among the rocks. Our men, outnumbered and out-gunned, left their two trucks, buried their ciphers and hid as best they could in caves and bushes. The Germans soon found the trucks and camped to await the patrol's return.

At midday another truck arrived with a load of Arabs and the New Zealanders heard the sounds of questioning followed by heavy beating. Then the Arabs were set to search the wadi. One of them passed so close to White, crouching in a bush of desert broom, that he must have seen him but gave no sign.

At dusk four of the patrol managed to get away and started to walk back to their base camp. Tinker, one of the four, stopped at some Arab tents for a drink. Hardly had he finished when a car drove up and while Tinker hid behind the tent the Germans questioned the Arabs who denied all knowledge of any " Inglizi " till the Germans drove away.

By dawn all four men were back at the rear base, arriving shortly before another enemy armoured car patrol which had been back-tracking them. The New Zealanders got away with their vehicles just in time. Thus Tinker rejoined us at Zella with six men missing, but we did not despair of seeing them again, for so often in L.R.D.G. history men had " walked out " and turned up days or weeks later.

And so it happened this time. What happened to four of the six I do not know, but two of them, Ellis and Sturrock, lay up all day and that night walked back to the base to find Tinker gone. During the night they separated in a search for water and did not meet again. At dawn Ellis, who told me this story, found himself in a position not new to L.R.D.G. men—five hundred miles from nowhere, with no food, no water and only the clothes he wore. But he knew that Rommel was retreating and that if he went due east there was a chance of being picked up, so for four days he walked eastwards, resting by day and moving by night when the cold made sleep impossible. Once he got water from some Arabs. On the fifth day he reached the Bu Ngem road, arriving into the middle of an action between German armoured cars and our own. This was soon over and the two German cars burning fiercely and Ellis walked over to an advanced patrol of the K.D.G.s. In a week he was back in Zella and a few days later Sturrock, after much the same experiences, turned up there too.

That was the end of the road watch for Middle East then signalled that we need not go on with it. Considering all things it was perhaps the most useful job L.R.D.G. ever did.

I wish Rommel could have read this chapter.

CHAPTER FOURTEEN

'ALAMEIN TO GABES

ON THE last day of August Rommel attacked at 'Alamein.

Axis hopes were high. Alexandria was only sixty miles away ; Mussolini had come over from Italy and Libya was being combed for a white Arab stallion on which he would make his triumphal entry into Cairo ; high officials of the new government for Egypt had been selected and Egyptian money printed ; Italian-Arabic phrase-books were selling well.

By September 3rd the offensive was over, broken up by the guns of the Eighth Army and the bombs of the R.A.F. The threat to Egypt had been removed and it was clear that the next move would be with Montgomery and that when that move came the Faiyum would be no place for L.R.D.G. For us, working on the southern flank of the Army when its advance started, Kufra was the proper base and by mid-October the whole unit was there. Then came the question of what part L.R.D.G. was to play in the coming offensive.

In the last six months Stirling's S.A.S. force had changed its character. From the small band of fifty odd experts in aircraft destruction with whom we had worked in the previous winter it had grown into a much larger force with its own transport, navigators and signals. With his heavily armed Jeeps and 3-tonners to supply them, Stirling no longer relied on us for transport across the desert ; the S.A.S. had become a sort of L.R.D.G. of their own. So it was decided to divide the desert between us, L.R.D.G. taking the western part of the country and leaving to the parashots the shorter range work to the east. Kufra was also the obvious base for them since with the Qattara passes, Siwa and Jaghbub in enemy hands and with the great barrier of the Sand Sea to the south of them, the next best line of approach to the coast was by Steele's route to Qaret Khod.

A year before this Lazarus with his Survey Section had been mapping the country between the two sand seas and at the end of one of the dune ranges which run southwards and peter out in the *serir* he had built a cairn for an astro-fix position—Howard's Cairn they called it (Howard was Lazarus's driver)—and it was a much-used rendezvous in the next fifteen months.

Here in October and November Mayne lived with his para-shot squadron, an existence which reminded one of Morgan or Kidd and the pirates of the seventeenth century, secure in the palm-fringed creek of some West Indian island, thrusting forth to raid the fleets of Spain. From Kufra their 3-tonners brought them supplies and water, for the nearest water was at Siwa, then in Italian hands. And from Howard's Cairn small parties of three or four Jeeps crossed the Sand Sea to the gravel desert beyond Jaghbub to attack the railway line which the Axis had put into use from Tobruk to Daba and other targets along the coast road.

Stories of their operations used to reach us at Kufra with the L.R.D.G. patrols which were using the Howard's Cairn route at the same time. Tales of trains mined, railway stations wrecked, road traffic shot up and aircraft burned on their landing grounds. Tales of Jeep patrols pushing out to the extremity of their petrol range and attacking the enemy from the back side of their line at 'Alamein; of someone (Scratchley, I think) taken prisoner there when the Axis line broke in October by an unbelieving British unit who scoffed at his story of having come from Kufra to Himeimat.

There was an echo of Moore's march and of the walk of the T2 men from Nofilia after one raid on the railway south of Sidi Barrani. The parashots had shot up the station staff and wrecked the buildings but when they withdrew and halted to collect their party one man, Sillitoe the navigator, was missing. When he had not come in by dawn they assumed he had been killed or taken prisoner and turned south to Howard's Cairn.

At daybreak Sillitoe found himself a mile or two from the railway, without food or water and with the alternative of going back to the station to surrender or of walking "home." With great courage he chose the second, and started southwards. Mayne's base was 250 miles away, but his patrols, after crossing the Sand Sea, used occasionally to lie up for a day or two in the scrub at Hatiet Etla, an old dumping ground of ours where we once kept a stock of food and water and where Lloyd Owen had hidden with Haselden before the September attack on Tobruk. Sillitoe guessed that here he might find some remains of food and water and set off on his 150-mile walk. In the end he reached Etla and by good fortune on the same day that another parashot party passed through.

In October and November L.R.D.G. patrols were going up to the Gebel Akhdar from Kufra with reliefs, food and other supplies for those various branches of Middle East who did their work inside Cyrenaica and whose names were carefully designed to mean nothing at all. Sweeting, returning from one of these expeditions in October, brought with him Guignol and also an L.R.D.G. survivor of the Barce raid. Guignol's job was the collection of escaped prisoners, baled-out airmen and others who found themselves stranded in enemy territory, and for this purpose he had organised a series of "cells" of friendly Arabs throughout the Gebel who collected any British they heard of, fed and sheltered them, and brought them back to his base to wait for an L.R.D.G. patrol and a passage back to Kufra or Siwa.

The survivor was Findlay of the Guards Patrol who had been with Dennis in the attack on the barracks at Barce on the night of September 13th. In the confusion of their withdrawal his truck had become separated from the rest, missed the road out of the town to the east, and at dawn was being chased across the plain towards the escarpment by a band of Italians. Off the road no car can scale that scarp so the crew set fire to their truck and vanished into the undergrowth with the Italians at their heels. By nightfall the hunt had died down and the next day Findlay, separated in the darkness from his companions, walked southwards and was guided by an Arab to Guignol's base.

Sweeting brought with him two other men, Gregory and

Urquhart, who had been picked up by Guignol's Arabs after they had escaped from the prison cage at Benghazi. Gregory, a New Zealander, had been captured in June when the N.Z. Division broke through south of Matruh during the retreat to 'Alamein. The New Zealanders, judged by so competent an authority as Rommel to be the finest British troops in the Middle East, had used their bayonets to some effect, but this, in the opinion of the Herrenvolk, was an unfair way of fighting, despicable, it appeared, by comparison with the mass murder by machine-gun of Central European Jews. So on the morning following the New Zealanders were separated from the other prisoners. " You," said the Huns, " will stand here in the sun and watch your fellow prisoners sitting there comfortably in the shade," and thus for forty hours they kept them without water. The rest of his captivity Gregory had spent in Benghazi, one of 4500 men, with one tin of bully and some scraps of bread as their daily ration, sleeping three to a blanket and with no hot meal since June. In the end he shammed sick, got transferred to the so-called hospital and escaped during the usual Italian panic in a R.A.F. raid.

Though the Axis forces were not driven out of Cyrenaica for the last time until December, 1942, the Intelligence branch at Middle East had been taking an interest in Tripolitania long before then. Their interest as it affected us was a request to carry men, stores and wireless sets to some point within striking distance of Tripoli and to take out reliefs and fresh stores from time to time.

It was not easy to select such a point. It had to be accessible to our patrols, remote from the thickly populated areas of Tripolitania, and yet near enough for the Intelligence party to do the last stage of their journey by camel or on foot. In the end Bir Tala was chosen ; there was water, Arabs believed to be friendly, and Lloyd Owen's journey to Scemech in December, 1941, had shown that the route was passable to L.R.D.C.

Guild made the first trip from Kufra at the end of August and left three men with their food and wireless sets at Bir Tala.

Three months later Tony Browne went up on the thousand mile journey from Kufra with fresh supplies and a relief wireless operator. The first man to go up had become very ill : he was, in fact, just " going bad " by degrees and when he got back to Kufra his body was a mass of sores.

Guild's journey was uneventful, but Tony's very different. On the way out he was caught by enemy fighters in the Wadi Tamet, about fifty miles south of the coast. The enemy were determined, diving down low over the cars, but T patrol fought back till their last round had gone. Pilkington who had been attached to us for a month from the Arab Legion and O'Malley, the navigator, were killed at their guns and two trucks were burnt out, but if they had not stood up to the strafing they would probably have lost all the cars in the patrol.

Tony had a lucky escape that day. He had been firing his gun till the ammunition began to run short and then handed it over to Pilkington while he climbed into the truck for more pans. As he was bending over the ammo. box the C.R. 42's came in again. Pilkington was killed but Tony escaped with a bullet graze which made him take his meals standing for the rest of the journey. He had lost two of his five trucks and one man was wounded besides the two killed, but he finished the job, sending one car back to Tazerbo with the wounded and going on himself with two to drop Flower and his supplies at Bir Tala.

Few men did more for L.R.D.G. than Tony. He joined with the first batch as a navigator, was then corporal, patrol sergeant, patrol commander, liaison officer at Middle East, instructor in navigation and general mentor to the Indian Long Range Squadron when it was being formed in Syria, guide and desert expert to an armoured car regiment at 'Alamein, guided the New Zealand Division in their " left hook " at 'Agheila—over-worked, blown up and twice wounded, his D.C.M. and M.C. were well earned.

They were brave men, with a cold, calculated two o'clock-in-the-morning bravery, these " spies " whom we took up to the back door to Tripoli in the autumn of 1942—Flower and his companions whose names, since they were not all of them British, had better be left unrecorded. In Cyrenaica it was a fair risk that 90 per cent of the Arabs would be friendly, but in Tripolitania, where Italian oppression was less recent and where the material benefits of their rule loomed larger, Arab feeling towards the British was unknown. From Bir Tala they moved up into the hilly country south of Tripoli and soon found a friend who never deserted them in the difficult days ahead.

This was Sheikh Suleiman of the Awlad 'Aal (I have changed his true name, having little confidence in what our present "co-belligerents" might do to him if Tripolitania is returned to them after the war). For many weeks Flower lived with the tribe in comparative safety but then the Italians began to suspect his presence in the hills. The other tribesmen were frightened that unless Flower left the district ruin would overtake them all and pressed Sheikh Suleiman to turn him out. But the Sheikh, refusing to break his word with one who had eaten his bread, packed up his tents, gathered his family and his animals and for weeks carried Flower with him from hiding-place to hiding-place, moving on as the Italians' search became more strict.

From their base in the hills Flower and his men worked their way north to Tripoli and to the airfield at Castel Benito, gathering information themselves and through Arabs whom they could trust. In Tripoli their best "contact" was Alfieri, owner of many lorries, whose transport contract with the Army gave him unlimited opportunity to learn what was passing through the port. They had many narrow escapes. X going down to Tripoli on one occasion, dressed as an Arab and with an Arab companion, was held up at a road block near Castel Benito and asked for his papers. He had none and things were looking unpleasant for him till the Arab, thrusting his own papers forward for inspection, started a lung-rending fit of coughing and the sentry, over whom he was spitting and spluttering, kicked them both with a curse along the road.

In the autumn of 1942, after an interval of nearly two years, we were operating again with the Free French in the Fezzan.

This was the third time the French had raided the Fezzan, counting as the first their participation in Clayton's attack on Murzuk. The second was in the spring of 1942. By January of that year the Eighth Army had taken all Cyrenaica and Tripoli seemed not far off. Leclerc, always ready for a fight, had been asked to move up into the Fezzan as soon as the Eighth Army drove westwards from 'Agheila, but that drive never came and by the end of the month Msus and Mechili had fallen and the enemy were nearing Gazala.

In December, 1941, Dick Croucher had taken R2 patrol from Siwa down to Tibesti to provide a wireless link between Leclerc and Middle East ; reliable communications would be vital for the operations then in prospect and only L.R.D.G. Signals could do the job. In pre-war days Croucher's journey would have been front-page news in the journals of geography but by the end of 1941 it was merely a routine L.R.D.G. trip. Southwards he went from Siwa to Tazerbo, then to Kayugi in the foothills of Tibesti, then through the mountains (I think for the first time with cars) to the French advanced base at Zouar. With the British retreat to Gazala the need for Leclerc's co-operation had disappeared and in February Croucher turned home. He was a good ambassador for us ; the French afterwards often spoke with affection for " le bon Grouchere, type assez sérieux," by which they did not mean " serious " but " sincere "—a quality not conspicuous in themselves which they admired in others. But Leclerc had no intention of losing the chance of a crack at the hated Italians, whatever the successes or failures of the Eighth Army might be. For weeks he had been preparing for this day, training his *tirailleurs* at Faya, putting his nondescript transport into shape, while the long caravans of camels plodded northwards from Fort Lamy with supplies.

In mid-February the French started northwards from Tibesti, a mixed force of motorised infantry, armoured cars, the méharistes of the Groupe Nomade Tibbu, a howitzer, some Lysanders— relics of the summer at Kufra—and a Glenn Martin bomber or two. With the Eighth Army out of the picture Leclerc's attack could be nothing more than a hit and run affair, strong enough to shake up the Italians and obtain useful information of their forces, but weak enough to leave him with some reserve of transport and petrol if the British advance into Tripolitania should take place after all.

He shook up the Italians all right.

On March 1st, in a blinding sandstorm, Dio with the Groupe Nomade Borkou took Tejerri. Dio had the howitzer with him and with this and his mortars soon drove the Italians out of the fort where their commander Bracchetti, a Saharan veteran long known to us, survived a direct hit with a shell which took off his right arm. For the rest of the day the French and Italians fought it out with rifles and hand grenades among the tamarisk bushes at point blank range, till by evening the enemy had had enough and retired into the desert. Two nights later Dio, flushed with success, pushed on to Gatrun. But as we had seen a year before the duller necessities of war such as good communications were never a strong point with the French and Dio, cautiously approaching Gatrun, found that Hous with another force had taken the place by storm two days before.

Meanwhile, pursuing Leclerc's plan of " penetration in depth with synchronised attacks," Geoffroi with his L.R.D.G.-like patrol had gone up north of Sehba to the cross tracks near Umm el 'Abid. The first evening his ambush was successful for he captured two lorries full of bombs and petrol, but next day the Italians had their turn and Geoffroi had a taste of the medicine they had given T patrol at Gebel Sherif, the successful co-operation between their Air Force and an Auto-Saharan Company hastening down from Hon. After a running fight of twenty miles Geoffroi turned south to Wau el Kebir.

On the night of March 5th he was before the small oasis. The palm groves seemed deserted and the landing ground unused. After dark, with one *goumier*, he crept up to the post. Here, too, there was no sign of life and they crawled through the wire and into the fort where the whole garrison appeared asleep. At once he sent back the *goumier* to bring up the rest of his men, but two hundred yards from the post a *tirailleur* stumbled and fell, letting off his rifle. The alarm was given and Geoffroi barely escaped to rejoin his patrol.

But Wau el 'Kebir had not seen the last of the French. de Guillebon, who had routed the Sciati Camel Company at Tmessa and was quite unaware of what Geoffroi had been doing, decided to make an assault on Wau el Kebir and attacked it on the 7th, two nights after Geoffroi's unsuccessful attempt. Over him de Guillebon had the advantage for he had with him two of those very effective weapons, the 81 mm. mortars.

" Our pieces were in position to fire at 17.20 hours. Registration of the two mortars had been done before night-fall. . . .

" At this moment the enemy had ceased fire. The screams of the wounded were heard. The order ' Cease Firing ' was given and the *ascaris* were harangued by a deserter and told that fire would be opened if they did not surrender. To this harangue there was no reply : fifteen rounds per piece were fired and the speaker took up the word again ; this time with success, and on the twenty times repeated statement that the French would not fire the garrison came out and surrendered."

Ten months later preparations were again being made at Zouar. · Men and stores were arriving from Faya and Fort Lamy ; Leclerc was there (now a General), with Ingold, a newcomer, in command of the force that was to advance into the Fezzan. In place of Croucher was Jim Henry with his Rhodesian patrol as the wireless link to Eighth Army.

In mid-December, 1942, Rommel withdrew from 'Agheila and Leclerc started northward from Zouar. Ten days before Christmas he occupied Wigh, a mile-wide hollow in the desert which, because of its good water, must be secured by any force which advances from the south into the Fezzan.

Leclerc had asked for fighter support for his operations, but

Middle East could not spare the aircraft and his few Lysanders
and Blenheims were no match for the Heinkels and C.R. 42's.
As a result, for the first ten days of their advance through that
open desert they had a very unpleasant time. I take from Henry's
diary his account of December 26th :

"Travelled all night, S2 patrol still leading. Arrived
in sight of Gatrun at daybreak. Two French trucks and S2
advanced towards the oasis to see what would happen. Enemy
opened up field artillery and Bredas of various calibres. Rest
of column came up and then moved slowly eastwards in
artillery formation until we were just out of range. French
75 mm. sent a few rounds back. Column then moved eastwards to a range of hills twenty miles away, dispersed and
held a council of war. The original plan was to shell Gatrun
sufficiently to shake up the garrison and then by-pass it,
leaving the main body to capture it. Just before lunch S2
patrol with a French patrol was sent out with the idea of
doing a recce of the northern part of the oasis, just out of
artillery range, and to lure out any Auto Saharan Coy and
lead them into range of the French 75's in position near the
hills. We got to within a couple of miles of the oasis when
we were attacked by six fighters and two bombers with M.G.
fire and bombs. Desert was good going so we fought back,
gradually edging off towards the hills and dodging bombs
during our spare moments. Saw a column of black smoke
rising several miles north of us. My gunner said it was an
aircraft burning though he had not actually seen the crash.
Soon afterwards ground strafing ceased but bombing continued for some time. During the fight we picked up one
Frenchman and four *ascaris* whose truck had been put out of
action. Checked up on the movements of the S2 trucks,
one unaccounted for, so circled back to look for it and found
it heading back to look for me. Had reached talking distance
when the bomber started work on us again ; kept visual
contact and returned to the hills. Carter came across with

information that two French trucks had been damaged and one *ascari* killed. A Frenchman in the patrol said he had seen the aircraft crash and since ours were the only trucks that fired Col. Ingold credited us with shooting it down and complimented us on the calm and organised way in which we had met the attack, saying that we had set an excellent example to the French troops."

For a week more the Rhodesians were bombed and strafed daily; Jackson and du Toit were wounded and one truck wrecked by bomb splinters and others hit.

But although in the air the enemy had the upper hand, on the ground the French had it all their own way. By the end of December, with Cyrenaica in British hands and the Eighth Army pressing towards Tripoli, the Italians in the Fezzan were beginning to lose heart. If they fought on in their isolated posts there was small chance of help reaching them; sooner or later their line of retreat would be cut off, so at fort after fort—Gatrun, Umm el Araneb, Murzuk, Sebha—they surrendered or fled northwards.

The garrison at Murzuk left in good time, pouring out on foot across the desert to the north-west. (Manerini, the general of the Saharan Command had ordered them to fight to the last man before himself hurrying away from Hon!) Mahé, our friend of Kufra days, was out on an air reconnaissance that morning and spotted this forlorn column trudging through the sand. As he dived to attack his gun jammed and he thought that he had lost the target of a lifetime, but on the ground the Italians were gesticulating and waving rags of white, so Mahé threw them a note telling them to stay where they were and flew off to find some ground troops to whom they could surrender.

While Leclerc was advancing into the Fezzan from the south L.R.D.G. patrols were doing what they could to help him by harassing the enemy in the north. The most useful thing would be to destroy aircraft, so Spicer and Nangle took their patrols through Henry's Gap and across the rough basalt country south

of Hon to try to raid the airfield there. But heavy rain and bad
going hindered them and when they finally got down to the outskirts of Hon they were met by heavy gunfire. And, as we saw
later, their chances of getting through the thick minefields round
the cantonments would have been very small indeed. But on
the road leading north from Brak to Shueref Wilder, Hunter and
Birdwood did more damage, laying mines and shooting up the
passing convoys.

At the beginning of December the Eighth Army was before
'Agheila and ready to push Rommel out of his positions between
the salt marshes and the sea. Though it was becoming clear that
he did not intend to make a firm stand there a frontal attack on
such strong positions was bound to be costly and Montgomery's
plan was to hasten the German withdrawal by a repetition of
that manœuvre so often used by both sides in the Libyan war,
the turning of the southern flank. This meant an advance through
the 'Agheila-Marada gap south of Ma'aten Giofer, across country
which we had first explored on the way to the Sirte desert in
July of 1941, and which the patrols had afterwards got to
know so well on their way to and from the road watch.

The New Zealand Division with the 4th Light Armoured
Brigade was chosen for the job and Tony Browne with R1
patrol was to guide them.

By the second week in December the force had gathered at
El Haseiat to which the New Zealanders had come by forced
marches across the desert from Bir Hakim. Here for four days
they waited, keeping a strict wireless silence, camouflaged in the
thick scrub and hidden by some lucky days of low cloud. On
the 13th they moved southwards, round the salt marshes at
Ma'aten Barbar where the T2 men had dug in vain for fresh
water on their way back to Aujila a year before, and then turned
north-westwards towards the coast. Now the movement of a
division, with its armoured cars, guns, lorried infantry, tanks on
transporters, ambulances and R.A.S.C. companies, across track-
less and badly-mapped desert is no light matter, particularly if

part of the move has to be made by night. General Freyberg took no chances, and before he left El Haseiat the N.Z. Provost Company with Browne to guide them had laid out the divisional axis along which the centre of the force was to move, marking it with black triangles of tin swinging from iron stakes and with hurricane lanterns in shaded petrol tins for the night march of sixty miles which took them across the Marada road.

On the 16th the division had reached the Via Balbia west of the Marble Arch, but though their outflanking movement was successful in hastening Rommel's withdrawal the greater part of his forces escaped westwards by taking a route near to the coast. Again with R1 patrol leading the New Zealanders moved to outflank him, swinging round south to Nofilia, but again the enemy rearguard got away.

At this time L.R.D.G. H.Q. was still at Kufra but the battle on the coast was moving quickly westwards and we should soon have to move too. It may appear strange that our H.Q. was often situated so far away from the country in which the patrols were working, but we had learned by long experience the value of a base at which the patrols could find some measure of comfort and where fitters, watchmaker, armourer, map draughtsman, signals instrument mechanic and the other technicians could work undisturbed.

The Italians had evacuated Zella and in Christmas week Oliver Poole and I took the H.Q. party up there from Kufra, a pleasant, uneventful journey of 600 miles, through the edge of the Rebiana Sand Sea to Zighen, then two days' easy going across the gravel to Oliver's Dump where we had built up a supply of petrol and water for the raids into the northern Fezzan, then northwards, with the basalts of the Harug seen as a dark line on the western horizon, through broken country to Zella, a mine-strewn hollow in the desert where a few hundred Arabs wring a precarious livelihood from the sandy soil. In the days of early winter the inner desert is at its best—the air at dawn clear, dry, exhilarating, the sun pleasantly warm at noon, and the stars at night, brighter than a northerner can imagine, lighting up the moonless sky.

The need to signal made the move of Group H.Q. a very leisurely affair, the scorn of the patrols who did their 250 miles a day. While at base Signals kept a 24-hour watch and on the move this must be restricted as little as possible, so we camped early and started late, with a long halt at midday with the three or four wireless trucks spread in a wide circle round the office caravan.

Rommel was being pushed steadily westwards and it was clear that his next big stand would be made beyond the Tunisian frontier in the gap between the Matmata Hills and the sea. Here, some years before the Nazi war, the French, fearing an Italian invasion from Tripoli, had built a strong defensive position along the line of the *wadi* which runs through the small town of Mareth.

Some weeks before Tripoli fell on January 23rd the Army Commander had sent for Prendergast to explain the part which he wished L.R.D.G. to play in the last phase of the advance to Tunis. It was his intention to make a holding attack against the fortified line at Mareth, while an encircling force turned the position by a " left hook " to the southwards and he wanted L.R.D.G. to reconnoitre the country over which this force would have to pass. (Among other visitors to Army H.Q. was the Frenchman who had built the Mareth Line, now in the difficult position of having to explain how to overcome his own excellent defences !)

At that time our base was still at Zella, for the Italians continued to hang on in Hon where the garrison of a thousand or more was too large for us to dislodge. Nangle with his Indians fought a skirmish on the outskirts of Uaddan on Christmas Day, and for the next fortnight he lived in the hills above the village, going down by night to discover if the Italians had left. On January 10th Hon was clear and L.R.D.G. moved there from Zella.

Now from Hon to the Tunisian frontier as the crow flies is four hundred miles, and it was clear that from there the patrols would not be able without refuelling to reconnoitre the country south of the Matmata Hills, zigzagging to and fro to make their "going" maps, and return to their base. The solutions to this difficulty were a series of dumps made by the Heavy Section in the desert country south of Gebel Nefusa, of whose existence the Italians never seem to have been aware, and a supply of petrol and food at Tozeur in Tunisia, arranged by Easonsmith in a flying visit to First Army at the beginning of the year.

All January and half of February our patrols and those of the Indian Long Range Squadron were going out from Zella or Hon. On January 12th T patrol crossed the frontier, the first troops of the Eighth Army to enter Tunisia. The information which the patrols were collecting might be needed by Army H.Q. at any moment, and therefore we could not wait till each party had returned to Hon with the map of its route. So at their midday halts and again in the evening they would signal the results of their work, giving their route from point to point by map reference and describing the terrain by the code Bagnold had worked out a year before.

The map which we gradually built up thus was not made without losses. Lazarus, crossing the track between Shueref and Mizda, fell in with a strong enemy column moving up to Tripoli from the Fezzan. In the scrap which followed the Rhodesians knocked out a German armoured car but lost half their own vehicles, and Henderson, the navigator, was killed. At nightfall three men were still missing but a week later they turned up at Hon, having walked eastwards till they met some friendly Arabs who set them on camels and brought them in. A week earlier Hunter was searching for a way, other than the existing roads which were sure to be guarded, down the precipitous northern face of Gebel Nefusa on to the coastal plain. East of Nalut he tried to get down the cliff with two Jeeps but one overturned, rolled down the slope and was wrecked. As they were recovering their guns and kit a Libyan soldier appeared offering assistance. Hunter explained in Arabic that they were a German party testing out new cars and while the man went to fetch help from his camp in the next valley made off hurriedly in the opposite direction.

It was Wilder who in the end found the route by which two months later the New Zealand Division made their last " left hook." By the middle of January, a week before Tripoli fell, he had reached a point thirty miles south-west of Medenine, and from a hiding place here sent out parties on foot to search the hills. But a few days' work showed that they were impassable so he turned to search farther southwards and a week later had found the pass which the Army came to know later as Wilder's Gap.

Meanwhile Tinker, Bruce, Rand, Spicer and the other patrols were covering the area west of the hills. Tinker with a couple of Jeeps pushed up to within 25 miles of Gabes but when he got back to his temporary base beyond Qasr Rihane he found his patrol had been shot up by enemy aircraft, two men wounded and most of his cars burnt out. While he had been away the survivors of a party of Free French parashots had come in to his camp, and Tinker was faced with the problem of getting home thirty-seven men, two of them wounded, in his five remaining Jeeps. So with three cars he went across the *shott* to Tozeur, borrowed more transport and returned to collect the twenty-five men who were following on foot.

Bruce's area was between the Shott el Gerid and the Grand Erg Oriental, the great sand sea of Southern Algeria, which a progress of fifty miles in three days in its confused and " choppy " dunes showed to be far less passable than the Libyan sand seas. Bruce had become expert in this work of "going" reconnaissance for at the end of December, when the front line stood at Buerat el Hsun, he had explored all the country south-west of Misurata over which XXX Corps later advanced to Tarhuna and on to Tripoli.

Before these operations in Tunisia began we had been warned that the Arabs of the country would probably be unfriendly and this proved to be true enough. Two years of efficient Nazi propaganda backed up by lavish bribery, and their long-standing dislike of the French had made their attitude to us very different from that of the Arabs in Libya. Arabs gave away the position of Tinker's base near Qasr Rihane ; they had betrayed David Stirling when he was attacked and taken prisoner near Gabes and on February 13th Bruce was twice ambushed by an Arab band. The Guards beat off both attacks, but in the first two men had been wounded so Bruce took his patrol into Tozeur, filled up with petrol and food a day before the Germans occupied the village, and took his wounded on to El Oued. With his return to Tripoli by the northern route now cut off he finally reached Hon by way of Touggourt, Fort Flatters and Ghadames, a sort of Cook's Tour through the Algerian Sahara which brought his mileage up to 3500 miles in the five weeks since he had started out.

During January and February the patrols had explored hundreds of square miles of country, had lost men, cars and equipment and used thousands of gallons of petrol. In the middle of March all this work bore its fruit.

The information we had collected showed that a " left hook " to outflank the Mareth Line was a possibility and the New Zealand Division was chosen to carry it out. From the beginning of the month, along the roads from Tripoli, supplies were pouring into the F.M.C.[1] at Dehibat. By night the R.A.S.C. companies lifted them forward to a second dump near Wilder's Gap, hurrying to be back at Dehibat again before dawn. In the wadis around the Gap the supplies were carefully camouflaged.

By the middle of March all was ready. A L.R.D.G. party under Tinker was to guide the force and it was only fitting that the Group's last task in Africa should be carried out by the New Zealanders who had begun its work two and a half years earlier, a thousand miles to the east.

On the 19th the New Zealand Division started westwards along the route which had been marked out by Bassett, Tinker's navigator, a couple of days before. From Wilder's Gap they moved up towards Gebel Tabaqa with El Hamma and Gabes as their final objectives. Rommel, appreciating the threat to his

[1] Field Maintenance Centre.

right flank, moved the 21st Panzer Division and two other divisions out west of Gabes to plug the gap. But Montgomery sent the 1st Armoured Division after the New Zealanders and on the afternoon of March 26th, with overwhelming support from the R.A.F. and the American Air Force, the two British divisions inflicted a defeat on the enemy which left Rommel with no alternative but to abandon the Mareth Line. On the 29th Gabes fell.

General Montgomery wrote this letter to Prendergast :

> MAIN H.Q. EIGHTH ARMY,
> M. E. F.
> 2 *April*, 1943.

MY DEAR PRENDERGAST,
          We are sending back the Indian Long Range Squadron to-morrow. They have done some useful jobs here—road recces, protective patrols for aerodromes, etc.—but I feel that there will be no further scope for them in the country we are now entering.

I would like you to know how much I appreciate the excellent work done by your patrols and by the S.A.S. in reconnoitring the country up to the Gabes Gap.

Without your careful and reliable reports the launching of the " left hook " by the N.Z. Division would have been a leap in the dark ; with the information they produced the operation could be planned with some certainty and, as you know, went off without a hitch.

Please give my thanks to all concerned and best wishes from Eighth Army for the new tasks you are undertaking.
> Yours sincerely,
> B. L. MONTGOMERY.

LT.-COL. PRENDERGAST, D.S.O.,
    O.C., L.R.D.G."

That was the end. The hilly country beyond Gabes was, as the Army Commander said, unsuitable for L.R.D.G. to work in and Prendergast took the unit back to Egypt for a re-fit and the rest it had well earned.

For two and a half years L.R.D.G. had been masters in the inner desert, moving through it as and when they pleased, causing the enemy losses out of all proportion to their own, and helping to make more true one of the few true sayings of the Leader of our enemies, who wrote of the " spirit of the broad masses " (of the British nation) " which enables it to carry through to victory any struggle that it once enters upon, no matter how long such a struggle may last or however great the sacrifice that may be necessary or what the means that have to be employed ; and all this even though the actual military equipment at hand may be utterly inadequate when compared with that of other nations."[1]

[1] Adolf Hitler, *Mein Kampf*. Unexpurgated edition, 1939. (Hurst & Blackett, Ltd.)

APPENDIX 1

GLOSSARY

A.F.V.	- -	Armoured fighting vehicle.
'Ain	- -	Spring.
Ascaris	- -	Native troops.
Barchan	- -	Crescent-shaped dune.
Bir	- -	Well, cistern.
Carabinieri	-	Italian police.
Dom Palm	-	Hyphæne thebaica.
Erg	- - -	Sand sea.
Fusti	- -	Fuel-drum.
Gebel, Jebel	-	Mountain, hill.
Ghibli	- -	Colonial bomber aircraft, Italian.
Gilf	- - -	Cliff, plateau.
Goum	-	Band of irregular troops.
Goumier	- -	Member of such a band.
Hammada	-	Stony desert.
Hatiet, Hatiya	-	Patch of vegetation.
Kebir	-	Large, big.
L.G.	- -	Landing ground.
Ma'aten	- -	Well.
Méhariste	-	Camel Corps soldier.
Mudir	- -	Native official.
Qaret, Gara	-	Hill.
Qibli	- -	Hot south wind.
Recce	- -	Reconnaissance.
Ril	- - -	Addra gazelle.
R.V.	- -	Rendezvous.
S.D.F.	- -	Sudan Defence Force.
Shott	-	Salt marsh.
Sirir, serir	-	Gravel desert.
Tibbu, Tebu	-	Inhabitants of Tibesti.
Wadi	- -	Watercourse, normally dry.
Zawia	- -	Religious centre, monastery.

APPENDIX 2

ROLL OF HONOUR

Arnold, Capt. P. L.	General List.
Ashby, Cpl. L. C.	Rhodesia.
Beech, Cpl. F. R.	2 N.Z.E.F.
Easton, Gdsmn. J.	Scots Guards.
Gravil, Dvr. M.	R.A.S.C.
Gurdon, Lt. Hon. R. B.	Coldstream Guards.
Henderson, Gnr.	Rhodesia.
Henry, Lt. J.	Rhodesia.
Hewson, Sgt. C. D.	2 N.Z.E.F.
Hopton, Gdsmn. A.	Coldstream Guards.
Jordan, Sgmn.	R.C.S.
Matthews, Gdsmn. G.	Coldstream Guards.
O'Malley, L/Cpl. N.	2 N.Z.E.F.
Rezin, Pte.	Rhodesia.
Riggs, Pte. R.	Rhodesia.
Yates, Cpl. G. F.	R.A.S.C.

APPENDIX 3

HONOURS AND AWARDS

D.S.O.

Clayton, Major P. A. - - -	General List.
Easonsmith, Major J. R. - - -	R.T.R.
Prendergast, Lt.-Col. G. L. - -	R.T.R.
Wilder, Capt. N. P. - - -	2 N.Z.E.F.

O.B.E.

Bagnold, Lt.-Col. R. A. - - -	R.C.S.
Steele, Major D. G. - - -	2 N.Z.E.F.
Shaw, Capt. W. B. Kennedy - -	Intelligence Corps.

M.B.E.

Barrett, Lt. D. - - - -	2 N.Z.E.F.
Heywood, Capt. G. B. - - -	Middlesex Yeomanry.

M.C.

Browne, Capt. L. H. - - -	2 N.Z.E.F.
Bruce, Lt. Hon. B. - - -	Coldstream Guards.
Easonsmith, Capt. J. R. - - -	R.T.R.
Holliman, Capt. C. A. - - -	R.T.R.
Hunter, Capt. A. D. N. - - -	R. Scots Fusiliers.
Lawson, Capt. R. P. - - -	R.A.M.C.
Mitford, Major E. C. - - -	R.T.R.
Morris, Lt. C. S. - - - -	2 N.Z.E.F.
Lloyd Owen, Capt. D. - - -	The Queen's.
Olivey, Capt. J. R. - - - -	Rhodesia.
Sutherland, Lt. J. H. - - -	2 N.Z.E.F.
Timpson, Capt. J. A. L. - - -	Scots Guards.
Tinker, Capt. R. A. - - -	2 N.Z.E.F.

D.C.M.

Bassett, Pte. D. M. -	-	-	-	2 N.Z.E.F.
Browne, Cpl. L. H.	-	-	-	2 N.Z.E.F.
Moore, Tpr. R. J. -	-	-	··	2 N.Z.E.F.

M.M.

Brown, Tpr. -	-	-	-	2 N.Z.E.F.
Cave, Tpr. A. H. -	-	-	-	R. Wilts Yeomanry.
Craw, Cpl. M.	-	-	-	2 N.Z.E.F.
Crossley, Cpl. J.	-	-	-	Coldstream Guards.
Dennis, Cpl. J.	-	-	-	Coldstream Guards.
Dobson, Tpr. T. B.	-	-	-	2 N.Z.E.F.
Dornbush, Tpr. C. -	-	-	-	2 N.Z.E.F.
Duncalfe, Gdsmn. R.	-	-	-	Coldstream Guards.
Ellis, Tpr. E. -	-	-	-	2 N.Z.E.F.
Fraser, Cpl. M. B. P.	-	-	-	Scots Guards.
Garven, Cpl. G. C.	-	-	-	2 N.Z.E.F.
Gibson, Cpl. L.	-	-	-	Scots Guards.
Gunn, Pte. D.	-	-	-	Seaforths.
Hutchins, Sgt. D. -	-	-	-	N. Somerset Yeomanry.
Jackson, Sgt. C.	-	-	-	Rhodesia.
Lewis, L/Cpl. T. J. -	-	-	-	2 N.Z.E.F.
Low, Pte. K. T.	-	-	-	Rhodesia.
McInnes, Cpl. I. H.	-	-	-	2 N.Z.E.F.
Sadler, Cpl. W. M.	-	-	-	Rhodesia.
Sanders, Gnr. E.	-	-	-	2 N.Z.E.F.
Sturrock, Pte E. C. -	-	-	-	2 N.Z.E.F.
Tighe, Pte. A.	-	-	-	R.A.O.C.
Tinker, Cpl. R. A. -	-	-	-	2 N.Z.E.F.
Tippett, Tpr. K. E.	-	-	-	2 N.Z.E.F.
Waetford, Cpl. C. -	-	-	-	2 N.Z.E.F.
Welsh, Gdsmn. M. A.	-	-	-	Scots Guards.
Wilcox, Tpr. L. A. -	-	-	-	2 N.Z.E.F.
Wilson, Sgt. -	-	-	-	Scots Guards.

B.E.M.

McLeod, S/Sgt. A. R.   -   -   -   2 N.Z.E.F.

MENTIONED IN DESPATCHES

Ames, Sgt. S. R.   -   -   -   -   R.A.S.C.
Arnold, Cpl. G.   -   -   -   -   R.C.S.
Arnold, Lt. P. L.   -   -   -   -   General List.
Ashdown, Capt. T. W.   -   -   -   R.A.O.C.
Atkins, Sgmn. R.   -   -   -   -   R.C.S.
Bagnold, Lt.-Col. R. A. -   -   -   R.C.S.
Ball, Sgt. C. G.   -   -   -   -   2 N.Z.E.F.
Ballantyne, Capt. L. B. -   -   -   2 N.Z.E.F.
Barrett, Lt. D.   -   -   -   -   2 N.Z.E.F.
Beech, Pte. R. F.   -   -   -   -   2 N.Z.E.F.
Bevan, S.Q.M.S. H. D.   -   -   -   Welsh Regt.
Carningham, Sgt. J. W. -   -   -   Warwickshire Yeomanry.
Cave, Cpl. A. H.   -   -   -   -   R. Wilts Yeomanry.
Clarke, Sgt. H. R.   -   -   -   -   R.A.S.C.
Croucher, Lt. C. H.   -   -   -   General List.
Davies, Sgt. A. M.   -   -   -   Intelligence Corps.
Davidson, Cpl. G. L.   -   -   -   2 N.Z.E.F.
Denniff, Lt. A. S.   -   -   -   R.A.C.
Dugan, Cpl. W. F.   -   -   -   R.E.M.E.
Gravil, Dvr. M.   -   -   -   R.A.S.C.
Hammond, Tpr. M. E.   -   -   -   2 N.Z.E.F.
Harcourt, Tpr. D.   -   -   -   2 N.Z.E.F.
Hickey, Cpl. G.   -   -   -   R.A.M.C.
Hough, Sgt. W. R.   -   -   -   Middlesex Yeomanry.
Hughes, Cpl. W.   -   -   -   R.C.S.
Hunter, Capt. A. D. N. -   -   -   R. Scots Fusiliers.
Jackson, Sgt. C. H.   -   -   -   Rhodesia.
Kendall, Cpl. F.   -   -   -   -   2 N.Z.E.F.
King, Cpl. A. T.   -   -   -   -   R.E.M.E.
Leach, Cpl. F. A.   -   -   -   Scots Guards.
Mather, Tpr. L.   -   -   -   -   2 N.Z.E.F.
McInnes, Pte. D. J.   -   -   -   2 N.Z.E.F.

McNeill, Pte. T. B.   -   -   -   2 N.Z.E.F.
McQueen, Lt. R. B.   -   -   -   2 N.Z.E.F.
Moore, Tpr. R. J. -   -   -   -   2 N.Z.E.F.
Murray, Cpl. J. R. -   -   -   -   R.E.M.E.
Penfold, S.S.M. M.   -   -   -   Coldstream Guards.
Pritchard, Pte. B. -   -   -   -   R.A.M.C.
Searle, Sgmn. A. D.   -   -   -   R.C.S.
Shaw, Capt. W. B. Kennedy -   -   Intelligence Corps.
Shepherd, Sgt. J. R.   -   -   -   2 N.Z.E.F.
Spottswood, Pte. R. O. -   -   -   2 N.Z.E.F.
Steele, Major D. G.   -   -   -   2 N.Z.E.F.
Stocker, Sgt. J. P. -   -   -   -   R.T.R.
Tatton, Sgt. F. W. -   -   -   -   R.A.O.C.
Tighe, Pte. A.   -   -   -   -   R.A.O.C.
Timpson, Capt. J. A. L. -   -   -   Scots Guards.
Tinker, Cpl. R. A. -   -   -   -   2 N.Z.E.F.

APPENDIX 4

PATROL COMMANDERS

L.R.P. Patrols.

R (New Zealand) - -	Capt. D. G. Steele.
T (New Zealand) - -	Capt. P. A. Clayton.
	Capt. L. B. Ballantyne.
W (New Zealand) - -	Capt. E. C. Mitford.

L.R.D.G. Patrols.

G1 (Guards) - - -	Capt. M. D. D. Crichton Stuart.
	Capt. A. M. Hay.
	Capt. J. A. L. Timpson.
G2 (Guards) - - -	Capt. J. A. L. Timpson.
	Lt. Hon. R. B. Gurdon.
	Lt. K. H. Sweeting.
	Lt. Hon. B. Bruce.
R1 (New Zealand) - -	Capt. J. R. Easonsmith.
	Capt. A. I. Guild.
	Capt. L. H. Browne.
	Lt. K. F. McLauchlan.
R2 (New Zealand) - -	Lt. C. H. Croucher.
	Lt. J. R. Talbot.
	Capt. K. H. Lazarus.
S1 (Rhodesian) - -	Capt. C. A. Holliman.
	Capt. J. R. Olivey.
	Capt. K. H. Lazarus.
S2 (Rhodesian) - -	Capt. J. R. Olivey.
	Lt. J. Henry.
T1 (New Zealand) - -	Capt. L. B. Ballantyne.
	Lt. J. Crisp.
	Capt. N. P. Wilder.
T2 (New Zealand) - -	Capt. C. S. Morris.
	Capt. N. P. Wilder.

	Lt. A. R. Crammond.
	Capt. R. A. Tinker.
Y1 (Yeomanry and other units)	Capt. P. J. D. McCraith.
	Capt F. C. Simms.
	Capt. D. Lloyd Owen.
Y2 (Yeomanry and other units)	Capt. D. Lloyd Owen.
	Capt. A. D. N. Hunter.
	Capt. E. F. Spicer.

Indian Long Range Squadron.

Indian 1	- - -	Lt. J. E. Cantlay.
Indian 2	- - -	Capt. T. J. D. Birdwood.
Indian 3	- - -	Capt. A. B. Rand.
Indian 4	- - -	Lt. G. W. Nangle.

APPENDIX 5

L. R. D. G. RATION SCALE

Daily

Bacon, tinned - - - - - - - - -	$2\frac{1}{2}$ ozs.
Bread - - - - - - - - -	16 ,,
Biscuits - - - - - - - - -	12 ,,
Cheese - - - - - - - - -	$1\frac{1}{2}$,,
Chocolate - - - - - - - - -	2 ,,
Curry Powder - - - - - - - -	$\frac{1}{8}$,,
Fruit, dried - - - - - - - -	$\frac{4}{7}$,,
Fruit, tinned - - - - - - - -	4 ,,
Herrings - - - - - - - - -	$1\frac{1}{4}$,,
Jam, Marmalade, or Golden Syrup - - - -	$1\frac{1}{2}$,,
Lime Juice - - - - - - - -	$\frac{1}{16}$ (bott.)
Margarine - - - - - - - -	$1\frac{1}{2}$ ozs.
Meat, Preserved - - - - - - -	6 ,,
Pickles - - - - - - - - -	1 ,,
Chutney - - - - - - - - -	$\frac{1}{4}$,,
Meat Loaf or Ham and Tongue - - - -	$1\frac{1}{4}$,,
Meat and Vegetable Ration (" M. & V ") - -	2 ,,
Milk, tinned - - - - - - - -	2 ,,
Mustard - - - - - - - - -	$\frac{1}{100}$,,
Oatmeal or Flour - - - - - - -	2 ,,
Onions - - - - - - - - -	2 ,,
Pepper - - - - - - - - -	$\frac{1}{100}$,,
Potatoes, tinned - - - - - - -	3 ,,
Salt - - - - - - - - -	$\frac{3}{4}$,,
Salmon, tinned - - - - - - - -	1 ,,
Sardines - - - - - - - - -	1 ,,
Sausages - - - - - - - - -	1 ,,
Sugar - - - - - - - - -	$3\frac{1}{2}$,,
Tea - - - - - - - - -	$\frac{3}{4}$,,

Vegetables, tinned	-	-	-	-	-	4 ozs.
Ascorbic tabs. -	-	-	-	-	-	1 tab.
Marmite -	-	-	-	-	-	$\frac{3}{28}$ oz.
Rum[1]	-	-	-	-	-	1 ,,
Tobacco or Cigarettes	-	-	-	-	2 ozs. per week.
Matches -	-	-	-	-	-	2 boxes per week.

Total daily weight (less containers) -   4 lbs. 2 ozs.
With containers, say   -   -   -   5 lbs.

[1] To be issued only under the authority of a Divisional or equivalent Commander. (In the first year or so, till supplies in the Middle East ran short, the rank of a Patrol Commander seldom fell below that of a Major-General !)

THE END

INDEX